Just Send Me Word

Just Send Me Word

A True Story of Love and Survival in the Gulag

ORLANDO FIGES

METROPOLITAN BOOKS
HENRY HOLT AND COMPANY
NEW YORK

Metropolitan Books
Henry Holt and Company, LLC
Publishers since 1866
175 Fifth Avenue
New York, New York 10010
www.henryholt.com

Metropolitan Books® and m® are registered trademarks of Henry Holt
and Company, LLC.

"In Dream" from *Selected Poems*, by Anna Akhmatova, translated by D. M. Thomas,
published by Vintage Books. Reprinted by permission of Random House, Ltd.

Library of Congress Cataloging-in-Publication Data

Figes, Orlando.
 Just send me word : a true story of love and survival in the Gulag / Orlando Figes.
    pages ; cm
 Includes bibliographical references and index.
 ISBN 978-0-8050-9522-7
1. Mishchenko, Lev—Imprisonment. 2. Mishchenko, Lev—Correspondence. 3.
Political prisoners—Russia (Federation)—Pechora (Komi) 4. Political prisoners—
Russia (Federation)—Pechora (Komi)—Correspondence. 5. Mishchenko, Svetlana. 6.
Mishchenko, Svetlana—Correspondence. 7. Fiancées—Soviet Union. 8. Fiancées—
Soviet Union—Correspondence. 9. Labor camps—Russia (Federation)—Pechora
(Komi) 10. Imprisonment—Soviet Union. I. Title.
 DK268.M585F54 2012
 365'.45092--dc23
 [B]   2011048355

Henry Holt books are available for special promotions and premiums.
For details contact: Director, Special Markets.

First U. S. Edition 2012
Printed in the United States of America
10 9 8 7 6 5 4 3 2 1

Contents

Preface   1

Just Send Me Word   7

Epilogue   285

Acknowledgements   291

A Note from Memorial   293

Sources   298

Notes   301

Black and enduring separation
I share equally with you.
Why weep? Give me your hand,
Promise me you will come again.
You and I are like high mountains
And we cannot move closer.
Just send me word
At midnight sometime through the stars.

Anna Akhmatova, 'In Dream' (1946)

Just Send Me Word

Just Send Me Word

Preface

Three old trunks had just been delivered. They were sitting in a doorway, blocking people's way into the busy room where members of the public and historical researchers were received in the Moscow offices of Memorial. I had come that autumn of 2007 to visit some colleagues here in the research division of the human rights organization. Noticing my interest in the trunks, they told me they contained the biggest private archive given to Memorial in its twenty years of existence. It belonged to Lev and Svetlana Mishchenko, a couple who had met as students in the 1930s, only to be separated by the war of 1941–5 and Lev's subsequent imprisonment in the Gulag. As everyone kept telling me, their love story was extraordinary.

We opened up the largest of the trunks. I had never seen anything like it: several thousand letters tightly stacked in bundles tied with string and rubber bands, notebooks, diaries, documents and photographs. The most valuable section of the archive was in the third and smallest of the trunks, a brown plywood case with leather trim and three metal locks that clicked open easily. We couldn't say how many letters it contained – we guessed perhaps 2,000 – only how much the case weighed (37 kilograms). They were all love letters Lev and Svetlana had exchanged while he was a prisoner in Pechora, one of Stalin's most notorious labour camps in the far north of Russia. The first was by Svetlana in July 1946, the last by Lev in July 1954. They were writing to each other at least twice a week. This was by far the largest cache of Gulag letters ever found. But what made them so remarkable was not just their quantity: it was the fact that nobody had censored them. They were smuggled in and out of the labour camp by voluntary workers and officials who sympathized with Lev. Rumours about the smuggling of letters were part of the Gulag's rich folklore but nobody had ever imagined an illegal postbag of this size.

The letters were so tightly packed I had to wedge my fingers between them to get the first one out. It was from Svetlana to Lev. The short address read:

Komi ASSR
Kozhva Region
Wood-combine
C[orrection] C[amp] 274-11b
To Lev Glebovich Mishchenko

I began to read Svetlana's small, barely legible handwriting on the yellow paper, which crumbled in my hands. 'So here I am, not even knowing what I should write to you. That I miss you? But you know that. I feel I am living outside time, that I'm waiting for my life to start, as if this were an intermission. Whatever I do, it seems like I'm just killing time.' I took another letter from the same bundle. It was one of Lev's. 'You once asked whether it's easier to live with or without hope. I can't summon any kind of hope, but I feel calm without it . . .' I was listening to a conversation between them.

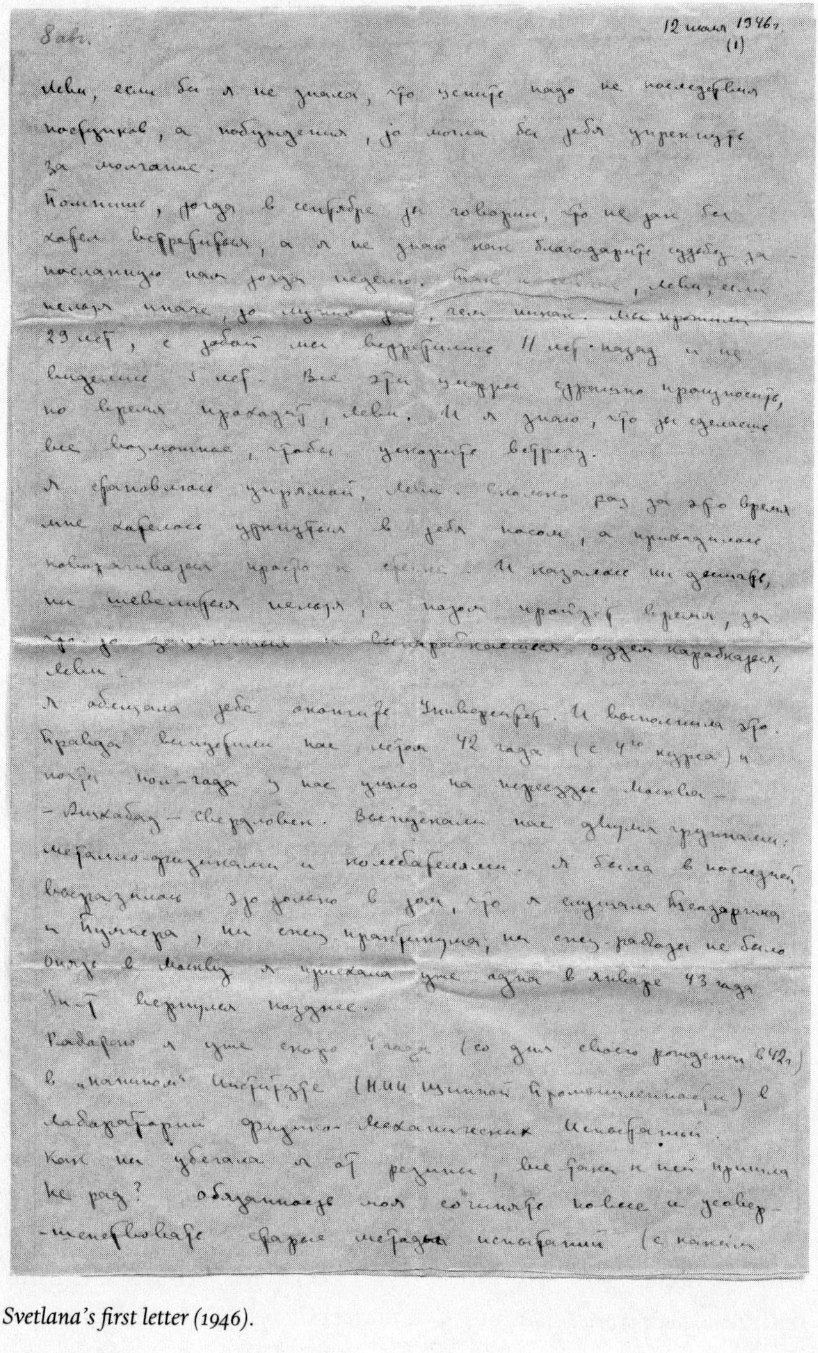

8 ч. 12 июля 1946 г.
(1)

Лева, если бы я не знала, что судить надо не последствия поступков, а побуждения, то могла бы тебя упрекнуть за молчание.
Помнишь, тогда в сентябре ты говорил, что не так бы хотел встретиться, а я не знаю как благодарить судьбу за посланную нам тогда неделю. Так и сейчас, Лева, если немного иначе, то лучше так, чем никак. Мне исполнилось 29 лет, с тобой мы встретились 11 лет назад и не виделись 5 лет. Все эти ужасные трудности, по-моему проходят, Лева. И я знаю, что ты сделаешь все возможное, чтобы ускорить встречу.
Я становлюсь упрямой, Лева. Сколько раз за это время мне хотелось уничтожить в себе память, а приходилось поворачиваться просто к стене. И казалось ни думать, ни шевелиться нельзя, а потом пройдет время, и [illegible] будешь карабкаться, Лева.
Я обещала тебе окончить Университет. И выполнила это. Правда выпустили нас летом 42 года (с 4го курса) и потом пол-года у нас ушло на переезды Москва — Ашхабад — Свердловск. Выпускали нас двумя группами: металло-физиками и колебателями. Я была в последней, несмотря на это только в том, что я слушала Ландсберга и Тамма, ни спец. практикума, ни спец. работы не было. Опять в Москву я приехала уже одна в январе 43 года. Ун-т вернулся позднее.
Работаю я уже скоро 4 года (со дня своего рождения в 42 г.) в „нашем" Институте (НИИ шинной промышленности) в лаборатории физико-механических испытаний.
Как ни убегала я от резины, все-таки к ней пришла не рад? Обязанность моя сочинять новые и усовершенствовать старые методы испытаний (с какой

Svetlana's first letter (1946).

As I leafed through the letters, my excitement grew. Lev's were rich in details of the labour camp. They were possibly the only major contemporary record of daily life in the Gulag that would ever come to light. Many memoirs of the labour camps by former

Lev's twenty-fourth (1946).

prisoners had appeared, but nothing to compare with these uncensored letters, composed at the time inside the barbed-wire zone. Written to explain to his sole intended reader what he was going through, Lev's letters became, over the years, increasingly revealing about conditions in the camp. Svetlana's letters were meant to support him in the camp, to give him hope, but, as I soon realized, they also told the story of her own struggle to keep her love for him alive.

Perhaps 20 million people, mostly men, endured Stalin's labour camps. Prisoners, on average, were allowed to write and receive letters once a month, but all their correspondence was censored. It was difficult to maintain an intimate connection when all communication was first read by the police. An eight- or ten-year sentence almost always meant the breaking of relationships: girlfriends, wives or husbands, whole families, were lost by prisoners. Lev and Svetlana were exceptional. Not only did they find a way to write and even meet illegally – an extraordinary breach of Gulag rules that invited severe punishment – but they kept every precious letter (putting them at even greater risk) as a record of their love story.

There turned out to be almost 1,500 letters in that smallest trunk. It took over two years to transcribe them all. They were hard to decipher, full of code words, details and initials that needed to be clarified. These letters are the documentary basis of *Just Send Me Word*, which also draws from the rich archive in the other trunks, from extensive interviews with Lev and Svetlana, their relatives and their friends, from the writings of other prisoners in Pechora, from visits to the town and interviews with its inhabitants and from the archives of the labour camp itself.

I

Lev saw Svetlana first. He noticed her at once in the crowd of students waiting to be called to the entrance exam in the tree-lined courtyard of Moscow University. She was standing by the doorway to the Physics Faculty with a friend of Lev's who waved him over and introduced her as a classmate from his former school. They exchanged only a few words before the doors of the faculty were opened and they joined the throng of students on the staircase to the hall where the exam would be held.

It was not love at first sight: both agree on that. Lev was far too cautious to fall in love so easily. But Svetlana had already caught his attention. She was of medium height, slim with thick brown hair, high cheekbones, a pointed chin, and blue eyes shining with a sad intelligence. She was one of only a half dozen women to gain admission to the faculty, the best for physics in the Soviet Union, along with Lev and thirty other men in September 1935. In a dark wool shirt, short grey skirt and black suede shoes, the same clothes she had worn as a schoolgirl, Svetlana stood out in this masculine environment. She had a lovely voice (she would sing in the university choir) which added to her physical attractiveness. She was popular, vivacious, occasionally flirtatious and known for her sharp tongue. Svetlana had no shortage of male admirers, but there was something special about Lev. He was neither tall nor powerfully built – he was slightly smaller than she was – nor as confident of his good looks as other young men of his age. He wore the same old shirt – the top button fastened but without a tie in the Russian style – in all the photos of him at the time. He was still more of a boy than a man in appearance. But he had a kind and gentle face with soft blue eyes and a full mouth, like a girl's.

During that first term, Lev and Sveta (as he began to call her) saw each other frequently.* They sat together in lectures, nodded to each other in the library, and moved in the same circle of budding physicists and engineers who ate together in the canteen or met in the student club near the entrance to the library where some would come for a cigarette, others just to stretch their legs and chat.

Later, Lev and Sveta would go out in a group of friends to the theatre or the cinema; and then he would walk her home, taking the romantic route along the garden boulevards from Pushkin Square to the Pokrovsky Barracks near Sveta's house, where couples promenaded in the evening. In the student circles of the 1930s the conventions of courtship continued to be ruled by notions of romantic chivalry, notwithstanding the liberalization of sexual behaviour in some quarters after 1917. At Moscow University romances were serious and chaste, usually beginning when a couple separated

---

* Russian names have a full and a shorter version (used by friends and relatives) and any number of affectionate diminutives. The short form of Svetlana is Sveta but she was also known as Svetochka, Svetik, Svetlanka, etc. In his letters from the labour camp Lev would often call her 'Svet' or 'Svetloe' (Russian words for 'light' – an association which he liked). From this point in the text we will know her as Sveta.

from their wider group of friends and he started to walk her home in the evenings. It was a chance to talk more intimately together, perhaps exchanging favourite lines of poetry, the accepted medium for conversations about love, a chance for them to kiss before they parted at her house.

Lev knew that he was not alone in liking Sveta. He often saw her walking with Georgii Liakhov (the friend who had introduced him

to Sveta) in the Aleksandr Gardens by the Kremlin Wall. Lev was too reserved to ask Georgii about his relations with Sveta, but one day Georgii said, 'Svetlana's such a lovely girl, but she's so intelligent, so terribly intelligent.' He said it in a way that made it clear to Lev that Georgii was intimidated by her intellect. As Lev would soon find out, Sveta could be moody, critical of others and impatient with people not as clever as herself.

Slowly, Lev and Sveta drew closer. They were brought together by a 'profound sympathy', recalls Lev. Sitting in his living room more than seventy years later, he smiles at the memory of that first emotional connection. He thinks carefully before choosing his next words: 'It was not that we fell madly in love with each other, but there was a deep and permanent affinity.'

Eventually they came to see themselves as a couple: 'Everybody knew that Svetlana was my girl because I didn't visit anybody else.'

There was a moment when it became obvious to both of them. One afternoon, as they were walking in the quiet residential streets near Sveta's house on Kazarmennyi Pereulok (Barracks Lane), she took his hand and said, 'Let's go that way, I'll introduce you to my friends.' They went to see her closest friends from school, Irina Krauze, who was studying French at the Institute of Foreign Languages, and Aleksandra ('Shura' or 'Shurka') Chernomordik, who was studying medicine. Lev recognized this as a mark of Sveta's trust in him, as a sign of her affection, that she let him meet her childhood friends.

Soon Lev was invited to Sveta's home. The Ivanov family had a private apartment with two large rooms and a kitchen – an almost unknown luxury in Stalin's Moscow, where communal apartments housing a family per room with one shared kitchen and toilet were the norm. Sveta and her younger sister, Tanya, lived in one room with their parents, the girls sleeping on a sofa that unfolded into a bed. Their brother, Yaroslav ('Yara'), lived with his wife, Elena, in the other room, where there was a large wardrobe, a glass-fronted cabinet for books and a grand piano used by the whole family. With its high ceilings and antique furniture, the Ivanov home was a tiny island of the intelligentsia in the proletarian capital.

Sveta's father, Aleksandr Alekseevich, was a tall, bearded man in his mid-fifties with sad, attentive eyes and salt-and-pepper hair. A veteran Bolshevik, he had joined the revolutionary movement as a student at Kazan University in 1902, had been expelled and imprisoned, and then had re-enrolled in the Physics Faculty of St Petersburg University, where he had worked with the great Russian chemist Sergei Lebedev in the development of synthetic rubber before the First World War. After the October Revolution of 1917, Aleksandr had played a leading part in organizing the Soviet production of rubber. But he left the Party in 1921, officially for reasons of ill-health, although in reality he had become disillusioned with the Bolshevik dictatorship. During the next decade he went on two extended work trips to the West, before moving with his family to Moscow in 1930. This was the height of the Five Year Plan to industrialize the Soviet

Union and the first great wave of Stalin's terror against 'bourgeois specialists', when many of Aleksandr's oldest friends and colleagues were rounded up as 'spies' or 'saboteurs' and shot or sent to labour camps. Aleksandr's foreign trips made him politically vulnerable, but somehow he survived and went on working for the cause of Soviet industry, rising to become the deputy director of the Resin Research Institute. In a household dominated by the ethos of the technical intelligentsia, all the children were brought up to study engineering or science: Yara went to the Moscow Machine-Building Institute, Tanya studied meteorology, and Sveta attended the Physics Faculty.

Aleksandr welcomed Lev into his home. He enjoyed the presence of another scientist. Sveta's mother was more distant and reserved. A plump, slow-moving woman in her mid-fifties who wore mittens to cover up a hand disease, Anastasia Erofeevna was a Russian-language teacher in the Moscow Institute of the Economy, and had the stern demeanour of a pedagogue. She would screw up her eyes and peer at Lev through her thick-rimmed spectacles. For a long time he was scared of her, but towards the end of Sveta's and his first year at the university an incident occurred that altered everything. Sveta had borrowed Lev's notes for a lecture she had missed. When he came to pick them up before the first exam, Anastasia told him that she thought his notes were very good. It was not much – a small, unexpected compliment – but the softness of her voice was understood by Lev as a signal of acceptance by Anastasia, the gatekeeper of Sveta's family. 'I took it as a lawful pass into their home,' recalled Lev. 'I began to visit them more frequently, without feeling shy.' After their exams, in the long, hot summer of 1936, Lev would come for Sveta every evening and take her to Sokolniki Park to teach her how to ride a bicycle.

For Lev acceptance by Sveta's family was always an important part of their relationship. He had no immediate family of his own. Lev was born in Moscow on 21 January 1917 – days before the cataclysm of the February Revolution changed the world for ever. His mother, Valentina Alekseevna, the daughter of a minor provincial official, had been brought up by two aunts in Moscow following the loss of both her parents at an early age. She was a teacher in one of the city's schools when she met Lev's father, Gleb Fedorovich Mishchenko, a graduate of the Physics Faculty of Moscow University who was then studying at the Railway Institute to become an engineer. Mishchenko was a Ukrainian name. Gleb's father, Fedor, had been a prominent figure in the nationalist Ukrainian intelligentsia, a professor of philology at Kiev University and a translator of ancient Greek texts into Russian. After the October Revolution, Lev's parents moved to a small Siberian town in the Tobolsk region called Beryozovo, which Gleb had got to know from surveying expeditions as a railway engineer. A place of exile since the eighteenth century, Beryozovo was far away from the Bolshevik regime and in a relatively wealthy agricultural area, so it seemed a good location to sit out the Civil War (1917–21), which brought terror and economic ruin to Moscow. The family lived with Valentina's aunt in a rented room in the house of a large peasant family. Gleb found a job as a schoolteacher and meteorologist, Valentina worked as a teacher too, and Lev was brought up by her aunt, Lydia Konstantinovna, whom he called his 'grandmother'. She told him fairy tales and taught him the Lord's Prayer, which he remembered all his life.

The Bolsheviks arrived in Beryozovo in the autumn of 1919. They began arresting 'bourgeois' hostages deemed to have collaborated with the Whites, the counter-revolutionary forces that had occupied the region during the Civil War. One day they took Lev's parents. Lev, four, went with his grandmother to see them in the local jail. Gleb had been placed in a large cell with nine other prisoners. Lev was allowed to go into the cell and sit with his father while the guard stood with his rifle by the door. 'Is that uncle a hunter?' Lev asked his father, who replied: 'The uncle is protecting us.' Lev and his grandmother found his mother in an isolation cell. He went to see her twice. On the last occasion she gave him a bowl of sour cream and sugar which she had bought with her prisoner's allowance to make his visit memorable.

Not long afterwards, Lev was taken to the hospital, where his mother was dying. She had been shot in the chest, probably by a prison guard. Lev was in the doorway of the ward when a nurse passed him with a strange red and palpitating object in her hands. Frightened by the sight, Lev refused to go into the ward when his grandmother told him to say goodbye, but from the doorway he watched her go up to the bed and kiss his mother on the head.

The funeral took place in the town's main church. Lev went with his grandmother. Sitting on a stool in front of the open coffin, he was too low down to look inside and see his mother's face. But behind the coffin he could see the painted faces of the colourful iconostasis, and in the candlelight he recognized the icon of the Mother of God directly above the coffin's head. He remembers thinking that the face of the Mother of God looked like his own mother's. Lev's father, released from prison for the funeral and accompanied by a guard, appeared by his side. 'He's come to say goodbye,' Lev heard a woman say. After standing by the coffin for a while, Lev's father was led away. Lev later visited his mother's grave in the cemetery outside the church. The mound of freshly dug earth was black against the snow and on top of it somebody had placed a wooden cross.

A few days later, Lev's grandmother took him to a second funeral in the same church. This time there were ten coffins lined up in a row in front of the iconostasis, each containing a murdered victim of the Bolsheviks. One of them was Lev's father. The prisoners in his cell must have all been shot at the same time. Where they were buried is unknown.

In the dry summer of 1921, when famine swept through rural Russia, Lev went back to Moscow with his grandmother. The Bolsheviks had temporarily called a halt to their class war against the 'bourgeoisie', and for the remnants of Moscow's middle class it was once again possible to make a living. Lev's grandmother had worked for twenty years as a midwife in Lefortovo, a district of small traders and merchants, and she and Lev now moved there to live with a distant relative. For a year they occupied the corner of a room – a bed and cot behind a curtain – while she did odd nursing jobs. In

1922 Lev was taken in by his 'Aunt Katya' (Valentina's sister), who lived with her second husband in a communal apartment on Granovsky Street, a stone's throw from the Kremlin. He stayed there until 1924, when he moved to the apartment of his mother's aunt, Elizaveta Konstantinovna, a former headteacher at a girls' high school, who lived on Malaia Nikitskaia Street. 'Almost every day, Aunt Katya came to visit us,' recalled Lev, 'so I grew up in a sphere of constant female influence and care.'

The love of these three women – none of whom had children of their own – could not have made up for the loss of his mother. Yet it produced in Lev a deep respect, even reverence, for women in general. This maternal love was supplemented by the moral and material support of three of his parents' closest friends, who all sent money to his grandmother on a regular basis: Lev's godmother, a doctor in Erevan, the Armenian capital; Sergei Rzhevkin ('Uncle Seryozha'), a professor of acoustics at Moscow University; and Nikita Mel'nikov ('Uncle Nikita'), a veteran Menshevik,* linguist, engineer and schoolteacher, whom Lev called a 'second father'.

Lev went to a mixed-sex school in a former girls' gymnasium in Bolshaia Nikitskaia Street (single-sex schools had been abolished in Soviet Russia in 1918). Housed in a classical nineteenth-century mansion with two wings, the school still retained much of its intelligentsia ethos when Lev started there. Many of its staff had been teaching in the school before 1917. Lev's German teacher was its former head; the teacher of the infants was the cousin of a famous Ukrainian composer; and his Russian teacher was related to the writer Mikhail Bulgakov. But in the early 1930s, when Lev was a teenager, the school shifted to a polytechnic curriculum with an engineering focus linked to Moscow's factories. Industrial technicians would lecture at the school with practical instruction and experiments to prepare the children for apprenticeships in the factories.

Sveta's school in Vuzovsky Lane was not far from Lev's. What would they have made of one another if they had met then? They

---

* The Mensheviks were a Marxist party opposed to the Bolshevik dictatorship.

came from very different backgrounds – Lev from the old world of the Moscow middle class, where the Orthodox values of his grandmother had influenced his upbringing, Sveta from the more progressive world of the technical intelligentsia. Yet they shared many basic values and interests. Both were mature for their age, serious, clever, independent in their thinking, with open and inquiring intellects shaped more by their own experience than by propaganda or social convention. That independence was to stand them in good stead. In a letter of 1949 Sveta would recall what she was like at the age of eleven – at a time when the campaign against religion was at its height in Soviet schools:

> It seems to me that I was more grown up than the other children at my school . . . Back then I was very worried about the issue of God and religion. Our neighbours were believers and Yara used to tease their children. But I stepped in, standing up for freedom of religion. And I solved the issue I had with God for myself – I concluded that without him we still can't understand eternity or creation, and that since I couldn't see the point of him it meant that he's not needed (not by me, that is, though he might be needed by others who do believe in Him).

Both Lev and Sveta were by this age the conscientious products of an ethos of hard work and responsibility. In Sveta's case it was the outcome of her upbringing in the Ivanov family, where she was put in charge of her younger sister, Tanya, as well as many household chores, while in Lev's it was neccessitated by his economic circumstances. He had to work his way through school to supplement his grandmother's small pension.

In 1932, when he was just fifteen, Lev had a night job working on the construction of the first Moscow Metro line, between Gorky Park and Sokolniki. He measured out the route across the streets and joined the digging teams made up largely of peasant migrants, who in those years were flooding into Moscow to avoid being forced by the Bolsheviks into collective farms. Lev became aware of collectivization's terrible consequences the following summer. As a cleaner on a rabbit-breeding farm he got to know a fellow worker who had arrived from the famine-stricken Ukrainian countryside. The man wrote sad poems about 'abandoned village homes, people dying, and corpses piled behind a fence'. Lev was struck by the poems' emotional power but was put off by their sensational subject matter. 'Why do you make up such terrifying scenes?' he asked the worker, who told him: 'I haven't made them up. That is my village. There is a famine there and no one has the strength to bury those who've died.' Lev was shocked. He had never really questioned Soviet power and its policies before. He had joined the Komomsol, the Communist Youth League, and believed in the Party. But the worker's words sowed a seed of doubt. Later that year Lev went to a collective farm near Moscow on a school trip organized by his biology teacher, a Bolshevik enthusiast, who used one of the abandoned houses on the farm to put on a play about the 'struggle against vermin'. The house had belonged to the village priest and his family, who had evidently been evicted during the collectivization of the village. Inside the house were the burnt remains of the priest's books, including a bible in ancient Greek, a language read by Lev's grandfather but no longer needed under the Soviet regime.

When he started at the university, in 1935, Lev was living with his grandmother (then aged eighty-two) in a communal apartment on Leningrad Prospekt in north-west Moscow. His eccentric 'Aunt Olga'* also had a room in the apartment and lived there with her husband. Lev and his grandmother occupied a narrow, dark room: there was a single bed for him on one side and a trunk on the other, on which his grandmother made herself a makeshift bed by resting her feet on a stool. By the window at the end was a desk and, above Lev's bed, a small glass-fronted cabinet where he kept his collection of chemical appliances and his books, mainly maths and physics

---

* She was actually the illegitimate daughter of Boris Tolmachev, the first husband of Aunt Katya.

books, though also classic works of Russian literature. When Sveta came to visit she would sit with Lev on his bed and talk. Aunt Olga kept a beady eye on their movements in the apartment's corridor. A strict church-goer, she disapproved of Sveta's visiting and made it clear to Lev that she thought something was going on. Lev would say, 'She's just my friend from the university,' but Olga would stand in the hallway by his door anyway, listening for 'evidence'.

The one place that Lev and Sveta could really be free was in the countryside. Every summer Sveta's family rented a large dacha in Boriskovo, a settlement on the Istra River 70 kilometres north-west of Moscow. Lev would visit them, sometimes cycling from Moscow, sometimes travelling by train to Manikhino, an hour's walk from Boriskovo. Lev and Sveta would spend the whole day in the woods, lying by the river, reading poetry, until darkness came and he had to leave to catch the last train or start on his long cycle back.

On 31 July 1936 Lev came out by train. There was a heatwave and he was sweaty after walking from Manikhino, so before turning up at Sveta's house he decided to have a quick swim in the river near Boriskovo. Stripping down to his underpants, Lev dived in. A poor swimmer, he stuck close to the riverbank, but the strong current carried him away and he began to go under. Catching sight of a fisherman on the riverbank, Lev cried out to him, 'I'm drowning, help!' The fisherman did nothing. Lev went under again and came up a second time, once more calling for help – before going under yet again. Too weak to save himself, Lev thought how stupid it would be to die so near to Sveta's house. Then he lost consciousness. When he came to he was sitting on the bank beside the fisherman. Struggling to catch his breath, Lev caught only a glimpse of his rescuer, who was standing behind him and telling off the fisherman for not jumping in to help him. The man left before he had a chance to find out who he was and thank him properly. Lev spent the day with Sveta and her family. In the evening Sveta and her sister, Tanya, walked Lev to the edge of the village to say goodbye and see him off to the station. In the village Lev recognized the man who had saved him; he was with an elderly gentleman and two women. Lev thanked the man and asked his name. The older man replied: 'I am Professor Sintsov and this is my son-in-law, the engineer Bespalov, and these women are our wives.' Thanking them again, Lev went on to the station, where the public radio system was playing Saint-Saens' *Introduction and Rondo Capriccioso*. Listening to David Oistrakh play the beautiful violin solo, he was overcome by a powerful sense of being alive. Everything around him seemed more intense and vivid than before. He had been saved! He loved Svetlana! And through the music he now felt that joy.

Life was full of precarious joys. In 1935 Stalin had announced that life was 'getting better and gayer'. There were more consumer goods to buy, vodka, caviar, more dance-halls and jolly films to keep the people laughing and sustain their belief in the bright and radiant future that would come when Communism had been built. Meanwhile arrest lists were being prepared by Stalin's political police, the NKVD.

At least 1.3 million 'enemies of the people' were arrested – and more than half of them were later shot – during the Great Terror of 1937–8. No one ever knew what this calculated policy of mass murder was about – whether it was Stalin's paranoiac killing of potential enemies, a war on 'social aliens' or, most likely, a preventive cull of 'unreliables' in the event of war at a time of heightened international tension. The terror reverberated throughout society. Every area of life was affected. Neighbours, colleagues, friends and relatives could be labelled 'spies' or 'Fascists' overnight.

The world of Soviet physics was particularly vulnerable, partly because of its practical importance for the military and partly because it was divided ideologically. The Physics Faculty at Moscow University was the centre of this split. On one side stood a group of brilliant young researchers such as Yury Rumer and Boris Gessen, who championed the physics of Einstein, Bohr and Heisenberg; on the other, an older group of teachers who denounced the theories of relativity and quantum mechanics as 'idealist' and incompatible with dialectical materialism, the 'scientific' foundation of Marxism-Leninism. The ideological split was reinforced politically,

the materialists accusing the followers of quantum mechanics of being 'unpatriotic' (i.e., potential 'spies') because they had been influenced by Western science and had travelled abroad. In August 1936, just before the start of Lev and Sveta's second year, Gessen was arrested on charges of belonging to a 'counter-revolutionary terrorist organization'; he was later shot. In 1937 Rumer was expelled from the university.

Students were expected to be vigilant. In the Komsomol they confronted fellow students whose relatives had been arrested, demanding their expulsion from the university if they failed to renounce those family members. Many were expelled from other faculties, but fewer from Physics, where there was a strong esprit de corps among the students. It was this communal spirit that saved Lev himself, following an incident in 1937.

Military training was compulsory for full-time students at Moscow University. They were obliged to join a reserve corps of officers that could be mobilized in time of war. In the Physics Faculty the students were prepared for command posts in the infantry. The training involved two summer camps near Vladimir. At the first camp, in July 1937, the main instructor had been recently promoted to the junior command of a regiment made up of non-university students. He enjoyed drilling the elite physicists by forcing them to run 200 metres, and then march an equal distance, repeated interminably. It was not in Lev's character to hold his tongue when he saw petty bullying by people in positions of authority. Eventually he exclaimed, 'We have idiots for commanders!' The remark was audible enough to be heard by the instructor, who reported Lev to the authorities. The matter went up to the Divisional Party Committee of the Moscow Military District, which expelled Lev from the Komsomol 'for counter-revolutionary Trotskyist agitation against the commanding ranks of the Workers-Peasants' Red Army'. The following September Lev returned to university. Fearing that there might be further consequences, he appealed to the Divisional Party Committee to revoke his expulsion from the Komsomol. He was called to the headquarters of the Military District, where the committee heard his version of events, repealed the expulsion and instead gave him a 'strict reprimand' (*strogii vygovor*) for 'un-Komsomol-like behaviour'. It was a lucky escape. Later Lev would discover that it was largely due to the courageousness of three friends from the Physics Faculty who had written an appeal to the committee and signed it with their own names. Lev was so well liked by the other students in his faculty that they were willing to take such risks in his defence. Their declaration of solidarity could easily have backfired and led to their own arrests, since a group of three was already enough to qualify as an 'organization' in the eyes of the authorities.

The episode brought Lev and Sveta together. Their relationship had cooled in the middle of their second year at university and they had not seen each other for a while. It was Sveta who had made the break, suddenly withdrawing from their circle of friends. Lev did not understand. Since the previous summer they had seen each other every day, and she had even asked him for his photograph. Many of their friends were getting married, and Lev must have hoped that they might soon be married too. Then, without warning, she had moved away. Looking back on this period, Sveta put it down to her 'black moods' – the depression from which she would suffer for much of her life. 'How many times,' she would later write to Lev, 'have I reproached myself for spoiling things between us and – God knows why – tormenting you.'

Once she saw he was in trouble, Sveta came back to Lev. For the next three years they were inseparable. Lev would meet her on her way to the university in the mornings. He would wait for her at the end of lectures, take her back to Leningrad Prospekt and cook for her or go with her to the theatre or the cinema and then walk her home. Poetry was an important element of their relationship. They would read together, send each other poems and introduce each other to new poetry. Akhmatova and Blok were Sveta's favourite poets, but she also liked a poem by Elena Ryvina which she recited to Lev one evening on a walk through Moscow's streets. The poem spoke of fleeting happiness:

The glow of your cigarette
first fades, then burns afresh.
We pass along Rossi's* street,
where the lamps burn in vain.

Our rare encounter is shorter
than a step, a moment, a breath.
Why, dear architect,
is your street so short?

Sometimes, if Lev had to work late and could not see Sveta, he would pass by her house at night. On one of these occasions he left this note:

Svetka! I came to see how you are and to remind you that tomorrow, which is the 29th, we would like to see you at our place. I decided not to just barge into your apartment because it's late – half past eleven – and two of your windows are already dark, and two others are dim; I might wake everybody and give them a fright. Come and see me if you're free. Greetings to your mother and to Tanya.

In January 1940, Lev's grandmother died. Sveta was by Lev's side when they buried her in the Vagankovskoe cemetery.

The next month, Lev became a technical assistant at the Lebedev Physics Institute (known in Russian as FIAN). He was still in his final year at university but he had been recommended by Naum Grigorov, a friend from the Physics Faculty who had just started at FIAN, and this was a chance to break into research. Named for Pyotr Lebedev, the Russian physicist who first measured the pressure exerted by light reflected or absorbed by a material body, FIAN was one of the world's leading centres of atomic physics, and in the vanguard of its research programme was the cosmic rays project, in

---

* Carlo Rossi, the Italian architect who built many buildings and ensembles in St Petersburg in the reign of Nicholas I (1825–55).

which Lev became involved. Because he was studying during the day, Lev often worked the evening shift in the laboratory. Sveta would stay late in the library and then walk the 3 kilometres from the Physics Faculty to FIAN on Miussky Square. She would sit on a bench in the courtyard and wait for Lev, who usually appeared at about eight o'clock to walk her home. On one occasion Lev was so

Lev on Mount Elbrus, 1940.

exhausted that he fell asleep in the laboratory and did not wake up until after nine. Sveta was still waiting for him on the bench. She laughed when he told her he had been asleep.

That summer Lev went on a scientific expedition to Mount Elbrus in the Caucasus. High up in the mountains FIAN had a research base where Lev's group could study the effects of cosmic rays closer to their entry point into the earth's atmosphere. Lev spent three months at the base. 'We climbed up and reached our shelter quite quickly yesterday,' he wrote to Sveta. 'I feel splendid, I've got a ferocious appetite and a host of unforgettable memories.'

Sveta, meanwhile, was on summer leave from the university and was working at the Lenin Library, which was then being built in a modern concrete block near the Kremlin. 'Do you know, there's a lovely square in front of the library now, and it's all been planted with shrubs and flowers,' she wrote to Lev. 'Who's going to give me a bouquet of flowers for my birthday?' Lev was due to return from the Caucasus on 1 September, ten days before Sveta would turn twenty-three, and he always gave her flowers on her birthday. Until then she would have to make do with letters.

3 August 1940

Levenka,

My first impulse when I got home today was to ask if any letters had come for me, but they all began to tease me about you, so I pretended that it was Irina's postcard I was waiting for. But then Tanya said – with so much emphasis – that there was no postcard from Irina that I knew there must be something from you, so I followed her from room to room (all the doors are still left open in our house so you can go round the rooms for as long as you like)* begging her to give me your letter. Mama eventually took pity on me and gave it to me.

Sveta wrote to Lev with her news. She had been offered a permanent job at the library.

They won't find anybody better than me. I know the layout of the rooms, the cupboards in the rooms and the shelves . . . I know the periodicals inside out, and with my knowledge of the Roman alphabet I can work out the month, year, name and price of any journal

* The rooms were laid out like this:

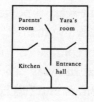

in any language except Chinese . . . I have a head on my shoulders which may not be filled with the finest brains but is not filled with cotton wool either . . . Vera Ivanovna said that I'd be group manager in a year. If I wanted to stay at the library my whole life, this would be a good start to a career. But I don't want to spend my whole life there so . . . on Monday I'll say no.

Lev, don't worry about my health. I told you that either my mood depends on my condition or my condition depends on my mood. At any rate, you'll be able to see from my handwriting that I'm calm and untroubled, which means that I'm not in any pain or ill with anything. Mama says that I have tuberculosis. Her reason – my weight loss. But you know, with the kind of diet I've had it would be difficult to expect anything else, and I don't have any other symptoms.

In June 1941, Lev was due to go with his FIAN colleagues on a second expedition to Mount Elbrus. On the morning of Sunday 22 June his team was at the institute, finishing its preparations for the trip. Lev was in excellent spirits. He had just passed his final exams at the university and had been told by the faculty committee assigning jobs to graduates that he was one of just four students chosen to go on to FIAN for research on the cosmic rays project. Sveta had returned to the Physics Faculty, now a year behind, and they were happy together. Lev and his colleagues were packing the final pieces of equipment when the leader of their team came in. 'We're not going anywhere,' he said. 'Have you heard the radio?' At noon that day there had been a special broadcast by Vyacheslav Molotov, the Soviet foreign minister. 'Today, at 4 o'clock in the morning,' he had announced in a trembling voice, 'German forces descended on our country, attacked our frontiers in many places, and bombed our cities – Zhitomir, Kiev, Sevastopol, Kaunas and others.'

The German assault was so powerful and swift that it took the Soviet forces completely by surprise. Stalin had ignored intelligence reports of German preparations for an invasion, and the Soviet defences were in total disarray. They were easily overrun by the nineteen Panzer divisions and fifteen motorized infantry divisions that spearheaded the German invasion force. The Soviet air fleet lost over 1,200 aircraft during the first morning of the war, most of them destroyed by German bombers while they were parked on the ground. Within hours German special forces had advanced deep into Soviet territory and were cutting telephone lines and seizing bridges in preparation for the main attack.

That afternoon the Komsomol of Moscow University called a meeting in the auditorium and unanimously passed a resolution to mobilize the entire student body for the defence of the country. Everybody wanted to sign up. By the end of June, more than a thousand students and teachers had enrolled in the 8th (Krasnopresnenskaia) Volunteer Artillery Division, including around fifty from the Physics Faculty. Lev was among them. 'There's a fair amount of confusion here at the moment,' he wrote to Sveta's family from the assembly point on 6 July, 'so I can't tell you anything definite about our prospects. The only thing that's more or less known is that we are going to be living and studying here until we're called up for military service by the draft board.'

Lev was shaken by the outbreak of the war. For the first few days he could not conceive what it would mean. His research, his life in Moscow, his relationship with Sveta – everything was now up in the air. 'We are at war,' he kept saying to himself in disbelief.

Although he had volunteered to go to the front, Lev was worried about taking a position of responsibility. Stalin's terror had left the Soviet forces desperately short of officers, and novices like Lev were being called upon to lead men into battle. After only two years of military training, Lev had reached the rank of junior lieutenant, which meant he could be placed in charge of a platoon of thirty men, but he had no confidence in his tactical abilities. In the end he was given the command of a smaller supply unit made up of six students and two older men from the university. He felt happier about being in a unit of students, inexperienced people like himself, who, he thought, would be more forgiving than a soldier from the working class if he made a mistake.

Lev's unit was to move supplies from the Moscow stores to a

communications battalion at the front. There were two truck-drivers, two labourers, a cook, an accountant and a storeman under his command. As they drove towards the front, they saw scenes of chaos that belied the propaganda of the Soviet press. In Moscow it had been reported that the Soviet forces were repelling the Germans, but Lev found them retreating in chaos: the woods were full of soldiers and civilians, and the roads blocked with refugees fleeing east towards Moscow. Untold thousands had been killed. By 13 July Lev had reached the forests near Smolensk, a city under siege by the Germans.

> Svetik, we're living in the woods and I'm doing household chores . . . I'm supposed to feed everybody here, including the most high-ranking officials, who don't so much ask for what they want to eat as just shout for it . . . There are some advantages – relative freedom during trips to stores. Sveta, there's absolutely nowhere for you to write to me – nobody here knows where we'll be from one day to the next. The only way of getting news from you is to call in and see you at home during one of our trips. I don't know when that will be.

On these journeys between Moscow and the front Lev would carry letters for the soldiers and their relatives. He would also see Sveta and her family in between his visits to the army warehouses. There was one trip in July when he missed Sveta but saw her parents, who 'fed and watered' him, as he put it in a letter that he left for her; and a second visit in early September, when Sveta had returned to the university. For Lev the connection to her family was almost as important as the time he spent with her; it made him feel that he belonged. On one of these last trips Sveta's father gave him a piece of paper on which he had written the addresses of four close friends and relatives in various cities of the Soviet Union: these were the people to whom he should turn for help in locating Sveta and her family if they were evacuated from Moscow while he was absent at the front. Although he had never said as much, the paper made it clear that Sveta's father saw Lev as a son.

There was one last visit to Moscow. Lev knew it was his final chance to see Sveta, because they had warned him at the supply depot that nothing more would be issued to his battalion. Telling his drivers that he would meet them later, Lev ran from the depot to Sveta's house. She was unlikely to be there – it was the middle of the day – but he went in any case to say goodbye to somebody. Perhaps Sveta's mother or her sister would be home. Lev knocked on the door. It was opened by Sveta's mother, Anastasia. Stepping inside the entrance corridor, Lev explained that he was in Moscow only for a few more hours and that he would then be leaving for the front. He wanted to say thank you and goodbye. Lev did not know whether he should kiss her; she had never shown much warmth or emotion. He made a bow and moved towards the door. But Anastasia stopped him. 'Wait,' she said. 'Let me kiss you.' She embraced Lev. He kissed her hand and left.

2

Lev set off from Moscow with three trucks carrying supplies for the Krasnopresnenskaia Volunteer Division. When he had left the division a few days before, it had been occupying a position near Viazma, between Moscow and Smolensk, but it was gone when he returned. The front had collapsed as the 3rd and 4th Panzer Groups attacked from the north and south with tanks, guns and aircraft in a rapid pincer movement encircling Viazma. Taken by surprise, the panic-stricken Soviet forces had dispersed into the forests. Without a radio, Lev had no idea how to find his division. No one knew what was going on. There was chaos everywhere.

Lev's men drove towards Viazma, hoping to locate their divisional command. It was getting dark and they had no map. One of the trucks broke down so Lev went on by foot. Walking on the road through the thick forest, he could hear guns ahead of him. In the early hours of the morning he came to a village where the remnants of his division were engaged in a fierce gunfight with three German tanks, which had moved out of the forest and on to the road. Soon the Soviet artillerymen abandoned their batteries (they had no ammunition left) and the tanks moved slowly forward, entering the village and firing with machine-guns at the houses. Lev, in a field between the tanks and the village, lay down and waited for the tanks to pass by him before running off into the forest. It was only then that he smelt the eau de Cologne: a bullet had smashed the bottle he had been carrying in his coat pocket to use as an antiseptic for minor wounds, but luckily he was unharmed.

Lev walked deep into the woods. Hundreds of Soviet soldiers who had lost their units were all moving in the same direction in between the trees. Lev did not know where he was going. All he had with him was a pistol, a spade and his knapsack. During the day he buried himself in the ground to hide from the Germans. By night he walked towards the east, or what he thought was east, hoping to rejoin the Soviet forces.

At the end of the third night, on 3 October, Lev found himself on the edge of a village occupied by the Germans. He decided to head away from it as soon as darkness fell. Retreating into the forest, he dug himself into a ditch, covered himself with branches and went to sleep. A sharp pain under his knee woke him. Peering through the branches, he could see in front of him what he thought was a single German soldier with a rifle. Impulsively, Lev got out his pistol and took a shot at him. As soon as he had fired he received a heavy blow on the back of the head. There were two soldiers: the one who hit him on the head had been poking him with his bayonet to see if he was alive or dead. Lev was disarmed and taken back to the village.

He was not alone. Tens of thousands of Soviet troops were trapped in the German encirclement of Viazma during the first week of October. Lev was brought to a transit camp, Dulag (*Durchgangslager*)-127, on the outskirts of Smolensk, where several thousand prisoners were crammed into the unheated buildings of a former Soviet military store. There Lev, like the others, was given just 200 grams of bread a day. Hundreds died from cold and hunger or from typhus, which spread in epidemic proportions from November, but he survived.

In early December Lev was part of a contingent of twenty prisoners transferred from Dulag-127 to a special prison near Katyn. The contingent was made up of educated people from Moscow, mostly scientists and engineers. They were imprisoned in a building that Lev thought must have been a school or possibly a clinic before the war. There were four large rooms on either side of a corridor – with up to forty prisoners in each – and a large room at the end where the guards lived. The prisoners were well treated: they were given meat, soup, bread; and their work duties were relatively light. At the end of the third week, Lev and his fellow Muscovites were joined by a small group of well-dressed Russians who were drinking vodka given to them by the guards. In a drunken moment one of them let slip that they had been trained as spies; they had just returned from behind the Soviet lines and were being rewarded for their work. A few days later they departed for Katyn.

Shortly afterwards, Lev and half a dozen other Muscovites were taken to the spy school in Katyn, where a Russian-speaking German captain proposed to turn them into spies and send them back to Moscow to gather information for the Germans. Only this, he said, would save them from almost certain death in Dulag-127, where they would be returned if they refused. Lev was determined not to work for the Nazis but he was afraid of saying so in front of the other prisoners lest he be accused of anti-German propaganda and given a worse punishment. So Lev said to the captain in German, a language he had learned at school and university: 'Ich kann diese Aufgabe nicht erfüllen [I cannot fulfil this task].' When the German asked why, he said: 'Das erkläre ich nachher [I will explain later].'

Taken by the captain to a separate room, Lev explained in Russian: 'I am an officer of the Russian army and cannot act against it, against my own comrades.' The captain said nothing. He sent Lev back to his holding cell. There Lev discovered that three other men had also refused to become spies. If Lev had spoken first, he might have been accused of encouraging their resistance.

The four refuseniks were put into the back of an open truck and driven down the highway towards Smolensk. A German guard sat with his back to the driver and played with his rifle all the way. The truck turned into the forest. Lev thought he was going to be shot. 'The truck was going very fast down a narrow forest road,' he recalled. 'I assumed they must be taking us to an execution ground. I thought: how will I conduct myself in front of the firing squad? Will I have sufficient self-control? Wouldn't it be better to kill myself? I could jump out of the truck, hopefully to smash into a tree, and if the soldier opened fire it would be even better.' Lev prepared to jump. But then he noticed through the trees a shed with a neat stack of metal barrels: they were stopping for petrol; they were not going to be shot. As the captain had threatened, the four men were taken back to Dulag-127. There they tried to stick together to protect themselves against recriminations by the other Soviet prisoners, who must have known that they had returned from the spy school.

A few weeks later, in February 1942, Lev was sent with a group of other officers to a POW camp near the Prussian spa town of Fürstenberg-am-Oder, 80 kilometres north-east of Berlin. Because they had come from the disease-ridden Dulag-127, they were held in quarantine in a wooden barrack, where six men died from typhus in the first few days. Otherwise the officers were treated well and conditions in the camp were generally good. Lev was interrogated by the commandant and two other officers. They wanted to know why he spoke German so well, and whether he was Jewish, because they claimed his comrades said he was. They were persuaded that he wasn't Jewish only when he recited the Lord's Prayer.

In April Lev was sent with a smaller group of Soviet officers to a 'training camp' (*Ausbildungslager*) on the outskirts of Berlin. The 'training' meant that they were lectured on Nazi ideology and the new German order for Europe – ideas they were supposed to pass on to their fellow Soviet POWs in other concentration camps. For six weeks they were made to listen to the lectures of their teachers, mostly pre-war Russian émigrés, who read closely from a script. Then, in May, the officers were dispersed to various camps. Lev was put into a work brigade attached to the Kopp and Gaberland munitions factory in Oschatz.

Oschatz was the centre of a vast industrial zone of POW labour camps (*Stammlager*, or *Stalag* for short) between Leipzig and Dresden. Lev was put to work as a translator for a military inspection unit before being transferred in August to one of the work brigades attached to the HASAG (Hugo Schneider Aktiengesellschaft) Factory in Leipzig. HASAG was a large complex of metal factories producing ammunition for the German army and air force. By the summer of 1942, it had several Stalags holding around 15,000 prisoners of various nationalities (Jews, Poles, Russians, Croats, Czechs, Hungarians, French) in two sectors, one named 'Russian' and the other 'French'. Lev was housed in a boxroom on his own in the French sector and assigned as a translator to a Czech called Eduard Hladik, whose role was to sort out conflicts among the POWs. Although his mother was German, Hladik considered himself Czech. After the German annexation of Czechoslovakia in 1938, he had been conscripted by the Germans as a guard in the HASAG camps. Hladik felt sorry for the POWs and could not see the sense of treating them so badly when they were working for a German victory. As a prisoner, Lev had to walk in the gutter when he accompanied Hladik through the streets of Leipzig; if passers-by insulted Lev, Hladik would defend him by saying: 'It's easy to curse a man who cannot answer back.'

Hladik saw in Lev someone he could trust. There was something in Lev's character that attracted people in positions of responsibility to him – his sincerity perhaps or maybe just the fact that he could speak with them in their language. The Czech befriended Lev and gave him German newspapers, forbidden to the POWs because they gave accurate reports on the military situation and – unlike the propaganda sheets they were given in the Stalags – described the Slavs as 'sub-humans'. On the pretext that he was taking Lev for disinfection outside the barracks zone, Hladik even took Lev to visit one of his friends, a socialist called Eric Rödel, who spoke a little Russian and had a radio on which he listened to Soviet broadcasts. It was a highly risky adventure because Rödel lived above a former SA (*Sturmabteilung*) officer. Rödel and his family received Lev as an honoured guest. 'The table was set with all sorts of luxuries,' Lev recalled. 'We talked for a long time . . . and then Eric turned the radio on, and I listened to the "Latest News" from Moscow with military bulletins from the Soviet Bureau of Information. The content of the programmes I can't remember now but – funnily enough – one phrase has stuck in my mind: "In Georgia the tea harvest has been collected." '

Eventually, the Germans became suspicious of Hladik. One of the other guards denounced him, accusing him of anti-German activity, and Hladik was summoned for interrogation. He was sent to the Norwegian front. Not wanting to continue working as a translator, Lev applied to the camp authorities to be relieved of his duties on the grounds that his German was not good enough to rule out the possibility of inaccuracies: 'I also said that I was incapable of doing propaganda work, because I lacked the skills of persuasion – I was just a scientist.' In November, he was sent back to the work brigade at the Kopp and Gaberland factory in Oschatz.

Conditions in Oschatz declined dramatically that winter. Working hours were increased, and there were beatings by the guards to squeeze more labour out of the exhausted prisoners. In the early months of 1943 there was an influx of new POWs into the work brigade. Most of them came from Ukraine, a territory occupied by the Germans where terror and the famine of the 1930s had alienated much of the population from the Soviet system. Their arrival was soon followed by a softening of the camp regime, part of a German effort to recruit the POWs into the Russian Liberation Army, the anti-Soviet force being organized by Andrei Vlasov. Vlasov was a former general in the Red Army who had been captured by the Germans in July 1942 and had then persuaded the Nazis to appoint him to head a liberation movement that would aim to sweep away the Communist regime. There was a group of Vlasovite recruiters in Oschatz, mostly pre-war Russian émigrés who 'wore some sort of undefined but non-German uniform', Lev recalled, and a smaller number of former Soviet junior officers. The officers had joined the Russian Liberation Army, or so it seemed to Lev, mainly to escape the terrible conditions of the POW labour camps, where Soviet prisoners were 'treated much more harshly and had fewer rights or means of self-defence than the prisoners of any other country'.

Lev was summoned several times and pressured by the Germans and the Vlasovite recruiters to join their army as an officer. On each occasion he refused. The Germans became suspicious. They began to question Lev about his activities as a translator at the HASAG camp. During a cigarette break in one of these interrogations the translator for the Germans took Lev aside in the corridor and warned him that they thought he was to blame for the Vlasovites' recruitment failure: Lev's was the only work-team in the camp that had failed to volunteer a single soldier for the Vlasovite army; and as the only Soviet officer in his work-team, suspicion fell on him.

Lev realized he needed to escape. Three other prisoners in his brigade had the same idea. They decided to make their attempt in June, when the crops would have grown just enough to supply them with food along their route to Poland, 150 kilometres away, where they reckoned that the population would be sympathetic and feed them. Their plan was to join up with the Soviet partisans in Belarus and eventually return to the Soviet Union. To prepare, they saved up dried bread and sugar; Lev made a compass and copied out a map lent to him by one of the German guards, who liked to talk to Lev about his family and tell him where he had been on his weekends. They even managed to obtain medicines: Lev deliberately cut his finger to get sent to the camp infirmary, where the doctor was a Russian POW. Without asking any questions, the doctor agreed to Lev's request for antiseptic, aspirin and bandages.

The prisoners made their escape on the night of 22 June 1943, the second anniversary of the German invasion. Climbing out of a barrack window they had partially dismantled previously, they scaled the wall of the courtyard and cut through the barbed-wire fence at the top with two sharpened metal strips Lev had made in the workshop. Jumping down into the field outside the camp, they ran through the darkness into the woods. The four men headed north, assuming that the Germans would first search to the east. They walked by night and hid by day. Their map was very rudimentary – the original from which it had been copied had come from a primary school textbook – so they had to make their way by the road signs. When they reached the Elbe River they followed it eastwards, Lev being too afraid to swim across, and, after skirting south of Dresden, kept on moving east towards Poland. 'We had dry rations,' Lev recalled, 'but soon we decided to keep these in reserve and feed ourselves by stealing from the outdoor cellars of the peasants' houses . . . It seemed wrong to me at first, but then I agreed.' After three weeks on the road they were captured near Görlitz, on the

Polish border, by a couple of German soldiers. Noticing the soldiers cycling towards them on the road and assuming that they would be carrying guns, they threw themselves into a ditch, but the soldiers used their lights to find them there. 'It was a stupid end to our journey,' recalled Lev. 'The soldiers were not even armed.'

Lev could not have known what he would have found if he had ever reached Poland or if he had crossed the German lines and somehow made it to Moscow. He had no real idea about the situation in the Soviet Union or about his chances of ever seeing Sveta and her family again. From the moment of his initial capture there had been no way of receiving reliable information from Russia. In Oschatz the prisoners were given pens and writing paper by the Germans, but they could write only to people in the German-occupied territories. Lev once wrote to Prague, to the wife of a fellow prisoner who had disappeared, asking if she had had news of her husband. The wife replied to Lev and even sent a parcel but told him that he was more likely to know about the fate of her husband than she was.

Sveta was equally in the dark. She had received no news of Lev since he had disappeared in the last days of September 1941. Everything had been uncertain then. No one knew if Moscow would survive. The city had been heavily bombed by German planes since July. Sirens sounded several times a day. The power stations had been hit, so there was no heat or lighting in apartment blocks, although burning buildings lit the sky at night. People lived in shelters underground. Untold thousands died. On 1 October Stalin ordered the evacuation of the government to Kuibyshev on the Volga. Panic spread as the bombing of the city became more intense. Huge queues formed at all the shops: there was fighting over food and widespread looting, which mass arrests did little to control. Reports of the German breakthrough at Viazma finally reached Moscow on 16 October. At railway stations there were ugly scenes as crowds struggled to board trains for the east. People cursed the Communists when they found out that the factory and Party bosses had already left. Workers fought with the police. Families packed up their belongings and moved out of the city by whatever means they could afford. Taxi drivers were charging 20,000 roubles to go from Moscow to Kazan.

Moscow University was evacuated in October. Sveta travelled with her family. Among the students on the train was Andrei Sakharov, the future Nobel laureate, who had joined the faculty a year after Lev and Sveta but was now in the same year she was after the break in her studies. Their first stop was Murom, an old provincial town 300 kilometres east of Moscow, where Sakharov stayed with a mother and daughter who turned the wartime chaos to their advantage: by day the daughter stole sugar from the shop where she worked and by night her mother entertained 'a succession of soldiers'. The town was overrun by wounded troops waiting for evacuation to the east. Many lay on stretchers in the station hall, even in the snow by the railway tracks. Women from the nearby villages came to the station to sell them food and tobacco. Others came to look for sons and husbands, asking the wounded soldiers who might know of their whereabouts or putting letters in their hands in case someone should come upon them in a hospital.

From Murom the students continued east to the Urals and then headed south across the frozen Kazakh steppe to Ashkhabad, the dusty capital of the Turkmen Republic, not far from the Soviet border with Iran. Here the Physics Faculty would recommence its work. The journey took a month. The railway cars, each with a stove and bunks for forty people, 'became separate communities', recalled Sakharov, 'with their own leaders, their talkative and silent types, their panic-mongers, go-getters, big-eaters, the slothful and the hard-working'. Sveta must have been among the quiet and industrious ones. In Ashkhabad, where lectures started in December, she needed to work hard to make up for the break in her studies before the war. She went to classes in chemistry and oscillation physics, a difficult theoretical subject for which there was no practical training, so she was buried in the library for long hours. She also worked as a dishwasher in a cafeteria to support herself and her parents. For much of that winter and the following spring Sveta suffered from malaria, a common disease in Central Asia at that time. 'It wore me out so much that it was even difficult for me to drink,' she would later write. Fighting off fever, exhausted and becoming 'quite jaundiced', she struggled to keep going. But she managed.

After her graduation, Sveta was assigned to the People's Commissariat of Munitions. But with her father's help she was transferred to the Scientific-Research Institute for the Resin Industry, then operating out of a chemical compound in Khromnik, near Sverdlovsk, where she worked in the 'physical and mechanical testing laboratory' as an industrial physicist from August 1942. The institute was working eleven-hour days, and Sveta found it had to find her place at first. As she later wrote,

I was in a strange, unfamiliar laboratory and didn't know what I should begin with, where I should perch myself. I was afraid of the machinery and didn't know anything about rubber. So I escaped to the library . . . where I spent half the day reading Russian articles and reports and the other half huffing and puffing over the English language. I joined an English-language club, although I hadn't studied it in Ashkhabad. Generally it was quite an uplifting period. After the fumes of Ashkhabad, the Afghan winds, the sand blown in from the desert as fine as dust, and the leaves that fell in August without any hint of a golden autumn, the Urals seemed like paradise on Earth – pines, birches, mushrooms, rain. I exchanged letters with the whole world . . . I received between 2 and 3 letters every day and I knew I'd be home soon.

The institute was already preparing to return to Moscow, where the German threat had passed after a Soviet counter-offensive during 1942. The Red Army was in urgent need of the institute's research expertise to boost the tyre industry. By January 1943, Sveta was back home. Much of the city Lev and Sveta had known as students had been destroyed or damaged by the war. Many of its buildings remained unheated, the lights were dimmed and often failed completely because of power cuts, sewers leaked, and the food shops were empty. 'It was very hard for everyone in '43 and '44,' Sveta later wrote. 'We were all cold and hungry and living in the dark.'

Sveta's parents had returned to Moscow with her younger sister, Tanya, in April 1942. They had aged noticeably. Anastasia was often ill with brucellosis, a painful stomach disease that left her exhausted, and at the age of sixty Aleksandr was also showing signs of slowing down. Sveta found them in a nervous state when she returned. There was plenty for them to worry about: they had not heard from Sveta's brother since he had left for the front (he had been captured by the Germans and imprisoned in a concentration camp on the Baltic Sea island of Usedom), while Tanya had been assigned as a student 'volunteer' to Stalingrad in September 1942.* Meanwhile they had Aleksandr's younger brother Innokenty ('Uncle Kesha') and his wife on their hands. The Leningrad couple had been in Moscow since the beginning of the war and would not return home until the siege of Leningrad was lifted in 1943.

From the family apartment on Kazarmennyi Pereulok Sveta had a long tram journey to the institute on the Highway of Enthusiasts, where she worked in an old laboratory on the third floor with windows looking out on to the factory smokestacks of east Moscow. The place depressed her. Many times she thought that she should run away or take a research post elsewhere, maybe even in another town, but she was 'afraid of losing touch with Lev'. Moscow was the only point of contact they had, the place where she hoped he would return.

Although she had not had any news of Lev, she had good reason to believe that he was still alive: in 1942 the NKVD had visited his Aunt Olga to ask if she had heard from him. They went through

---

* Tanya had been pressured into volunteering by the military authorities, which desperately needed nurses for the front. To refuse would have put not only Tanya but her family in danger of arrest.

the belongings in his room, which was still being kept for him as someone who was serving in the army. Some of the spies who had been recruited by the Germans in Katyn had evidently entered Soviet territory and been arrested. Under interrogation one of them must have mentioned Lev and recounted the incident when he had spoken with the captain in German. The NKVD was probably working on the assumption that Lev was spying for the Germans in Moscow. After Sveta returned to the capital they summoned her for questioning practically every evening. They knew that he would come to see her if he was already in the Soviet capital. Claiming that Lev was a spy, they tried to force her to cooperate with them in catching him, threatening serious consequences if she refused. It was frightening to be summoned to the Lubianka, the NKVD headquarters; the memory of the Great Terror was fresh in people's minds. But Sveta was not easily frightened. To defend her relationship with Lev, she was ready to defy the Soviet authorities. Eventually she got fed up with their badgering and, in a moment of characteristic bravery and headstrong foolishness, told the NKVD men to leave her alone. 'Getting a bit angry because these same relatives [code for NKVD men] kept pestering me, I said that I was not yet your wife and that the matter would only be cleared up when we met – not just for an hour but for good,' she later wrote to Lev.

Sveta was meanwhile writing to the military authorities asking them for any information about Lev. News came shortly after her twenty-sixth birthday, 10 September 1943. 'All my relatives had come for my birthday,' she later wrote to Lev.

My father's brother from Moscow and his family were there, his brother from Leningrad with his wife, my cousin Nina with her husband and their baby, and so on. Everything was great and everybody was having a good time. We drank to the health of all those who weren't with us, of course. And then everything happened all at once – a message came about the death of Tanya (Uncle Kesha intercepted it and didn't show it to Mama for a long time).

Tanya had died of appendicitis in a military hospital in Stalingrad. Later more bad news arrived: Aunt Olga had been notified officially by the military authorities that Lev 'had gone missing' at the front. It was the kind of terrible announcement that struck fear into millions of families still recovering from the terror of the thirties, when so many people 'disappeared'. Those three words ('propal bez vesti') could mean almost anything: capture by the enemy (equivalent to treason under Soviet wartime law); worse, 'desertion' to the other side (a crime by 'enemies of the people'); or death without the body's being found. So many soldiers had been killed that Sveta must have feared the worst for Lev.

It was so painful and distressing that I decided I would never celebrate my birthday again unless you were with me. You know, the existence of a dwarf-star is desperately painful, for it has lost the whole of its electron shell and preserved only its nucleus; in my breast it was just as empty and just as painful, as though my heart had withdrawn into itself. It was impossible to breathe. For months on end I couldn't talk to anyone, couldn't go anywhere, couldn't read. As soon as I returned home I would turn my face to the wall. And however much I cried in the evening, during the night or in the mornings the pain never eased.

Struggling to cope with her longing and anxiety for Lev, Sveta poured her feelings into poetry. Two of her poems have survived. The first is dated 'Winter 1943', not long after 'that terrible day' in September when she heard that Lev had disappeared. 'It was what I needed to say to someone,' she would later write of the poem, which expressed her sadness about losing him:

> For a long time I stood on the threshold,
> But then I made my mind up and set off.
> In the road, amidst the crushed stone,
> I found a symbol of peace and happiness –
> A horse-shoe to hang over your door.

I brought it to share my joy with you,
But the war threw us on to separate paths
Along which we have to wander on our own.
Through what forests have you forced your way?
Which stones bear the traces of your blood?
Here instead it is the spectre of a lonely old age
That hangs over me ever more menacingly.
What keepsake will you leave me with?
The bitter impression of a long-vanished dream?
Or will you let another woman touch your heart
With passionate words in September?
Can I not trust you? Who else if not you –
A youth who is a stranger to me now?
My circle of friends grows ever smaller,
Which of you will reach the end with me?

The second poem was shorter. It too was written that winter. Even more than in the first, there is a note of hopelessness in Sveta's prayers for Lev's return:

It's not for me to judge you, who are under fire,
With whom death has already spoken more than once,
But to pray night and day,
That the Mother of God keep you safe for me.

I would pray for this. But the A B C of prayers
Was not taught to me by my mother and father
And I couldn't find a path to God
In joy, sorrow, or in grief.

But Lev was not dead. He was a prisoner in one of Hitler's harshest labour camps, a Stalag in Leipzig where Soviet POWs were marched under heavy guard to work every day at the Pittler ammunition factory. Lev had been sent there from the Mühlberg prison camp, where he had been held after being caught on the Polish

41

border in July 1943. The regime in the Pittler factory was punitive. Armed guards stood by all the doors in the workshops, and the German foreman carried a revolver, ready for use at any time. During the winter of 1943–4 the work regime became increasingly severe as the German army's need for ammunition grew with every new defeat on the Eastern Front. Productivity declined as the POWs became more exhausted and undisciplined, prompting the Gestapo to investigate and root out potential leaders of a slave rebellion.

Lev was interrogated several times. One day in May 1944 he was arrested in a group of twenty-six prisoners and sent to the main prison in Leipzig, where they were all kept in a single cell with a toilet pan and basin by the door. They were held there for a month without being let out of the cell. On 4 July, they were transferred to Buchenwald, the notorious concentration camp near Weimar, where they were held in a quarantine barracks consisting of long, unbroken rows of sleeping shelves four tiers high. There were prisoners of every nationality – French, Poles, Russians, Yugoslavs – each one designated by a different badge on his striped uniform. Lev, like the other Russians, had a badge marked with an 'R' on a red triangle.

After a month in quarantine, the Pittler group was dispersed to various auxiliary camps linked to Buchenwald. Lev was sent to a work brigade in the Mansfeld munitions factory near Leipzig and then to Buchenwald-Wansleben, an abandoned salt mine at Wansleben-am-See, where he arrived in the first week of September. The mine was being converted into a series of workshops, 400 metres underground and safe from Allied bombing, where bits of engines for Luftwaffe planes were to be assembled by the prisoners. 'For each of these rooms dozens of inmates died,' recalled a French prisoner involved in digging tunnels into the salt mine. Lev worked there for the next seven months. The regime was hard, with eleven-hour shifts and harsh discipline. 'For any misdemeanour or falling-off in the work-rate prisoners were given twenty lashes with a rubber club, which, though excruciatingly painful, left no marks on the body.'*

Even worse horrors were to come. In April 1945, as the Western Allies pushed through Germany, Buchenwald-Wansleben was evacuated by the Nazis. At 5 p.m. on 12 April the long march began. The surviving prisoners left the camp in a convoy flanked by open trucks, each holding six armed SS guards. They walked north-east through open fields on the road towards Dessau, though Lev and those around him did not know where they were going at the time. It seemed to them that they were marching back to Buchenwald (in the opposite direction) and therefore heading for the crematorium, where tens of thousands of the Nazis' murdered victims had been burnt before. Dressed in rags, the prisoners began to fall along the way from exhaustion – only to be shot by the Germans. 'I remember that at 8 p.m. we suddenly heard much shooting coming from the end of the column,' recalled the French prisoner. 'The SS were shooting all the inmates who were too weak to walk or who did not walk fast enough.'

Lev decided to escape. He told Aleksei Andreev, a prisoner from the Pittler group who was marching by his side. 'Ahead of us on the road to the right I saw something burning,' Lev recalled. 'A bombed-out German lorry was on fire. I said that if we made a run for the bushes beyond the lorry as we marched past it, the guards in the truck behind us would not notice because of the flames. Andreev agreed.' Running from the column, the two men threw themselves into the bushes behind the burning lorry and waited for the rest of the long column to pass them. Then they crawled into the field, dug themselves into the furrows and covered themselves with dry grass to conceal their striped prison uniforms. Lev was terrified. As he

---

* A punishment technique designed to circumvent the Geneva Convention, which supposedly protected POWs (though not Soviet ones) in German concentration camps.

recalled, it was the only time during the entire war when he was overwhelmed by fear.

At night they moved into the woods. They could hear the firing of guns ahead of them. Much of the forest had already been destroyed by shelling. Through the trees they saw a shining light – a searchlight – and by the side of it they could make out the shadows of some tanks. They were US tanks.

From the darkness an American appeared. He shouted at them: 'Throw away your weapons!'

Lev shouted back in English: 'We have no weapons.'

'Who are you?'

'We are Russian officers. We escaped from a concentration camp.'

Lev explained that they had been in Buchenwald and now wanted to return to the Soviet Union. The American took them to a nearby house. There were five tank drivers staying there. They let the Russians sleep on the floor with them and shared their rations, which Lev, who had been living on bread and gruel, thought 'tasted as good as restaurant food'. The next morning they sent Lev and Aleksei on their way to Eisleben, the town they had just liberated, where they said they would be helped by the US military authorities.

At Eisleben the two were interrogated by a US army major, who spoke to Lev in German. When he found out that Lev was a nuclear physicist, he tried to persuade him to emigrate to America and could not understand when Lev refused. 'But why not?' he said. 'In Russia you have Communism, and with Communism there is no democracy.' In a manner that revealed how far his political opinions had altered in the war, Lev replied that there was 'no Communism in Russia', but there was 'just enough freedom for a clever person to get by'. Lev tried not to engage in a political discussion. The real reason for his refusal to seek a better life in America had nothing to do with politics: he just wanted to go home, to the people whom he loved. All he had in the world was there – 'Svetlana and her family, Aunt Olga and Aunt Katya, Uncle Nikita: these were the people who were dear to me,' Lev recalled. He had no idea if Sveta was alive or whether she had waited for him all this time, but he knew he had to follow where his heart led him. 'Even if I had only one small chance that she was alive, how could I turn my back on that and go to America?'

The major gave the Russians a coupon for a hotel being used for liberated POWs. The Burgermeister of the town, a former Communist, took them to a shop to buy them coats and hats and order them new suits, all paid for by the town. For the next two months Lev and Aleksei remained in Eisleben. The window of their room looked on to the house where Martin Luther had been born. These months were like a holiday. There were four free canteens for the US military personnel and liberated POWs in Eisleben, and after years of hunger in the concentration camps, Lev made sure to eat each meal in every one of them. 'We ate twelve times a day!' The only problem he now had was getting to each of the four canteens in time for the meals. This frenzy of feeding lasted several days, until Lev had overcome the fear of starvation.

In early May there were victory parades by the US troops in Eisleben. Shortly afterwards, Red Army representatives arrived to organize the repatriation of the Soviet troops. On the day of the Soviets' departure, 8 June, the Americans arranged an open-top lorry decorated with the Soviet and US flags and a banner reading 'Happy Return!' The lorry took the men to the Elbe River at Torgau, where they crossed over into the Soviet zone of occupation. They were not received with the same friendly attitude by the Soviet authorities, who treated them as prisoners. The returning soldiers were divided into groups of thirty by the Soviet armed guards and taken off by lorry to Weimar, where they were put into a prison block attached to the headquarters of the 8th Guards Army. The prison was administered by a special NKVD unit known as SMERSH (an acronym for 'Death to Spies!'), whose task it was to root out Soviet soldiers who had collaborated with the Germans.

Lev's good luck had run out. He was imprisoned in a room with eight other men. They were stripped and body-searched; all their personal belongings were taken from them. Lev lost the possession he had cherished most and carried in his pocket for the past four years: the list of addresses he had been given by Sveta's father. It was just a scrap of paper but the only thing that connected him to her.

During the day the men were forced to sit on the floor but forbidden to lie down or sleep. The interrogations took place at night. Each man in turn was taken out for questioning and brought back after three or four hours to snatch some sleep before the morning wake-up call. Lev was interrogated for more than a month. The SMERSH investigators accused him of spying for the Germans. Their only evidence came from one of his fellow POWs, who had heard Lev speaking German with the captain in Katyn. Lev confirmed that this was true. He admitted that he had worked as a translator but insisted he had never been a spy: he had worked against the Germans, not for them. Naively, Lev clung to the belief that if he told the truth he would be allowed to go home. He believed in Soviet justice. Wasn't that what he had been fighting for? What happened next shattered his belief. After several nights, the interrogating officers threatened to shoot him unless he agreed to sign a confession. Lev refused. They beat him. 'I was not afraid of dying,' he recalled, 'but sometimes I despaired because I was afraid that the people I had loved might believe I was guilty.'

Lev thought frequently about Sveta. It seemed to him unlikely that he would survive to be with her. On 10 September 1945, Sveta's twenty-eighth birthday, at this low point of his interrogation, Lev gave up hope of seeing her again and resigned himself to 'say good-bye' to her.

In the early morning hours after a particularly stressful night of questioning, Lev was sleeping lightly when he had a vivid dream. This is how he described it:

I was dozing after an interrogation, it was almost daybreak, and I had a dream. It was very clear, very well-defined, as if I were walking somewhere on my own. I turned around and saw Sveta behind me. She was dressed in white, kneeling on the ground beside a little girl who was also dressed in white, and she was adjusting something on her dress. It was very bright, very clear, and then I awoke.

Having failed to get Lev to sign a confession, his interrogators tricked him into signing an admission of his guilt. Assuring him that he would be found innocent by the military tribunal, they got him to sign a protocol of the interrogation which Lev did not fully check. He trusted the interrogating officer who showed him the document and took his word that it said what he claimed. The officer read the statement out to him, and Lev simply signed it. That signature, ten small letters at the bottom of the page, would change the course of his life. Perhaps he was tired. Perhaps naive. What Lev did not know was that the officer had read only parts of the protocol to him – not the bits admitting to the treason charges – which Lev then signed. It was only at the trial that he realized his mistake.

On 19 November 1945, a three-man military tribunal of the 8th Guards Army in Weimar sentenced Lev to death for treason against the motherland, under article 58-1(b) of the Criminal Code reserved for Soviet servicemen. The sentence was immediately commuted to ten years in a corrective labour camp of the Gulag – a concession often made by Soviet judges in the interest of a system built on slave labour. The trial had lasted all of twenty minutes.

In December, Lev was transferred to a military prison in Frankfurt an der Oder. He was then sent back in a convoy under guard to the Soviet Union, where he began the three-month journey north to the Pechora labour camp.

3

The convoy travelled slowly north by train from Minsk to Vologda, Kotlas and Pechora, deep in the forests near the Arctic Circle, where Lev was to serve his long sentence. Cattle trucks were used for the prison train. A double tier of bunks made of wooden planks lined each wagon on either side of the sliding doors. In the middle of each truck was a 'toilet' in the form of a wide-open pipe protruding from the floor and letting out on to the tracks. The wagons had been built for twenty cows or a dozen horses, but sixty prisoners were crammed into each. 'Politicals' like Lev – mostly soldiers who had been caught up in the German zone of occupation – were mixed in with common criminals. Organized and violent, the criminals quickly took possession of the small iron heaters. Lev and the other prisoners, all of whom had been arrested in their summer clothes, huddled together, trying to derive warmth from one another's bodies in the unheated corners of the draughty carriages.

The prisoners were fed 200 grams of bread a day and salted fish, but they were given almost no water. Many of them became ill or even died from thirst. The dead and dying were thrown out of the carriages. No one understood why the guards deprived them of water. There were lots of Gulag rules about the proper care of prisoners on a convoy, and it made no sense to let them die if they had economic value as slave labourers. The most likely explanation is that the guards simply could not be bothered to lug heavy water buckets to the carriages. But there may also have been an element of cruelty whose rationale was linked to the guards' own system of profiting from hierarchy and control. The guards employed the criminals to beat the politicals and steal from them in exchange for better rations and water. They told the criminals that they were 'our people' who were being only 'temporarily detained', whereas the politicals were 'enemies of the people' who deserved to be beaten. Lev was shocked by the criminals' brutality. He thought they were 'no longer human beings but a new biological phenomenon, cynical and cruel to the point of sadism'. The guards were little better. They would come into the carriages once or twice a day to carry out a 'search'. Ordering the politicals to one side, they would beat them with whatever came to hand – iron bars, hammers, mallets, wooden planks and sticks – to show the criminals how it was done. In one search Lev was badly hurt in the kidneys and, in another, bashed so hard about his head that one of his eardrums burst.

Beyond Kotlas the train slowed to a jogging pace, and every now and then it stopped to eject another dead or dying prisoner. The track had been poorly built by Gulag prisoners and did not allow for faster speeds without risk of accidents. All along the line there had once been labour camps filled with prisoners to build the railway. Looking through the tiny windows of the cattle truck from his corner of the upper bunk, Lev could see their physical remains: barbed-wire fences and watch-towers between the pine trees. At Mikun', Ira-Iol' and Kamenka, the prisoners were taken off the train and marched under convoy to a 'sanitary point', where they were made to strip in the freezing cold and pass through disinfecting showers. Those with swollen legs or cracked and flaking skin around the hips, the first signs of pellagra (a disease caused by vitamin deficiency), were not allowed back on the train. Perhaps they were taken to a hospital. Perhaps they were shot.

After travelling for three months, Lev's convoy arrived in Pechora in March 1946. It was not yet spring. The dark Arctic winter lasted nine months this far north. The river was still frozen and there was snow on the ground. The prisoners were exhausted from their long journey. Even Lev, a strong man who had grown accustomed to the deprivations of the German concentration camps, was thin and weak. Many of the prisoners were so frail, some no more than skin and bones, that they were barely able to climb down from the carriages on to the track.

The prisoners were taken to the transit camp, the point of arrival in the labour camp, an area near the railway station fenced by barbed wire, with three barracks for the prisoners, an isolation block (for punishments), an infirmary with a cemetery, and a small working yard. The men were showered, head-shaved and de-liced, and then sorted into groups – the sick (mainly from pellagra and scurvy) going straight into the infirmary and the rest assigned to various labour tasks and installations according to their physical condition. Lev was selected for the wood-combine (*Lesokombinat*), the main industrial zone of Pechora, where timbers floated down the river from smaller labour camps or colonies in the forests further north were hauled up from the riverbank and turned into furniture and housing for the Gulag settlements on the railway line between Kotlas and the important mining area of Vorkuta.

The railway was the be all and end all of Pechora, the key to the Gulag's colonization and economic exploitation of the North. In the nineteenth century, the region had been forest thinly populated by the Komi tribes. The discovery of enormous coal, oil and mineral deposits in the Pechora and Vorkuta basins in 1929–30 had transformed the North into an area of supreme industrial and strategic importance for the Soviet Union. Hitherto the country's major fuel supplies had come from the Donbass and the Caucasus in the south-east. But these areas were vulnerable in military and political terms (in 1918–20, the newly born Soviet Republic had lost them to the Whites and their Western allies in the Russian Civil War). Opening up the immense coal reserves of Vorkuta would not only help the country to industrialize but guarantee its fuel supply in the event of another foreign invasion: the remote Arctic region was practically unassailable.

For a while the Soviets toyed with the idea of using the rivers to transport coal from Vorkuta, but the route was long and indirect and the Pechora and Ust-Usa rivers remained frozen for nine months of the year. Then, in 1934, they committed to the building of a railway connecting Leningrad to Kotlas, Ukhta, Pechora and Vorkuta (see map on p. 288). By 1939, labour camps and smaller Gulag colonies had been set up along the entire length of the projected line. According to the census of that year, there were 131,930 prisoners (18,647 of them women) in these labour camps and colonies. All the work was done by hand – the cutting of the trees, the levelling of the land, the laying of the tracks – and went on around the clock. During the long hours of darkness, which in winter numbered more than twenty, the building sites were lit by bonfires made of scrapwood collected by prisoners too weak to work on the railway. In the three months of summer it was light all day and night.

The German invasion added urgency to the construction of the railway line. By the end of 1941, the Germans had occupied most of the Donbass, which produced 55 per cent of the Soviet Union's coal, and in 1942 they steadily advanced into the Caucasus, threatening the country's oil supplies. Finishing the railway to Vorkuta became a top priority, a matter of the country's survival, and immense pressure was put on Gulag bosses to complete the line in record time. By 1942, 157,000 prisoners were working without break on the railway, sleeping in unheated tents or out in the open in freezing temperatures, all of them exhausted and hundreds dying every day from cold, hunger and disease. To speed up the completion of the line they put the rails directly on the ground without stabilizing stones or sand, went round lakes and swamps rather than carry out the necessary land reclamation, and even laid tracks on the ice (bridges could be built later). The line had so many dangerous curves and slopes that trains often crashed, leading to arrests for 'sabotage'. The crucial bridge across the Pechora River – between Pechora and Kozhva – was built in such a hurry (with temporary wooden girders instead of steel and iron) that the first trains to cross it in 1942 could not go faster than 5 kilometres an hour without serious risk of falling off from the vibrations. Nonetheless, coal from Vorkuta could at last get through to Soviet towns and industries – 200,000 tons of it a month by 1945.

Pechora developed as the main industrial hub of the region. Its location at the intersection between the railway and the Pechora River placed it at the centre of the Gulag's wood-processing, railway-servicing and shipbuilding industries. Established as a Gulag settlement in 1937, Pechora was a small ramshackle town of about 10,000 prisoners and free citizens by the time Lev arrived in 1946 (see map on p. 289). Near the railway station was a shanty-town of crooked narrow lanes and squalid dugouts known as 'Shanghai' because of its 'Asiatic' appearance and the Chinese immigrants who had settled there. The main part of Pechora was between the station and the wood-combine, the industrial zone behind barbed wire, which occupied the riverbank. From the transit camp, Lev would have marched down the long main avenue, Soviet Street, in a convoy flanked by guards with dogs towards the wood-combine, whose main entrance was at the end of 8 March Street (named for International Women's Day). Soviet Street was a wide dirt track with wooden boards for a pavement. There were no street lights, only the searchlights of the watch-towers around the prison zones; practically no cars or motorcycles, only horses, which the camp bosses used to get around; no stone buildings, only wooden houses, half-buried in the ground for better insulation against the Arctic winds; no inside toilets (except in the house of the commandant of the labour camp); and no running water in anybody's house, only wells, sheltered in small pavilions to keep the water from freezing during the long winter, when temperatures regularly dropped to minus 45 degrees centigrade. There were hardly any shops and only one small post office (which sold vodka) in the Shanghai area.

Passing through the gates of the wood-combine, Lev entered the industrial zone, his prison for the next ten years (see map on pp. 290–91). It was a large rectangular area the size of a village, 52 hectares, surrounded by a high barbed-wire fence and watch-towers with searchlights. Inside were about fifty buildings, mainly 'temporary wooden structures' that seemed to have been built without any planning and 'randomly positioned' in the zone. There were various workshops, a drying unit, wood-stores, saw-mills, stables, canteens, barracks, a club-house for the guards and free workers, a settlement of single-storey houses sunk into the ground, a wash-house, a fire station with a horse and cart and a light railway with a loading area. Ahead of him, towards the river, Lev could see the red-brick chimney of the power station towering above the camp.

The men of Lev's convoy were counted in the railway's loading area, where the finished products of the wood-combine (units of furniture and pre-fab housing) were loaded on to trains. Then they marched into the barracks of the 2nd Colony, or work brigade (*kolonna*), which was located in a special prison sector with its own barbed-wire fence and guard-house inside the industrial zone.

There were ten barracks with about 800 prisoners in the 2nd Colony. All the barracks were the same: long single-storey wooden buildings with two rows of double-decker bunks holding two men at each level (in Gulag parlance they were known as *vagonki* because they were like the bunks in sleeping cars on passenger trains); in the passage-way between the rows of bunks were tables, benches, and wood-burning heaters. The 40-watt bulbs hanging from the ceiling gave off a dim yellow light. The mattresses and pillows were filled with wood shavings. Lev's barrack had the advantage of always being warm because the guards allowed the prisoners to bring in scraps of wood for the heaters. The barrack was not locked at night and prisoners were free to come and go (there was an outside toilet block), provided they did not approach the barbed wire (if they did they would be shot).

Lev took his place on the lower storey of a bunk by the window at one end of the barrack. It was the oldest barrack in the colony. One of his neighbours was a young 'political' from Lvov in western Ukraine, a small and slender man with an expressive face and lively eyes called Liubomir (or 'Liubka') Terletsky. He would become Lev's most precious friend, much loved for his fine intelligence, poetic temperament, wit and sensitivity. Terletsky had been at Pechora for six years and so could help Lev settle in. He had been arrested at the age of eighteen, in 1939, shortly after the Soviet invasion of Lvov. In his home the NKVD officers had found a map, a compass and a rucksack (Terletsky was a keen walker) and had taken these as evidence of espionage for the Germans. Beaten into a confession, he was sentenced to be shot. For two months he sat in a prison in Kiev waiting for his execution, before his sentence was commuted to ten years' hard labour in the camps. Terletsky almost died on the convoy to Pechora. He was put to work in a team collecting firewood and scraps from the riverbank and hauling them by cart 500 metres up the hill to the power station, where the wood was fed into the steam engines producing energy for the wood-combine. Terletsky could not handle the heavy work. The stokers at the power station, seeing that he was dying from exhaustion, took pity on him, allowing him to rest while they did his work for him. It was a lucky break: at the power station Terletsky was spotted by the head of the Electrical Group, Viktor Chikin, a prisoner himself, who was impressed by his intelligence and got him put into his team of electricians at the power plant.

In the bunk next to Lev's was Aleksei ('Lyosha') Anisimov, a fellow Muscovite and student of the Moscow Institute of Transport Engineers. He was a shy and quiet man, much liked by Lev, who described him as 'a wonderful fellow' in his letters to Sveta. Anisimov had been arrested in 1937 and given fifteen years for 'anti-Soviet activity'. The 2nd Colony was mostly made up of 'politicals' like Lev, Terletsky and Anisimov. Many (eighty-three to be precise) had been caught in the German zone of occupation and arrested as 'spies' or 'collaborators' on their return to the Soviet Union or else had been swept up in the mass arrests that accompanied the Soviet reinvasion of these territories in 1944–5.

The other colonies at the wood-combine were populated by different categories of prisoner. The 1st Colony (located in a separate sector outside the industrial zone) was made up of 'special exiles' (*spetspereselentsy*), workers sent by administrative order to the Gulag, of which there were about 500 in the camp in 1946. The 3rd Colony (by the river) was made up of criminals and other prisoners who had been singled out for punishment. 'It is next to us but much stricter,' Lev would write. 'Prisoners are sent there if they break the rules, and the next step is a penal convoy.' Conditions in the 3rd were 'appalling', according to a report by the camp administration looking into riots in the colony in 1947. The prisoners had no bedding, the basins were broken, and there were rats.

Lev was assigned to a general labour team, hauling wood from the riverbank to the wood-combine. The work meant dragging heavy timbers up a hill to the log-conveyor, where, with the help of capstans, winches and cables, they were hauled up to the saw-mill.

It was back-breaking work which involved standing in freezing water for hours at a time. In the summer, when it was light all night, the mosquitoes were unbearable. Before the prisoners went to work they would cover up their hands and faces with bits of cloth.

Like the rest of his team, Lev received the standard uniform: a cap with ear-flaps, a wadded pea-jacket, heavy cotton trousers, gloves and winter shoes made of the same material as the jackets. There was no fur or lining in the shoes and no way of drying them in the damp and airless barracks, so his feet were always wet.

The twelve-hour shifts started before dawn; prisoners received rations of 600 grams of bread a day if they fulfilled the quota, but only 400 grams if they did not. To fulfil his daily quota Lev had to haul a minimum of 60 cubic metres of timber (enough to fill a small garage) from the river to the wood-combine. If he exceeded his quota, he got 800 grams and, as a bonus, 'a rye-flour pie with a filling that had no particular taste or with no filling at all', as he recalled. Every morning the prisoners were given a bowl of thin porridge, a cup of tea, a lump of sugar weighing 15 grams (it was measured carefully) and a piece of herring; for lunch, they normally received a bowl of cabbage soup with a bit of meat or fish in it; and for dinner, another bowl of porridge with more tea. It was not enough to sustain someone in the hauling teams for long. Sickness and death-rates were very high. In 1945–6, more than one-third of the camp's 1,600 prisoners were ill in the infirmary, a compound made up of isolation barracks outside the main prison zone of the wood-combine, in which at that time there was only one doctor. According to a prisoner who was then working in a grave-digging team, they were burying a dozen prisoners every day in the cemetery behind the infirmary. The working conditions of the hauling teams were so inhumane that even some of the guards became uneasy. 'We don't seem to care if they live or not,' complained one at a meeting of the Party in the wood-combine. 'We let them stand in freezing water until they get ill, and then we let them die in the infirmary if they can't work any more.'

Hauling team at the wood-combine.

After three months in the hauling teams, Lev himself was close to exhaustion. He was broken psychologically. Terletsky later said that, when he first saw him, Lev 'looked like a peasant who had been run over by a tractor.' There was no trace left of the energetic boy who had dived into the Istra River ten years earlier.

Encouraged by Terletsky, Lev would go to the wood-drying unit to warm himself after his shift. There were no guarded convoys inside the industrial zone – prisoners were left to find their own way to their jobs – so if Lev was working on the log-conveyor or near the saw-mill he had some time at the end of every day to stop by at the drying unit on his way back to the barracks of the 2nd Colony, where the prisoners were counted in through the guard-house. It was on a visit to the drying unit that Lev was rescued from work that was likely to kill him.

The head of the research laboratory attached to the drying unit was Georgii Strelkov, a veteran Siberian Bolshevik of the Civil War and senior Soviet industrialist who had been the head of the Minusazoloto Gold-Mining Trust in Krasnoyarsk, part of the People's Commissariat of Heavy Industry, until his arrest in 1937. Concerned by reports of starving prisoners at the Kolyma gold mines in the far north-east of Siberia, he had sent two ships with food supplies which had been intercepted by the NKVD, emptied of all food and loaded up with new prisoners instead. The NKVD did not care how many people died and accused Strelkov of wasting food. He was charged with 'counter-revolutionary activity'. Sentenced to be shot, Strelkov was given a reprieve: twenty-five years without rights of correspondence in the Pechora labour camp. His expertise was so highly valued by the Gulag authorities in Pechora that they let him lead experimental work at the wood-combine, although, as a prisoner with a twenty-five-year sentence, he should have been engaged in heavy manual labour. They permitted Strelkov to live on his own in the laboratory, rather than in the barracks, because his presence was so frequently required to resolve some technical problem or other inside the industrial zone. He was even allowed to wear a suit instead of a uniform.

Strelkov was strict and firm but also kind. Thanks to his authority at the wood-combine, he had been able to save many prisoners from complete exhaustion in the hauling teams by getting them transferred to the drying unit or workshops – even though his interventions often brought him problems with the camp authorities. Strelkov was not afraid. He knew that he was needed by the Gulag bosses, and for years he had managed to work the system to his advantage. In 1942, the wood-combine had received orders from the Gulag administration to find a way of turning sawdust into a yeast-based feed for animals. Strelkov was in charge of the research. After eighteen months of experimental work, the head of the wood workshops, a prisoner called Boris Serov, took two jars of the promised feed to a big meeting of the Gulag bosses in Abez, the administrative centre of the Pechora camps, to mark the anniversary of the Revolution. The jars were received with a thunderous ovation from the delegates. On returning from Abez, Serov was told by one of Strelkov's assistants that the two jars had been filled with ordinary barley flour.

In 1946, the drying unit was in desperate need of new technicians with engineering expertise. The high-pressure steam heaters were not drying the timbers fast enough to maintain the necessary volume of supply for the workshops to meet their planned targets, and there was growing pressure from the Ministry of Internal Affairs, or MVD (which had taken over the running of the Gulag from the NKVD in March 1946), to improve their performance. Having learned that Lev was a scientist, Strelkov invited him to join the drying unit as a technician, putting him to work in the steam-room. Lev's job was to turn the timbers to allow the covered parts to dry. The room was kept at a minimum temperature of 70 degrees centigrade, so he had to go in with his hands and face covered and could not stay more than a few minutes at a time. It was hard physical labour but, compared with hauling timbers from the river, a 'paradise' for Lev.

For the first time since he had arrived in Pechora, Lev was able to keep his shoes and clothes dry. He was warm all day. He was not bothered by aggressive guards. Perhaps even more important for his morale, when he was not working in the steam-room, Lev could visit Strelkov in his laboratory. There Strelkov had organized a spacious living area, 30 metres square, in which he kept a cat ('Vasily Trifonych') and entertained his friends with lively conversation, cards and chess, music from a radio he had built, vodka he had brewed in the scientific flasks and precious vegetables he grew in window-boxes heated by wood-steamers he had specially adapted for the task. There were even flowers growing under heated glass – which so impressed the head of the wood-combine that he gave his imprimatur to Strelkov's newest fantasy of developing a flower farm.

Moving to the wood-drying unit gave Lev his first opportunity to write letters. That had not been possible before. When he had been working in the hauling teams, he would get back late to the barracks – he would be hungry, dirty, wet and cold, totally exhausted and in no state to write in the short time before lights went out following the evening meal. He had no paper or pen in any case. But

Strelkov and his cat in the laboratory. The picture on the wall is Ilya Repin's Volga Barge Haulers, *in Soviet times a symbol of Tsarist oppression.*

after working at the drying unit, Lev had time to write; he could get what he needed from Strelkov.

Lev had resolved that he would not write to Sveta or Olga. On Sveta's last birthday, he had despaired of seeing her again. The ten-year sentence and the convoy to Pechora must have reinforced his hopelessness. What was the point of writing to a woman he had not heard from for five years? She might be dead. She might have given up on him and married someone else. It might be awkward for her to receive a letter from a prisoner. The last thing he wanted was to put her into danger by contacting her. Lev had chosen not to inter-fere in Sveta's life. A victim perhaps of that sense of worthlessness that comes from years of being a prisoner, he felt he did not have the right to claim her love.

Then, for some reason, he changed his mind. Maybe the com-panionship of Strelkov and his friends lifted Lev's spirits. Maybe, as he would himself explain it later, he 'surrendered in a moment of weakness' to the desire to find out what was happening to her. Lev did not dare to write to Sveta directly, but wrote instead to Olga ('Olya') to ask after her:

2 June 1946

Dear Aunt Olya! You cannot have expected to get a letter like this. I don't even know if you're alive and well. So much has happened in the past five years. Forgive me for writing to you, but you were always dear to me – so I now ask your help. I wanted to write to Aunt Katya as well, but I cannot remember the number of her apartment.

I am in a correctional labour camp of the MVD, where I am serving a ten-year sentence. In 1945 I was convicted of treason against the motherland. How, what and why – that would be long and difficult to write in a letter . . .

Conditions here are good, if you don't count the northern climate. The only thing that's hard is that for five years I have not known anything about the people who were close to me, people I have always loved. If you answer me, write to me about Aunt Katya, Vera [Olga's sister-in-law], Mikh. Iv. [Olga's husband]; how is Nikita, how is S.'s family? Do not tell them anything about me but write to me what you know about them.

I want to think that you are fine. I wish you all the best with all my heart – you, Aunt Katya, Mikh. Iv. and everyone else. I've been thinking constantly about you all during these long years.

All the very best,
L. Mishchenko,

My address: Komi ASSR, station Pechora, Wood-combine, Postbox 274/11, L. G. Mishchenko.

Lev received a reply from Olga on 31 July. It was his first contact with anybody from the world he had left. The letter was upsetting: Olga told him about the deaths of many of his friends and relatives during the war, including Sveta's sister, Tanya. But she also wrote that Sveta was alive and well. The next day he wrote back to Olga:

No. 2   Pechora, 1.VIII.46

My dear Aunt Olga, yesterday, 31.VII.46, I received your first letter. The 31st has often been a joyful date for me.* How that letter stirred my emotions, how much happiness its warmth of feeling brought to me – I cannot find the words to express that. I wasn't counting on anything from you, I couldn't hope for a letter such as yours. I'm so happy that you are alive but sad to learn that you're unwell and lonely. There have been so many bitter losses in our lives . . . It was very painful to learn about Tanya. It is a blessing that all is well with the rest of S.'s family. I cannot tell you how happy I am that S. is alive, that her life is full and meaningful. From the bottom of my heart I wish her every happiness. I'm glad you're still in touch with her. Write to me about her, whatever you can find out. Which institute is she working in, and with whom? What is her specialization? Has she passed her doctorate? My feelings towards her remain the same, despite all the time and distance separating us.

I am writing this to *you* and not to her because I do not want to burden her. Let her live her life calmly, without my complicating it, without my overshadowing it with memories of the past and thoughts about my current existence.

By the start of 1946, Sveta had given up all expectation of seeing Lev again. Everybody else had returned from the war, so she must have assumed that he was dead or had gone missing for ever. For months, she 'could not sleep', she 'would not eat' and she 'drove her parents to despair'. She 'longed for even just a word' from Lev. It 'would have changed everything'. But as time passed she became more despondent and lost hope. And then she heard from Olga.

At once Sveta wrote to Lev

* Lev was saved from drowning in the Istra River on 31 July 1936.

12 July 1946   (1)

Levi, if I didn't know that actions should be judged by their motives and not by their results, I would reproach you for your silence.

You remember that September when you said you didn't want us to meet like that, whereas I was grateful for the week that was given to us? It's the same now, Lev: if it can't be otherwise, this way is better than nothing. We are both 29 years old, we first met 11 years ago, and we haven't seen each other for 5 years. It is terrible to spell out these figures, but time passes, Lev. And I know you will do all you can so that we can meet before another five years pass.

I'm becoming stubborn, Lev. How many times have I wanted to nestle in your arms but could only turn to the empty wall in front of me? I felt I couldn't breathe. Yet time would pass, and I would pull myself together. We will get through this, Lev.

I promised you I would finish university and I kept my promise. We graduated in the summer of 1942 (after the fourth year of courses) but were relocated for almost six months – from Moscow to Ashkhabad to Sverdlovsk . . .

Soon I will have been working in the physical and mechanical testing laboratory at 'Papa's' Institute (the Scientific-Research Institute for the Tyre Industry)* for four years (since my birthday in 1942). No matter how much I tried to avoid rubber, I still came back to it. Aren't you glad? My job is to come up with new and better testing methods (there are too many details to put in one letter, so I'll tell you about it bit by bit). My manager is very good but he's not really an administrator and the two of us together supervise 42 young women quite unsuccessfully. There's a new postgraduate course in our institute and the first candidate is – Svetlana Aleksandrovna! I passed my exams (in May and June) with flying colours, better than anyone at the university (mainly because of my background in sciences rather than because of my talents) . . . Are you happy, Levi?

---

* Formerly the Scientific-Research Institute for the Resin Industry.

I should be on holiday from 1 July, but our academic secretary is keeping me here until I hand in an article for the journal. I'm torturing and tormenting myself, trying to picture how I'll ever get it done (it's about experiments on the plasticity of rubber and rubber composites). Mama and Alika [Sveta's nephew] have already been at the dacha for a month – it's on the Istra again but a little bit closer to Moscow this time. Alika is already six. He knows how to read and is fascinated with capital letters. He's inherited all of Yara's skills and talents. He draws, sets up 'experiments', talks about the way words are spoken and written, and already knows a lot of poems. He is building a herbarium and collecting beetles, flies and caterpillars, and he sings songs – clearly taking after his aunt! His little head is as round as a button, he's blond with big black pupils but blue irises (also from his aunt). Yara came home last November. We hadn't heard anything of him for more than three years. At the moment he's still quite gaunt. Tanya was in the army (from May 1942) and died in hospital from appendicitis on 2 September 1943. I think about her, just as I think about you, all the time, but I can't talk about it. Mother and Father have got older, of course. Father is currently working at the Ministry of Rubber Industries, and Mother busies herself around the house – brucellosis is wearing her out . . .

Levi, write and let me know if I can send you any small parcels. If I can, then what do you need? Any fiction or physics books? The sooner this letter gets to you, the sooner I'll get a reply, so I'm finishing it now.

All the best, Levi.   Svet.

Lev received the letter when he went to get the post for his barrack after work on a Thursday evening, 8 August. He recognized her writing on the envelope. Opening the letter, he found a photograph of her inside. Lev read the letter over and over again that night. He did not go to bed but paced around outside, the white night of the Arctic giving him his reading light. The sun had been up for two whole hours when Lev began to write at half past five the next morning:

Pechora, 9.VIII.46   No. 1

Sveta, Svet, can you imagine what I'm feeling now? I can't put a name to it or measure the happiness I feel. The 8th has always been an important date in my life (you see, I've become a fatalist) – and now it has become a joyful date. I went to get the letters for our block and was not at all jealous of those who received letters, because I didn't expect anything for myself. I had got a letter from Aunt Olga on the 31st and didn't expect anything else until the start of September. And then suddenly – my surname! And, as if it were alive, your handwriting! For three years I had managed to keep safe a tiny scrap of paper with your handwriting – it was all I had of you – until it was confiscated in the full search at Buchenwald on 3.VII.44. I lived with the hope that you were still alive and that I'd see you again. But on your last birthday, which I celebrated at a difficult moment in the interrogation, I resigned myself to saying goodbye to you . . . I carried on denying myself any hope, not only of our ever meeting again but even of my ever hearing anything about you.

Sveta, if you could only imagine, understand, what an interrogation really is! It's not just a question of the physical sufferings – I never experienced those – but what it feels like in the soul! Did you know that there's something worse than death? It's mistrust. But I'm getting off the point. And so, anyway, I said goodbye to you. But I couldn't hold out without you. Eight months later, I wrote a letter to Aunt Olya – just on the off-chance, without much hope. And I asked her about you. And then on the anniversary of that foolish day on 31 July 1936 when I nearly drowned and had to be pulled out of the Istra on my way to see you in Boriskovo, I was saved again. I had never expected such an affectionate, warm-hearted and maternal letter; in fact I hadn't expected a letter at all . . . Aunt Olya wrote all about you! You – alive! And it turns out you even visit her, which means that you couldn't have decided to erase me from your memory. What more could I wish for? I had only wanted to find out about you, without interfering in your life. And then, suddenly, yesterday, or rather today, because although it's now 6 o'clock in the morning on 9 August, I still haven't gone to bed, so for me it is today – and anyway there is no night in the Arctic – suddenly a letter came. Not only the handwriting, not only the words written by you, but what words, what a letter! And a photograph as well. And it's all for me? For me? Svetka, Svetka, I'm not in a fit state to say more . . .

Let's move on to something else. You ask about a meeting . . . Svetka, it's almost impossible. 58-1(b) is a terrible figure.* I don't have any illusions about this. But I promise you I'll do everything I can to improve the sentence.

I'm so happy that you're taking control of your life at last, Sveta, that you're strong and in good spirits. It's good that you have a serious job, and that they value you. You have a fine mind, Sveta, you're so intelligent! Now, now, don't screw up your nose – it's praise from an unauthoritative source. Sveta, Sveta, you are so close to me – it feels as if the last five years never happened, although it's also distance that separates us now, 2,170 kilometres of it. And to me you look practically the same – an imperceptible something, hardly noticeable in the photograph, says your heart has aged a little, that is all . . .

You ask about books. I've missed books terribly over the years. It has been very difficult to get hold of any and therefore I've read shamefully few . . . Do you remember the Akhmatova and the Blok? I longed for Pushkin and your favourite, 'The Stone Guest' – I remember bits you recited to me once while we were walking, arm in arm, beneath the lights of the Tver Boulevard. *La Traviata* is another thing I cannot hear without emotion, if somebody is whistling it, or if I hear it on the radio . . .

Sveta, as you said, we'll get though this . . .

I need to stop now. I wish you all the best. Don't send anything except letters – letters – letters! . . .   Lev

---

* Lev was sentenced under Article 58-1(b) of the Criminal Code.

4

The Gulag had elaborate rules for the sending and receiving of letters. These rules altered over time, as circumstances changed, and were applied with varying degrees of strictness in each labour camp. How many letters a prisoner received depended on his sentence and on how well he met his production quotas.

In the wood-combine prisoners were officially allowed one, censored letter every month. This was better than in other camps, where the allowance was as few as four a year. In his letter to Aunt Olga on 1 August 1946, Lev told her that there were 'no restrictions' on how many letters or packages he could receive:

> Letters and printed matter [*banderoli*] get here in 2 to 3 weeks, but there have been cases of their getting here from Moscow in 7 or 8 days. They are not held up long by the censors . . . If you write, remember to number your letters in order, so that I can check if they have all arrived. There's no need to send me anything, except perhaps paper and pencils.

What Lev said was not entirely true. He often gave a reassuring picture of conditions in the camp. In fact, letters were delivered to the camp only two or three times a month, so a prisoner was likely to get several at a time. But this was still fairly good, and certainly much better than in the Gulag camps of the 1930s, when prisoners could go without a letter for several years. Censorship was relatively light – most of it by the wives of camp guards and other officials who often did not read through the letters properly but merely blacked out the odd harmless phrase to show that they were doing their job. But the prisoners did not know that and exercised self-censorship in their writings.

Nor was it so simple with parcels or printed-matter rolls. Sending them was a complex bureaucratic procedure that involved travelling to Mytishchi, or some other town outside Moscow, because parcels to the Gulag labour camps could not be sent from the Soviet capital, and standing for hours in long queues to have one's package checked and registered. Parcels were not accepted if they weighed more than 8 kilograms. When they arrived at the camp there was an equally complicated process for receiving them. At the wood-combine parcels were collected from an MVD office where the guard on duty unpacked all the items and often helped himself to what he wanted before giving the rest of the contents to the prisoner. Because food and money and warm clothes were nearly always taken by the guards, Lev discouraged friends and relatives from sending them, asking only for books, though here too vigilance was required, as foreign literature was likely to be confiscated, especially if it had been published before 1917. As Lev warned Sveta in his first letter:

> So if you or Aunt Olya are going to send me books, make sure they are cheap. The cheaper the edition and the more tattered the book the better, as then you won't have wasted so much money if they get lost. And if you send any foreign-language literature, make sure it's a Soviet edition and not from an antiquarian store, which may result in a misunderstanding with the censors and my not receiving it.

Lev's first letter had not arrived when Sveta wrote to him again, on 7 August: 'My dear Lev, I spend all day wondering if you've received the letter I sent on 12 July. Have you got it?' Lev had not (he got it the next day, on the 'important' 8th). Sveta received his first letter on the 23rd, shortly after she got home from the dacha. 'I too have become a fatalist,' she wrote to him that afternoon.

> When I was writing my first letter you were writing your second, but I sent my second when you were receiving my first, and I was writing my third when I received your first – and *La Traviata* was playing on the radio!

Lev wrote his second letter to Sveta on 11 August, wanting to make sure it got to her in time for her birthday on 10 September, and received her reply to his first letter that very day. 'It was a present for me,' he wrote to her that evening, 'although on this date all the presents ought to be for you.'

Their conversation had begun. But it was a halting and frustrating one. 'I got your letter of the 26th today,' Sveta wrote to Lev on 6 September,

> and your letters of the 8th and 11th before that, but I still haven't received your letter of the 21st. It's difficult to talk, Levi, when the interval between our letters adds up to months. By the time you get my thoughts, you might already be in a different mood.

The delays were not the only frustrations. Their awareness of censorship also put limitations on their conversation. They were not sure how clearly they could express themselves without getting into difficulties. Lev could only intimate as much when he wrote of 'defined boundaries' in his third letter:

> Sveta, you know that I'm never lazy when it comes to writing letters. And you'll believe me if I tell you that in my thoughts I'm talking with you for no less than 16 hours in every 24. And so you will understand that if I don't write to you often it's not for lack of wanting to but because I don't know how to write to you within defined boundaries.

Lev thought carefully about what to put in his letters and composed them in his head for days before actually writing them. Afraid that the other prisoners would use them for cigarette paper if he left them in the barracks, he carried unfinished letters in his pocket, so they were often creased and crumpled by the time he finished them.

Much of his meaning had to be read between the lines – with coded words for MVD officials ('uncles', 'relatives'), the Gulag system ('umbrella'), or bribe-money ('vitamin D': from the word for money, *den'gi*), and literary allusions (especially to the nineteenth-century satires of Nikolai Gogol and Mikhail Saltykov-Shchedrin) to convey messages about the absurdities of daily life within the camp. The names of friends and relatives were never written out but given as initials or concealed through nicknames.

Lev's initial fear was that Sveta might be endangered by receiving letters from a prisoner. In his first letter he had suggested writing to a poste restante. 'There's no need for any kind of poste restante,' Sveta had replied, 'we know all our neighbours.' Later she would change her mind, suggesting that he omit her name from the address on the envelope 'so as not to attract attention' from the neighbours when they saw it in the mailbox by the entrance to their block. But for the moment she was open about writing to a prisoner, and all her family and closest friends were supportive.

Sveta also composed her letters carefully. She would write a draft, correct and copy it to make sure that she got her thoughts down right, and said nothing that could endanger Lev. She was unsure that her letters would get through, so keeping drafts was an extra measure of security. She wrote in small, barely legible handwriting on blank sheets or on the most narrowly ruled writing-paper she could find, cramming as much as possible on to the page. In each letter she inserted some blank sheets so that Lev could write back to her. She wrote at night when she was on her own.

> I need to be at home to write letters and alone as well (or for every-one to be sleeping), for my head not to hurt, for me not to want to sleep, and for me to be in a tolerable mood. All these 'fors' don't always coincide.

Sveta filled her letters with news and details of her daily life, family, work and friends. She lived for Lev through her letters. Outwardly her language seems to lack romantic sentiment. It has the some-what dry and spare linguistic character of the Soviet technical intelligentsia – the milieu in which she had been raised – whereas Lev's is closer to the more expressive language of his grandmother and the Russian gentry of the nineteenth century. Sveta acknowledged that she did not like to gush. She was a practical person, emotionally generous, often warm in her affections, but far too honest and plain-speaking to succumb to romantic illusions.

> Sentimental words about love (both lofty and cheap) produce the same effect on me as commerce. Mine to you, just as yours to me. From them stem never-ending grievances. In my mind, I always hear that line: 'Give and don't reach out for its return – this is the key to opening all hearts.'

The lack of sentimental words in her letters was deceptive. The Sasha Chorny poem Sveta quoted ('For the Patient') expresses perfectly the love she gave to Lev by writing to him every day:

> If the best decide to end their plight,
> Heavy-footed hyenas will scour the world whole!
> Fall in love with the instinctive joy of flight . . .
> Unwrap every corner of your soul.
>
> Be a brother, a sister, a wife or a husband,
> A doctor, a nurse, or a master of arts,
> Give freely – but don't reach for it back with trembling hand:
> This is the key to opening all hearts.

Sveta wrote to Lev with a running commentary about her life. She described what Moscow looked like on her way to work and added little details about her clothes that connected her to Lev:

> Muscovites wear whatever they have left – a fur coat or a wadded jacket (a favourite of the morning commuters with whom I travel to work). Factories start at 8, institutes at 9, and ministries at 11 . . . I don't have a winter coat – the old black one having fallen prey to my passion to destroy, a characteristic of all two-legged animals, and reused for a good suit at Mama's insistence . . . My summer grey-green coat is still alive . . . And do you know what else is still going? The shoes we

bought. They've been everywhere with me and now I wear them to the institute because they're so light . . . That's all I have to say about the way we live – which is not as well as I think you imagine.

Lev yearned for news about Moscow. He loved to hear about it from Sveta. In the camp he spent many hours reminiscing about the city with fellow Muscovites like Anisimov and Gleb Vasil'ev, a mechanic in the metal workshop who had studied at the same school as Sveta and had just completed his first year at the Physics Faculty of Moscow University when he was arrested in 1940. From the bleak northern landscape of Pechora, Lev wished his letters would carry him away to the Moscow of his dreams:

It's grey and overcast today. Autumn has crept up silently, deceptively, and has thrown its persistent, web-like veil over Pechora, over the forest, over the houses on the embankment, over the buildings and chimneys of our industrial plant, over the impassive, severe pines . . . In Moscow you have an autumn worthy of Levitan and Kuindzhi,* a golden season where leaves fall and dry ones rustle underfoot. How far away it all seems. And yet I imagine that everything in Moscow must be as it was – the people are as they were, the streets unchanged. And that you are also as you were. And I don't want to think that what I can still see is an illusion, that it will disappear. Oh, how many 'ands' I've written on this page, and how little logic. This is not a letter but an incoherent bundle of feelings.

Sveta counteracted Lev's nostalgia with a more realistic portrait. 'No gold has been seen in Moscow yet,' she wrote on 10 September. 'Moscow is not as you imagine it at all. There are too many people. It's unpleasant on the trams. People are irritable. They swear and even fight. The metro is always full. The stations where you change lines can no longer cope.'

* Isaac Levitan (1860–1900) and Arkhip Kuindzhi (1842–1910), Russian landscape painters.

As she had promised in her first letter, Sveta told him more about her work. The institute was a large complex of workshops and laboratories employing 650 people, 120 of them engineers, 50 researchers and technical assistants, and the remainder labourers – fitters, builders, mechanics. Many of these workers lived with their families in the old wooden barracks built for the experimental rubber factory that had been there before the war. In the laboratories where Sveta worked they were testing new methods of manufacturing tyres from synthetic rubber (sodium butadiene). Her work involved a lot of research and teaching as well as learning English to keep up with the latest developments in the West, which she would need to discuss in her disseration, 'On the Physical Mechanics of Rubber'.

Sveta's research had military applications and so was deemed a 'state secret'. She had access to 'closed' materials – confidential information about Soviet technology, Western publications and so on. Maintaining contact with a prisoner was therefore full of risks for her. If it was discovered that she was writing to a prisoner, she would almost certainly be expelled from the institute and probably arrested on suspicion of divulging state secrets to a convicted 'spy'. Of all her colleagues at the institute, only two knew about her relationship with Lev: her close friend Bella Lipkina, three years younger than Sveta, who worked with her in the laboratory; and her boss, Mikhail Tsydzik, a chemist 'on the grey side of 50', who was an old acquaintance of her father. Sveta and Tsydzik got on well. He was always kind to her, protected her in a paternal way and relied on her help with administrative chores, since he was often in poor health. 'I can talk with him easily and freely about everything and everyone,' she explained to Lev.

Sveta was fortunate in many ways, yet her heart was clearly not in her research:

I've learned that it's very difficult to bang away from 9 till 6 or 7 o'clock without respite. Usually when you're working you spend time on one thing, then another, you do some teaching, then you give advice to someone about how best to test something, then you do some studying . . . and then you talk a little about some concert or a book . . . But here we've been working as if we were on an assembly line: I write, Mik. Al. [Tsydzik] reads, a girl copies, a second girl draws, I read again as the girls are poor at punctuation, and then we sign the document . . . and send it to the Academic Secretary and the registration office. That's how we dashed off three scientific methodologies . . . The one on frost resistance was my first piece of work and now, in addition to the methodology, we've also written 'A Project on the All-Union State Standard for the Determination of Frost Resistance Using the Impact Fracture Method'. It will probably spend more than a year making its way around various agencies and committees. It's my job to write about elasticity at high and low temperatures. But I'm already bored to death by it.

Sveta had a busy schedule: English lessons after work on Mondays and Thursdays, technical training on Tuesdays and Fridays, lectures on high polymers on Wednesday evenings, and compulsory lectures on 'Diamat' (Dialectical Materialism) on Saturdays. On Sundays she went food shopping with her ration card (meat, eggs, sugar, dairy products and sometimes even bread continued to be subject to wartime rationing) or travelled out of town to the dacha allotment where her family grew vegetables.

Sveta sought distraction in her social life. Yet it did not always bring her joy. So many people she and Lev had known in their student days had been killed during the war. 'I don't often meet with our old friends from the university,' she wrote to Lev, 'it's just too painful.' Most of her girlfriends were already married with small children – a source of envy for Sveta – and she found it bittersweet to go to places she had visited with Lev. 'Today, after lectures,' she wrote to him, 'the Academic Secretary suggested that we walk along the Moscow riverbank. We got as far as the Stone Bridge and crossed it to go through the Aleksandr Gardens to the Lenin Library Metro. It made me feel so sad.'

Sveta did her best to put old friends in touch with Lev. She knew it would be good for his morale to hear from them. The first to write was Aleksandr Zlenko on 19 September; he had been with Lev in the Leipzig POW camp.

> Dear Lev, hello! It turns out you are still alive? I don't know if you're healthy, but it seems you are alive? I received a postcard from Svetlana telling me that you had resurfaced, but nothing else except your address and something about medicines (ask her yourself)!

Naum Grigorov, Lev's friend from the Physics Faculty, sent a letter with a photograph of his recently born son, a risky thing for him to do, since he was a member of the Party and a researcher in subatomic physics at Moscow University. Then a letter came from Evgenii Bukke, Lev's oldest friend (they had shared a desk from their first year at school) and a colleague at the Physics Institute. It was soon followed by a letter from Evgenii's mother, the actress Ksenia Andreeva, that gives an insight into Sveta's state of mind towards the end of the war. Despairing of ever seeing Lev again, Sveta had distanced herself from Evgenii's family, which at first had puzzled Ksenia:

> I was very surprised and offended by Svetlana, who suddenly stopped coming to see me, and I could not explain it. I even went to the university to try to find her, but that was very difficult because I knew nothing except her name. I thought something had happened to her. But now I understand why she did not come.

Lev was worried that many of his friends and distant relatives would not want to correspond with a prisoner. 'I'm afraid of being an unwanted guest,' he wrote to Sveta on 23 October. 'Not everybody perhaps finds it pleasant to receive greetings from our corner of the world . . . Maybe you feel you are the better judge of that, but I'm afraid that you may be mistaken, for not everybody shares your feelings.' Sveta was annoyed with Lev for harbouring such doubts. In her fifteenth letter she gave him a 'dressing-down':

On to the matter of umbrellas.* Tell me, Levi, if a person knocked on your door, would you let him in, even if he wasn't very close to you and regardless of where he had come from? Of course you would. So why do you have the right to think worse of others than you do of yourself? I know that's not what you have in mind, but that's what it amounts to. Maybe it's because I've been spoilt a little, and maybe it's not a good thing, but I don't find it hard to accept favours or concern and help, sometimes even considerable help, and I don't try to pay for it. My conscience allows me to do this because I will do the same (or would if the need arose), not necessarily for the same person but for somebody else. Levi, you need to be kinder and go easier on people – the same goes for certain events and issues. Humiliation is to blame, as well as pride, Lev. Forgive me for giving you advice and lecturing you on common truths while I sit here at home.

Lev replied in his sixteenth letter, on 14 November. Her words triggered an outpouring of anguished thoughts he had not disclosed before. Five years of imprisonment had made him doubt whether he mattered to anyone:

I read your dressing-down, Sveta, and it was hard for me to agree with you. If I were in your position, I would probably have said the same, but being here sometimes makes you think differently and look at things in such a tortured and suspicious way that it drives you mad. Psychic trauma is to blame – it can turn a lot of things inside out . . . Do you understand? Do you believe me? . . . When you've been seeing with your memory, and only your memory, for five years, not knowing whether something (or someone) from the past still exists and not knowing how they are living or have lived, everything that you suppose to be true is supposed in ignorance. It's not out of pride or humiliation that you suppose the worst, Sveta, but out of ignorance, which is the root of doubt. And then all the logic that you bring to bear, the natural logic even I can use, is can-

* A code word for the Gulag.

celled out . . . Yet from the moment I received Aunt Olya's letter, everything suddenly started to become clearer. Every word was like a resurrection. I'm now writing quite wildly, not as I should be; I'm scratching my right ear with my left hand and I'm not making anything simpler. Forgive me, Svet.

Lev was uplifted by the knowledge that his friends had not abandoned him. 'It's very good, Sveta, really very good, that our fate has not offended any of our friends,' he wrote after she had sent him greetings from her old schoolmates Irina and Shura.

But even more than knowing he had friends who cared for him, it was Sveta's love that sustained Lev. He lived through her letters. 'Your two letters make up my entire library,' he wrote to her in October, when he was still waiting for a third, 'they are with me constantly and are a substitute for everything I'm missing – people, music, books.' The arrival of a letter would always excite him, as he later confessed to Sveta:

> When I see my name on the envelope and it's written in your hand, I always feel the same sensation – a mixture of disbelief, astonishment, joy and certainty – when I realize that it really is for me – and really hers. Yours, that is. There's been no point to this confession – and now I am afraid that, having thought about it logically, you'll start to send me empty envelopes.

Lev would read her letters before he went to sleep – 'covering my head with the blanket so that my idiotic blissful smile would not cause those around me to doubt my sanity and get me carted off to the infirmary'.

Sveta's letters gave him hope. She said that was her aim – to make him feel wanted – in the letter he received on her birthday:

> Listen, Lev, in order to decide whether to be part of life or not you need to have left it, but a five-year absence doesn't mean you've left it at all: it's clearly not enough for the people who watched you

grow up, and it's not enough for me either. Maybe for colleagues at university and work you are just a memory, but life is life, and you're my life because not a day goes by when you're not on my mind morning, afternoon and evening.

Lev replied by acknowledging that they had exchanged roles. Before the war, he had been the one instilling optimism in Sveta, but now it was the other way around. Succumbing to despondency, he thought there was 'little ground for optimism' – no hope that he might be released or that they might meet before the end of his sentence. Sveta replied on 15 October:

You're right that I'm trying to breathe some optimism into you. But isn't that my main goal at the moment? You're also right that conditions are more complicated and therefore more difficult and that I have far less to deal with than you do. But the idea that the ultimate goal is hopeless – Levi, I just don't know how to think like that . . . Does hope depend on persistence? Yes, I rather think it does. There's a saying: by doing nothing you get nowhere. I understand that it's difficult for you to do anything, but maybe hope and desire will develop over time. And if not, we'll just have to live and wait. I won't try to convince you that my life is easy and happy, but it's certainly easier than yours: I have a home, and art, and science, and friends. It was Vera Inber,* I think, who wrote, 'Why everything, when only one is necessary?' These days I would change everything for one thing; both of us would. All I want is for us to be together. Levi, forgive me if my letters cause you pain and don't always lift your mood. And if I sometimes write nonsense, there's nothing to be done – a long time ago it was foretold, by the lines on my palms, my handwriting and various other signs, that my heart rules my head.

As if that were not enough to give Lev hope, three weeks later, in her eighteenth letter, Sveta sent him this:

---

* Russian poet (1880–1972).

Levi, I have always believed you – in everything. It was so before, has been all these years, and is still the case now. It's true, no one can vouch for the future. Yet even now I believe in our future, though I cannot picture it clearly to myself. All that matters is that we can be together. As for everything else, I think I have become wise enough not to let anything trivial or beyond our control spoil the most important thing. I notice you mentioned 'virtue' once again. Have you any idea, Levi, how angry I was about your virtue back then, when I was a first-year student? . . . How many times during these years have I reproached myself for spoiling things between us and – God knows why – tormenting you. And how painful it was for me to think that perhaps I would never get the chance to ask your forgiveness . . . You know, Levi, not so long ago during a conversation about life in general, about its difficulties and hardships, a girl said that I was the happiest of them all – she meant because the two of us haven't yet spoilt things for our-selves or for each other (when others spoil it for you it's not so bad). And I didn't protest. It's true, Levi – they don't have you, which means they cannot be the 'happiest'. So there you are, it's confirmed by logic and dialectics. People have tried to prove to me so many times, in word and deed, that a loving couple cannot be happy in a hovel unless it's insulated and equipped with limitless electricity and gas, and other such comforts, but I haven't given up yet, Levi. I would only need to see that you are there when I wake up in the morning and then, in the evening, to tell you everything that had happened in the day, to look into your eyes and hold you close to me. A fine 'only', isn't it? For the time being, it would be enough simply to receive your tenth letter. The point of all of this is that I want to tell you just three words – two of them are pronouns and the third is a verb (to be read in all the tenses simultaneously: past, present and future).

Lev was overwhelmed. He thought for several days about how he should reply to Sveta's declaration of love. At last, on 1 December, he sat down in the machine room of the power station and got out a precious sheet of paper to start his twenty-second letter. But the right words would not come.

I need finally to start this letter somehow. I've been sitting here in front of a blank piece of paper for ten minutes now, I've dipped the pen several times, but it has dried from lack of use. Sveta, I don't even know what to call you or what to write, although I'd intended to unburden myself of everything. You are entirely to blame, with your 18th letter, after which I couldn't sleep and there was nothing coherent in my head – except you.

Lev felt blessed by Sveta's love. He felt he had been saved. He had nothing to offer her, not even hope that he would return, yet she gave herself to him. Lev felt profound gratitude that she would wait for him, a prisoner, that she loved him in spite of everything. But he was also troubled by a sense of guilt and shame. He did not want to be a burden to Sveta – or to anyone else. That is why he had first written to Aunt Olga rather than to her. And why he had been afraid of 'knocking on the doors' of friends and relatives. Sveta understood. As she had told him, 'humiliation is to blame, as well as pride'.

The two of them would often battle over Lev's self-abasement. Sveta would lovingly assemble parcels and send them off to him, only to have him protest that he needed nothing, only letters, paper, pens and a few books, and urge her not to waste her money or precious time on him. Sveta would not be deterred:

As for the parcels, don't try to stop them. For us at the moment it's the only thing that brings any kind of satisfaction (all the others in our lives may be necessary, but they don't bring any kind of joy) . . . Mama has asked me to tell you what was in the parcel that was sent on the 20th . . . Here's the list: a white shirt, warm socks, lined trousers, a towel and headscarf, soap, toothpaste, a brush and comb, slippers, thread and buttons, two tins (up to a kilogram) of tinned food and a box of chocolates (with strange packaging, as I told you, but Papa insisted on it because of the rats), paper and a textbook, pencils, pens and ink, glucose and ascorbic acid (vitamin C to the unenlightened) – eat it, for God's sake.

Lev continued to protest. He felt not only that he was a burden but that he had become as helpless as a child:

> Sveta, it's obvious that God, or maybe someone else, is punishing me for your disobedience. I told you not to bother with parcels at all . . . I'm responsible for 90 per cent of the things depriving you of time and strength – even you can't deny that. It causes me a lot more distress than you probably think . . . There's absolutely nothing I'll be able to do in return . . . At 30 years of age I have ended up, through no will of my own, in the same position as a child whom people spoonfeed, *when to care for them should be my duty* . . . What could be more agonizing than this? Please excuse the harshness of my words, but I need to be candid.

Lev was seldom harsh or candid. In his early letters he was always careful to give Sveta a positive impression of his situation in the camp. Self-pity was not in Lev's character. Stoicism was. His main anxiety was not about himself but about Sveta and how it might affect her if he described his living conditions in detail. He never wrote of cold or hunger – on the contrary, he insisted he was warm and had enough to eat – and hardly ever wrote about the guards, whose treatment of the prisoners was often cruel and violent. The archives of the wood-combine reveal that there were several random killings of prisoners by guards during Lev's first six months in the camp – cases where a group of guards got drunk and shot or beat to death a prisoner. It is inconceivable that Lev was unaware of any of these incidents – rumours of them circulated in the camp – but he never mentioned them in his letters.

Instead he wrote about the beauty of the northern sky – his greatest visual relief from the prison zone and the only part of the world they could now both see:

> The autumn here is beautiful. The sky is clear, the days are warm, the morning freshness of the first cold spells has a calming and invigorating effect. The northern lights are already fighting with the stars.

Their bright, luminous curtains, which look as if they have been woven together from the beams of blue, red and green searchlights, shimmer in the sky, ever changeable, wonderful and enticing. They're a symbol of human happiness, light, tranquil, always dreaming of the future – thank God for that – yet impossible to reach.

Lev mourned the time they were losing. 'Sometimes when I write to you, Sveta,' he reflected in his eighth letter,

I look at the people around me in the camp, all of them living in circumstances and surroundings so different from what they were used to once. Their spiritual outlook has changed beyond recognition. This is not a matter of ageing, of changes a person must go through with age – it would be bad if they didn't. You once said, and quite correctly (you were sitting at your table with 'Principles' or 'Thermodynamics', I've forgotten exactly, but I remember it was evening and a table lamp was buzzing, and I was standing near the piano) that without changing over time people would not become themselves . . . What can I say about you, Svetushka? That I see you every day, that I know how you used to be and how you are now . . . and that although I will regret every greying hair on your head, although every additional crease in the corners of your eyes will hurt me, these things must occur, and when they do they will not take anything away from how I feel about you, they will only add something – something new but yours. Does it really matter if this is called old age? You were my world and always will be, and whatever you were, for me you will always be my Svet, my light.

'Time is moving on and people are changing, it's true,' Sveta agreed. 'But are they really changing for the worse?'

I don't know, Lev, it seems to me that every age has its good side. The question of age and the passing of time worried me most between the ages of 17 and 19. It seemed to me then like half my life, the best half, had already passed, but once I was with you, I never thought about my age again. My life was good and it seemed that it would go on being good or not change a lot. I've probably aged over the past five years, it's difficult for me to judge, but at least I haven't become old (to grow older and be old are different things). If I'm concerned about age at all, it's at a more banal level, a purely physical one. I would like to preserve my youth and as much beauty as I was given – as a gift to you.

Meanwhile, Lev kept her informed about how he was counting down the 3,360 days that remained of his sentence before he could hope to see her 'greying hair'. He sent Sveta his carefully censored commentary on the main events inside the prison camp. The big news of that first autumn was his transfer from the drying unit to the electric power station of the wood-combine. He had no training or experience as an electrical engineer, but his scientific background was deemed sufficient to qualify him to work on the high-voltage power cables. There were few engineers in the labour camp and the administration cared little for the safety of the prisoners it used for such dangerous work. 'I've finally managed to get moved to a job I like more,' he announced on 2 September.

I have been transferred to the Electrical Group as a fitter. I like the work and the people here are much better, although the job is more difficult physically. I'm working with pleasure and don't even notice the days of the week. Today's the 2nd, a Monday, isn't it? I'm going to have to study a bit more because in the past I've only worked on wiring and a little on electrical installations in factories, but now I'm working on the overhead cables. If you find an electrical installation manual or some kind of textbook on electrical engineering, please send it.

Lev owed the move to his friendship with Nikolai Lileev, a prisoner he had met on the convoy from Frankfurt. Lileev had been so ill with scurvy when he arrived at Pechora that the only work for which he was deemed fit was in the power station, where he recommended Lev to Viktor Chikin, the head of the Electrical Group.

Chikin was himself a prisoner. He had been arrested in 1938 and sentenced to fifteen years in Pechora because a fire had broken out at a power station in Vologda on his watch. His expertise as an engineer was so highly prized that he was put in charge of electrical maintenance at the wood-combine. The labour camp had many prisoners like Chikin and Strelkov who worked as specialists and administrators. Indeed, in 1946, more than half the responsible positions on the production side of the wood-combine were occupied by prisoners. Lileev's recommendation came at a good time. The wood-combine was falling far behind its production plan. There was a particular problem with shortages of electricity: the power station was unable to supply the drying unit, saw-mill and workshops with more than half their requirement; the three generators (worked by steam-engines burning wood) were operating at only a quarter of their 700 kw capacity and were constantly breaking down; accidents and fires were a frequent occurrence; and there was a chronic need for electricians, engineers, mechanics and chemists. To increase productivity, the MVD decided to recruit or train 212 more specialists from among the prisoners. Lev was one of them.

Working in the power station was a privileged position for a prisoner. It was easy by Gulag standards, a world apart from the back-breaking labour of the hauling teams. There were eight-hour shifts instead of the normal twelve, an effort by the camp administration to cut down on accidents caused by fatigue. For those on duty there was little to do but check the running of the plant and carry out repairs, which left them a lot of time to read, write letters and play cards, dominoes or chess. It was always warm in the power station, and there was a shower room for stokers and machinists where Lev could wash himself and his clothes in hot water – an important advantage because it meant he did not have to go to the wash-house, where clothes were often stolen and the water was cold. There were no guards inside the power station and no convoys to escort the prisoners to work, so Lev and his friends in the Electrical Group were free to move around the industrial zone. They could visit the voluntary workers who lived in houses by the power station; go to the club-house of the wood-combine, a place out of bounds for other prisoners, where films were shown, there was a radio (tuned only to the Pechora Gulag station), and vodka and tobacco could be bought from the nearby shop; stop by Strelkov's laboratory to see their friends on their way home from work; and pass in and out of the barracks zone more or less as often as they liked. 'Going through the guard-house between the barracks and the rest of the industrial zone,' recalled Lileev, 'all we had to do was to say our surname and prisoner number. A guard would mark down the time of our departure and the time of our return in a notebook kept on a special desk. Sometimes an inspector would try to tighten things up a bit, but on the whole everything was quite relaxed.'

In the autumn of 1946, Lev was working the day shift from 8 o'clock in the morning. Because he started later than the other prisoners, he would get up after them, at 6 a.m., and eat his breakfast in the canteen while the work convoys were being counted by the guards in the railway yard. Many of the convoys had an hour's march to their work site and an hour's march back afterwards; but Lev could walk to work in eight minutes. Lunch was brought to him while he was on duty at the power station. During the hours when all he had to do was keep an eye on the machinery, Lev composed his letters to Sveta. 'Right now in my den the commotion of the day is settling down,' he wrote on 30 October:

> the working day is over; no more installations to do until tomorrow. In an hour my relief worker will arrive. You can't hear your own voice over the noise of the machines but that doesn't bother me, I'm used to it. Through the windows, a dark blue twilight turned into black night an hour ago, and darkness is the master of Pechora now.

There was no ventilation in the generator room ('It's like a banya here – hot, damp and steamy') so it was a problem to keep the paper dry. But writing in the power station was easier than at night in the barracks, where the din of the prisoners was more intrusive than the machines in the generator room, and the light from the lightbulbs hanging from the ceiling was 'so dim and yellow', as Lev explained to Sveta, 'that it would be difficult to write at all without placing the kerosene night-lights on the table'.

After work, Lev had free time until the evening meal and the final roll call before bed. Normally he spent these precious hours in the laboratory, where Strelkov liked to entertain his friends from the Electrical Group. 'At the moment work is done,' Lev wrote to Sveta on 2 September, 'and I'm enjoying the hospitality of the manager of

Lev in the laboratory.

the laboratory. I'm sitting in cultural and "scientific" surroundings among jars, weights, flasks and test tubes and I'm writing to you in complete silence, pleasantly disturbed only by the sounds of a mazurka on the loudspeaker.' Strelkov was particularly fond of the electricians, who were all his young admirers. 'The time we spent in the laboratory was the happiest in our lives,' remembers Lileev. 'We used any opportunity we could to go to Strelkov's. We often spent our lunch breaks in the laboratory. Sometimes – if our work shifts fell at the same time – we even managed to meet there for some-body's birthday or some other anniversary.' Strelkov's laboratory was a refuge where they could store their letters, parcels and other precious belongings, which would otherwise be stolen by the guards or by their fellow prisoners in the barracks. It offered them a few hours' respite from the harsh conditions and boredom of the camp. The electricians went there to drink and smoke, tune in to a concert on the radio, play cards and chess, read or write their letters or just listen to Strelkov, who was 'an excellent raconteur with a colossal store of all sorts of information, incidents, events and things that he has read,' Lev explained to Sveta. 'I listen to his stories with my mouth open.'

There were half a dozen electricians who regularly gathered at Strelkov's. One of them was Liubka Terletsky, Lev's bunk-mate in the barracks, who also worked with Lev during the day shift in the power station. Lev enjoyed the company of Terletsky. He felt protective towards the young Ukrainian, whose health had been destroyed in the six years he had already spent at Pechora. 'Liubka is a wonderful, very special boy,' Lev wrote to Sveta on 15 November.

He looks about 24 years old, is intelligent, and has a sense of humour and pleasant character. As a schoolboy in Lvov he studied physics and taught himself electrical engineering . . . He loves Russian lit-erature and misses reading Polish . . . He has lived through a lot, and if you spoke to him you would understand why for six years he has not dared to write to his parents, although he thinks about them all the time. He is such a modest, honest, decent person, yet he demands even more from himself. He has lost all hope, it seems, and believes that once someone has been here 'he cannot make himself whole again'. Sometimes when I listen to him speak, I think I am listening to myself. He says there is logic in my thoughts. But the only logic I can live by, Sveta, is contained in your letters.

The Muscovite Lyosha Anisimov, Lev's other bunk-mate, was also part of Strelkov's circle, along with Gleb Vasil'ev, the twenty-three-year-old mechanic who had been to the same school as Svetlana in Moscow. 'Gleb is good at mathematics and knows his poetry,' Lev wrote to Sveta, 'and he has a talent for reciting it, which is cherished here. He doesn't advertise it but keeps it for "domestic consumption", which I also like.' Lev enjoyed talking about Moscow with Gleb, whose wife and son lived there with her mother. He described his friends in so much detail that Gleb almost came to know them all. He would tell Gleb the news from Sveta's letters about Moscow. But he said very little about her. 'I can't share you with anyone,' Lev explained to Sveta. 'You are mine!'

The twenty-two-year-old Oleg Popov, half-Latvian and half-Russian, was another member of the group. 'Oleg is wonderful,' Lev told Sveta. 'He speaks Russian with a slight accent and does not know some words, but to listen to him learning new words is a real pleasure.' Lev derived a curious satisfaction from his 'daily conversations with Oleg, sometimes in English, about all sorts of trivial things that don't amount to much but matter nonetheless.' He liked Oleg's 'naive intelligence' and thought of him as 'an original (in the best sense)'.

Finally, in the group that congregated at Strelkov's, there were 'the two Nikolais': Litvinenko ('Nikolai the younger'), a twenty-one-year-old political prisoner from Kiev; and Lileev ('Nikolai the elder'), aged twenty-four, from Leningrad, who had recommended Lev to Chikin. Lileev, like Lev, had been arrested by SMERSH in 1945 and given a ten-year sentence for treason against the motherland. He had been forced to work as a translator and then as a prefect for the Germans in a concentration camp. Having met on the convoy to Pechora from Frankfurt, the two men were particularly close. 'He is more modest and straightforward than the younger Nikolai . . . who has a more practical approach to life and a talent for arranging it to his advantage, with the result that he can sometimes appear insincere – a quality you know I do not like,' Lev wrote to Sveta. Lileev was 'simpler and more direct', sometimes to the point of 'tactlessness', a weakness which Lev did not mind at first but found increasingly annoying as time passed.

'It's no longer such a boring world, good Lord!' Lev wrote to Sveta, paraphrasing Gogol,* on 18 November. In the company of Strelkov and his other friends there were joyful moments even in a place as God-forsaken as the Pechora labour camp. 'Generally speaking, the day hasn't been too bad at all,' Lev wrote to Sveta:

Strelkov (centre) in his laboratory with Lev (on his right), Konon Tkachenko, a chemical engineer at the power station (on Strelkov's left) and the 'two Nikolais' standing behind them (Litvinenko on the left and Lileev on the right).

After work I spent an hour with Strelkov in the laboratory listening to a broadcast of *The Oprichnik*† on the radio. It gave me the greatest of pleasure . . . At 7 o'clock I set off for 'home' and in a few minutes was enjoying dinner in silence. Then – almost as though I were at home – I decided to go to the banya. Forgive my poor writing. Although birches are not very abundant in our part of the world,

* From 'How Ivan Ivanovich Quarrelled with Ivan Nikiforovich'.
† An opera by Tchaikovsky.

there were enough green birch twigs, and Lyosha Anisimov forced me to pay tribute to the customs of the Moscow banya. Good tea is required after a good banya, but Nikolai [Lileev] insisted we abandon these outdated customs. So, under the canopy of a 150 watt lamp with a dark-blue crêpe-de-Chine lampshade, we drank mocha coffee together. (This is in their barracks. We, unfortunately, live elsewhere, about 20 m away, where we have only 40 watt bulbs. It's what we use as a yardstick for domestic comfort.) You see what kind of gourmets we are here – we won't put up with any coffee substitutes. And while breathing in the tropical fragrances emanating from the tin mugs, we spoke fondly of Moscow, Leningrad and Novosibirsk. After this, although it was already late by local standards – 9 o'clock – we went outside to breathe in the frost and gaze up at the stars. But the stars were covered by the clouds and the moon was barely visible. We wandered along the lanes between the pines and our barracks, which are freshly bleached and plastered in a country manner, with smoke coming from the chimneys and the eyes of the windows yellow from the lights inside. Only the 11 o'clock signal [for lights out in the barracks] reminded us of the time. Within five minutes we had moved from under the imaginary roof of the Maly Theatre in Moscow to under our blankets. That's how we live here.

Winter set in early in 1946. The wood-combine was not prepared. There were insufficient boots, hats, gloves and wadded jackets for the prisoners, and many of the buildings were in disrepair. The early freezing of the river meant shortages of wood because it was no longer possible to float the timbers down from the labour camps and colonies connected to the wood-combine.

In mid-December, as the temperature dropped to minus 35 degrees, the delivery of letters also slowed to a virtual halt. Lev sent his last letter of 1946 on 25 December. He had not heard from Sveta for two and a half weeks, and was desperately worried because she had been ill with a high temperature. 'Sveta, I am drowning in a sea of despair and cannot swim to the surface – no letters have arrived.' On 9 December, Lev had written what he thought would be his final letter to reach Sveta before the New Year. It was his twenty-fourth. 'What do I wish for you – for us?' he had written, equating his own wishes with her well-being. 'For myself, all I want is more letters . . . and if I can wish for something else, it would be for you to start the year in better health, in good spirits, with a light heart, in spite of everything, and with friends.' Lev was planning to spend New Year's Eve drinking tea with Strelkov, who was looking gaunt from a recent intestinal disease and two operations that had not improved his condition. 'He's putting a brave face on it,' Lev wrote to Sveta on the 25th, but 'only those who don't know him well are deceived by his self-control. I can see it in his face . . . Sveta, try to send something that will help his intestinal pains.' It was typical of Lev to think of helping others and not ask for anything himself.

Meanwhile Sveta was succumbing to despair. She wrote to Lev on New Year's Eve. She had not yet received his letter of 9 December. Wanting to connect to him, she had decided to stay at home that night and write to Lev instead of going out. 'I'm tired of spending holidays without you,' she wrote.

I hardly ever enjoy myself anywhere, and you can believe me when I say that, apart from Irina, no one really notices. Anyway, I made Alik [Sveta's nephew] happy – we turned on the Christmas tree and drank a festive tea at the table . . . It's almost midnight and Alik's only just fallen asleep. He's still scared to go to sleep . . . The Christmas tree is lovely – strong and green right up to the ceiling. Not one branch is dying yet. Yara hung a little silver nut on each of the top six branches, and on the very top there is a red star (of course). We still have the decorations from our old apartment in Leningrad, although I've given away a fair amount to other people for their trees. The Christmas tree seems to bring more pleasure to grown-ups (because it brings back memories). Alik was more interested in the reflection of the lights in his grandmother's glasses ('where do they all come from?') and the ABC book he got as a present . . . We played word games together (Is it feminine or masculine? What kind of letter is it?) . . . I am happy, too, because I have been writing to

you. This will be the first letter of the New Year – the clock has already chimed – and I'm going to put a '2' on the next letter right away. Tomorrow, I'll go book-hunting in the shops. I've got a lot of books still waiting to be sent, but I'm scared to send a lot of books at once, and for the time being we don't even have a small box or anything to make one with, and without a box they won't be accepted . . .
I don't remember whether I told you that I bought a rather lovely collection called *Classical Poetry* put together for the children of workers? In farewell, I'm treating you to some Aleksei Tolstoy from that book:

> Don't ask why, don't question it,
> Don't calculate with reason:
> How I love you? Why I love you?
> What I love you for? And for how long?
> Don't ask why, don't question it:
> Are you a sister to me? A young wife?
> Or a little child?

> I don't know and don't understand
> What to call you, how to call you.
> There are many flowers in the open field,
> There are many stars shining in the sky,
> But I can't name them
> Or recognize them all!
> I didn't ask how I came to love you,
> I didn't calculate or question it,
> I just fell in love with you,
> I followed my own wilful head!

Well, Levi, that's everything for now.
The New Year has been met and it's time to go to sleep.
All the best.

Svet.

1 January 1947

5

A significant proportion of the people working in the Gulag system were not prisoners at all but free workers who were paid. There had always been a contingent of free workers in the labour camps, but in the post-war years their numbers increased, particularly in the timber-hauling and construction sectors, where jobs that large teams of prisoners had done by hand were gradually mechanized. This necessitated the recruitment of paid workers with the skills and expertise to operate the new machinery. By the end of the 1940s, more than a quarter of the Gulag's workforce in construction was made up of free workers.

Most of them were former prisoners who had served their sentences but had nowhere else to go. There were millions of these workers in the post-war years, when the eight- and ten-year sentences of the Great Terror came to an end. Bureaucratic obstacles prevented many of them from leaving the Gulag. Typically, the MVD would refuse to issue them exit papers thereby compelling specialists and qualified technicians to go on working for the labour camps. Others stayed because they had no home to return to, had lost contact with their families or had married someone in the Gulag.

The Pechora wood-combine had 445 free workers in 1946. Most of them were employed by the MVD as managers and specialists. They lived with their families in various locations – some inside the prison zone, where there was a settlement of houses for free workers not far from the power station, others outside the zone, although they worked inside it. Living conditions were not much better than those of the prisoners. Many lived in overcrowded dormitories or barrack houses, where they shared a single room with as many as six other people. According to a report discussed by the Party leaders of the wood-combine in October 1946, the free workers inside the zone had just 1.8 square metres of living space per person – not much more than the 1.5 square metres allowed for each prisoner by Gulag regulations. The single-storey wooden houses had no running water or sanitary provision; most had leaking roofs; and all of them were missing basic furniture (in a labour camp that manufactured it). The settlement itself was in a squalid corner of the camp without outside lighting, washing blocks or toilets, and only one well for water. The place was littered with the rubbish of the wood-combine – sawdust, bark and kindling – which posed a fire hazard and encouraged rats.

Remains of the settlement inside the industrial zone – the chimney of the power station is in the distance on the right.

Although the free workers played important roles in the administration of the wood-combine, they were generally closer to the prisoners – with whom, as former prisoners themselves, they sympathized – than they were to the MVD or Party leaders of the labour camp, who were suspicious of them. 'We are surrounded by disaffected people who have been opposed to Soviet power,' argued

Comrade Vetrov, the Party secretary of the wood-combine, at a meeting to discuss the free workers in December 1945. 'We must be more vigilant and increase our agitation among the voluntary contingent.'

The camp administration was particularly worried by the intermingling of the free workers and the prisoners. Inside the camp there was no real segregation between the settlement – which contained the houses of the free workers, the administrative buildings, the staff canteen, the club-house and the shop – and the rest of the industrial zone, where prisoners like Lev were free to go about without a guard during their shifts. In 1949, the two areas were divided by a barbed-wire fence with passage in and out of the settlement controlled through a guard-house, though even then the fence was not complete, and prisoners could get into the settlement relatively easily by crossing the wasteland between the power station and the outer fence near the river. But before the fence was erected there was no more than a makeshift guard-house to control access to the settlement. Prisoners came and went regularly. They were often to be seen in the club-house drinking with the free workers. There were numerous reports of free workers – and indeed of guards and Party members – cohabiting with the prisoners and even having families with them. The MVD was constantly calling for the tightening of security to meet Gulag regulations but its efforts were undone by lack of funding, the terrible conditions endured by everyone, human weaknesses and sympathies: minute freedoms were allowed to develop at the system's edge.

Many of the free workers were involved in the smuggling of letters for the prisoners – sometimes for a monetary or material reward but more often simply out of friendship or solidarity. They took letters out of the prison zone by hiding them in their clothing and sent them off from the town's post office in the Shanghai area. Conversely, they received letters sent to their own addresses and smuggled them into the prison zone. Either way, these illegal letters got round the Gulag censors, although it was still advisable for prisoners and their correspondents to write in ways that avoided incriminating anyone if the person carrying the letter was caught by a guard. The MVD was well aware of the smuggling and frequently resolved to stamp it out. Its concern was not just that the prisoners were writing candidly about conditions in the camp and undermining the secrecy of the Gulag system but more immediately that they were being sent forged documents and money to help them prepare an escape.

By 1947, Lev had a growing circle of free-worker friends ready to mail and receive letters for him and Sveta. Not all his letters were sent illegally but he used this channel when he wanted to write to Sveta about something important. The system appears to have become fully operational between March and June. On 1 March, Lev still had to wait for somebody to smuggle an important letter out:

> My darling Sveta, I need to write to you a letter about all kinds of things. But I just don't know when I'll be able to send it; I'll do so only when I'm sure, assuming the opportunity arises, that it will fall into your hands and your hands alone. It's true that waiting for this opportunity, once the letter is written, is also rather dangerous. I'm planning to write about two issues – the minimaxes [the question of appeals against Lev's sentence] and the possibility of a meeting.

By 14 May, Lev was sending letters through the 'new system', which still had teething problems: 'This is to tell you that the new system of sending letters has temporarily stalled – and two letters have been waiting to be sent for a fortnight.' And on 2 June he was able to confirm: 'My letters seem to be more punctual with the new system because they no longer have to pass through tar [code-word for camp censor] and so there is not so much danger of their getting stuck.'

At this stage, the chief smuggler of Lev's letters was his 'namesake' Lev Izrailevich, a small Jewish man with lively eyes and a round, balding head. He lived in Kozhva, a sprawling settlement on the other side of the river from Pechora, where he worked as a railroad dispatcher. 'I've become acquainted with an interesting gentleman,' Lev wrote to Sveta on 16 May.

I still haven't asked his name, but we talked agreeably . . . He's an intelligent, cultured man. It turns out he's from Leningrad and studied at the Polytechnic (he was stopped from finishing) and until 1937 was a journalist . . . He knows all the Leningrad big-shots and captains of industry.

Before his arrest in 1937, Lev Izrailevich had been the academic secretary of the popular journal *Science and Technology* and had written several books intended to bring science to the Soviet masses, including *How to Make Things with Your Hands: A Practical Guidebook with 40 Drawings* (1927), which showed readers how to make a range of things from microscopes and cameras to simple household items such as clothes hangers. After his release from the Pechora labour camp, Izrailevich had settled in Kohzva, where he lived in one of the wooden houses half-buried in the ground for insulation. Working as a dispatcher, he often came to the wood-combine on contract jobs as a technician and repairman. He had a pass that allowed him in and out of the industrial zone at any time. A keen photographer, he earned extra cash taking photographs of prisoners and sending them to their families.

The smuggling system worked like this: Sveta would send her letters for Lev to his 'namesake' along with a consignment of photographic paper, chemicals and other materials for which Lev Izrailevich had asked; delivering the letters to Lev in the wood-combine, Izrailevich would pay him for these materials and pick up any letters for Sveta. In this way, Sveta was able to get not only letters and packages to Lev but also money that would otherwise be stolen by the guards. Lev's letters describe the system's operation:

[16 June] I saw Izrailevich again recently. He's still earning money through photography, although he's always running out of developer and the resources of our laboratory are too meagre for us to really be able to help him. By the way, he suggested that, if anyone needs to write me a letter or send me a telegram, using his address

96

will get it to me quickly and safely: To L. M. c/o Lev Yakovlevich Izrailevich, Freight Office, Kozhva Station, Komi ASSR. He can always call us on the telephone at the electric station.

[24 July] L. Y. [Izrailevich] is really grateful for your efforts. There's no need for $HgCl_2$ in a form other than pharmaceutical powder, although nitric acid would be better . . . He also asked for 6×9 film and glazed paper – any size – soft and hard. He'll cover the expense, of course . . . I'm so happy that I can now receive all your letters . . . The only thing we need to make this possible is photographic materials. He said something about sodium carbonate and sodium borate. They are (at least, they were) cheap but difficult to send as around a kilogram is needed, so don't count this as a definite order.

[23 August] Yesterday I[zrailevich] brought two letters – from 10 and 12–14 August, [nos.] 46 and 47, but the earlier ones have not yet turned up . . . I wrote to you that you should use not the address of the electric station but only the address of I[zrailevich], otherwise your letters will go missing, like the earlier ones.

In one of her letters Sveta had asked Lev whether it was necessary to write 'For Lev' on the envelope addressed to his 'namesake'. Lev replied: 'In future, as I have written, do not write to the electric station. My namesake is the correct address, and thanks are due to him: you can write without the "for".'

Lev enjoyed the company of his namesake. The two men shared an interest in mathematics and science, and Lev always found their conversations interesting.

I learn from talking with him. Apart from the sheer pleasure of it, what I like most is that, while he may know less than me, he thinks mathematically and comprehends things better than I do, and if I get ahead of myself he is sure to correct me, so between the two of us we can usually work things out.

But, more than mathematics, it was photography that united the two Levs. Izrailevich took hundreds of photographs of the prisoners – an exceptionally rare phenomenon in the Gulag. Lev sent Sveta several photographs of himself and his friends. At first he was afraid that he had changed so much after nearly six years in the camps that she might not even recognize him. 'The other day an opportunity turned up – quite unexpectedly – to have my photograph taken,' he wrote to Sveta in April.

> I've enclosed the result, which is fairly similar to the original. G. Ia. [Strelkov] is at the front. It might be worth explaining that, of the other two, I'm the one on the right. You can see from these pictures that I'm quite healthy and thus my requests for you to calm your worries about me are completely well-grounded . . . I sent the same picture to Aunts Olya and Katya – at Aunt O's address (poste restante). I sent only one. If the opportunity presents itself, I'll try to correct my negligence and send them another one, but I don't love my face to the extent that I want to distribute lots of copies.

Sveta wrote back about this photograph (which has been lost), the first she had seen of Lev since 1941:

> Aunt Katya came to see us today. She still hasn't received your photograph, but she liked my copy. She says that you have a fine expression and merry eyes. In my opinion this is only because without stronger lenses she just can't make out that your expression is exactly the opposite. But all things considered, you look much more yourself than I had thought you would. Bad light has cast a shadow on your face, so half of it is gloomy, and seems to be not quite yours. But Sveta is grateful to your namesake all the same.

There were several other free workers who smuggled letters in and out of the wood-combine for Lev and the other prisoners. One was Aleksandr Aleksandrovsky, a grey-haired man in his mid-fifties who worked in the provisions department. Born near Voronezh in

1892, Aleksandr had fought in the First World War and joined the Reds in the Russian Civil War. In 1937, he was arrested after speaking out in public against the repression of Marshal Tukhachevsky, a Civil War hero. Sentenced to five years in the Pechora camp, he remained as a free worker after his release, living with his younger

Aleksandr and Maria with their younger son, Vladimir.

wife, Maria, who had been evacuated to Pechora from the town of Kalinin during the war. She worked in the telephone exchange on Soviet Street. The couple lived with their two young sons in a dugout by the river, but in 1946 they moved into one of the barrack houses in the settlement inside the industrial zone. The house was very cramped inside. The walls were made of plywood. They had a tiny kitchen (without running water) and two small rooms but just a single bed. The boys slept on the floor. There was a garden at the back of the house where they kept some chickens and a pig.

Aleksandr and Maria were good friends of Strelkov. They often entertained him and his followers from the Electrical Group in their home. They sympathized with the political prisoners, and did everything they could to help and support them. Maria listened in on official conversations at the telephone exchange and so was able to warn the prisoners of planned convoys and other punishments. The two of them sent and received letters for the prisoners. 'My father would hide the letters in his shirt and take them in or out of the prison zone,' recalled their son Igor, who liked to collect the stamps. (Lev encouraged Sveta and his aunts to send different types of 'interesting stamps' because 'there is a keen collector here'.) 'My father had a pass for the industrial zone and was never searched,' Igor continued. 'He was not afraid of anyone. He used to say: "Let them try to punish me!"'

A machine operator at the wood-combine, Stanislav Yakhovich was another of the voluntary workers involved in smuggling letters for the prisoners. The first time Lev met him at the power station, they nearly got into a fight. Yakhovich had taken Lev's clean gloves and returned them covered with dirt and grease. It was Lev's first week at the power station, so he was eager to show that he was not a person to be pushed around. He had been in the army and was strong. He knew that his survival depended on his ability to defend hismelf. So he jumped on Yakhovich and threatened to 'smash his face' if he took his gloves again. Yakhovich said nothing; he just smiled. He was much bigger than Lev and could see that Lev was not a violent man, despite his fighting words. The two men became friends.

Yakhovich was a Pole from Lodz who spoke Russian with a slight accent. He had graduated from a technical college, married a Russian from Orel and had two children, a son born in 1927 and a daughter in 1935. He worked as a machine operator until 1937, when he was arrested, almost certainly because of his Polish origins (enough to make him a 'Polish nationalist'). Sentenced to eight years in the Pechora labour camp, Yakhovich remained there after his release in 1945, living now with a woman called Liuska, another former prisoner, in a room in one of the barrack houses on

Wood-Combine Street just outside the barbed-wire fence of the industrial zone.

Having spent so long in Pechora, Yakhovich had a profound sympathy for the prisoners and did what he could to help them: running errands, bringing food and delivering letters, at great risk to himself. He had a special feeling for those prisoners who, like himself, had been separated from their wives. In 1947, he would travel to Orel to try to persuade his wife and daughter to come and live with him in Pechora.

On one occasion, Lev gave Yakhovich a bundle of Sveta's letters that he had been storing underneath a floor plank in his barrack. Lev wanted Yakhovich to take them out of the camp for safekeeping, until someone could be found to carry them back to Moscow, where Sveta collected them. Lacking a stamp from the camp censors, the letters were illegal, so if they were found during a search by the guards they would be confiscated and destroyed. Lev would be punished in the isolation block or transferred to the 3rd Colony, where conditions were appalling and prisoners were sent on a penal convoy if they broke the rules again. Yakhovich took the tightly packed bundle of letters, stashed them inside his jacket and headed towards the main guard-house on his way out of the camp. But the guard noticed the bulge in his jacket. Stopping Yakhovich, he asked him what it was. 'What, this? Just papers,' Yakhovich replied. 'Show me,' the guard said. Yakhovich took the packet out. 'But those are letters,' the guard said. 'Well, so what?' Yakhovich said. 'Someone chucked them out, so I'm taking them to the toilet block to use as paper.' The guard waved him through.

As the network of smugglers developed, Lev became more confident of avoiding the censors and began to write with greater openness. The first issue on which he wrote in this new mode concerned something that had bothered him for several months: a vendetta against Strelkov that exposed the darker side of human nature in the camps. Strelkov's expertise as a mining engineer had given him a powerful position as the head of the laboratory that tested and controlled production methods in the wood-combine.

No one else could do Strelkov's job. But his 'obstinate persistence' (Lev's words) in getting his own way had alienated several of the Gulag bosses, who resented being told what they could or could not do by a mere prisoner when they were themselves under pressure to meet the production plan. In 1943, Strelkov had clashed with Anatoly Shekhter, the deputy director of the forestry department of the Pechora railway: Strelkov had stopped him from building with materials that did not comply with technical requirements. The matter had gone all the way to the highest Gulag authorities, who had found in Strelkov's favour. But Shekhter had not forgotten the incident, and had presecuted Strelkov ever since, finding fault with everything he did.

In December 1946, Shekhter spent some weeks at the wood-combine to inspect its work. Taking advantage of this opportunity to advance his own career, the head of the drying room – a prisoner called Gibash, 'known to everyone as a liar and racketeer', according to Lev – wrote a vicious denunciation accusing Strelkov of refusing to release wood for the workshops on the grounds that it was not dry when in fact it was. Gibash sent a sample of the wood for tests in a neighbouring laboratory, which found them to be dry, though it was widely suspected that he had dried the sample before sending it. On the basis of this denunciation – which in the language of the Great Terror had accused Strelkov of 'subversively delaying the release of dry material and wrecking the plant's plan' – Strelkov was removed from his job and hauled before the MVD on charges of 'sabotage'. Strelkov appealed to the Department of Technical Control, more wood samples were tested, and he was eventually rehabilitated in his post. But Gibash came up with new charges, and the case dragged on until the early weeks of 1947, when Lev wrote to Sveta:

> I didn't want to write about this, it's so very sad, but you're the only person I can share it with . . . What makes people want to ruin others who are in the same position as them? Gibash isn't a human being at all – he lost the right to that description long ago . . . During

the whole of this saga I have genuinely admired Strelkov's com-
posure and self-control. Sometimes I want to write to his wife or
daughter and tell her what a wonderful person they have. Of course,
that's stupid, they know it better than anyone, and I wouldn't accomplish anything except indiscretion, but I'm afraid I'll do it all the
same. His daughter is a student at Moscow State University of Railway Engineering and lives with her husband, their baby son, and her
mother on Pravda Street. The authorities are going to do something
about the Strelkov business but it's too slow and God knows whom
they'll decide for. Sometimes the most idealistic people are forced
here into the darkest alleys – I have become an utter sceptic and have
faith only in the past.

Good news came on 28 January, when the Pechora Gulag administration in Abez passed a resolution reinstating Strelkov. A few weeks
later, Gibash was sent to Vorkuta, the coal region further north.

The Strelkov incident had set off something inside Lev. He began
to write more frankly to Sveta about how he was affected by conditions in the camp. What disturbed him most was the way the camp
system brought out the worst in almost everyone: petty rivalries
and animosities were amplified by the cramped conditions and
struggle to survive; ill-will festered and easily erupted into violence.
'My darling Sveta, I need to tell you about all kinds of things,' Lev
wrote on 1 March.

I don't have much to say to bring you comfort, Sveta, maybe I should
not be writing this at all. You once said that it's not always good or
necessary to finish painful sentences. But having started, I need to
finish. Can you see that the hardest thing for us to bear is not the
material hardships at all? It's two other things – the lack of contact
with the outside world, and the fact that changes in our personal
situation can happen any time and unexpectedly. We have no idea
what will happen tomorrow, or even in the next hour. Your official
status can change, or you can be sent elsewhere any minute for
the most trivial reason, and sometimes for no reason at all. What

happened to Strelkov, Sinkevich (he had to leave today) and a multitude of others is proof of this.

It's interesting here (in a tragic sort of way) because everything in normal life is magnified. Human shortcomings and defects and the consequences of people's actions take on huge significance. There are virtues too, of course, but inasmuch as they don't play a great part in normal circumstances to begin with, here they become so much rarer that they start to disappear. Ill-will turns into hostility, hostility takes the form of wild hatred, and pettiness becomes meanness, eventually leading to some crime. Abruptness becomes an insult, suspicion slander, money-grabbing robbery, indignation rage, sometimes ending in murder . . .

Any remotely positive activity becomes pointless and unnecessary, from both a selfish angle and a general one. The most one can hope for is something quite dull, like the duties of an usher in an out-of-the-way provincial theatre, which at least leaves you 16 hours a day for your personal life and brings in a little money too . . .

Oh Sveta, it's such a sunny day today that it seems all this nonsense I have written is of no use to anyone.

'Being sent elsewhere' was Lev's great fear. What he meant was a penal convoy despatched to another camp or forest colony where conditions would be worse. Lev was afraid not of the 'material hardships' but of losing 'contact with the outside world', by which he meant Sveta. On a convoy the guards were bound to take his things ('everything will vanish – printed material, written material, letters, photographs', he had explained to her) and he might end up in a place where he would not be able to write. This was Sveta's fear as well – that at any moment Lev might disappear and she would lose touch with him. There were convoys every month from the wood-combine. The camp administration used them to punish certain prisoners and break up groups considered dangerous. What determined whether a prisoner was chosen for the convoy was usually arbitrary and often came down to no more than a guard's or manager's disliking him.

Falling ill was Lev's other fear. The arrival of prisoners from other camps and colonies – who 'nearly always look much worse and frightfully unwell' – served as a reminder of how easily he could get sick:

Dystrophy – consumption – is normal in our camp. There's also scurvy, but with some know-how and experience it's fairly manage-able, because the summers are green and if you can't get vitamin C by eating lemons, there's enough of it in pine needles and all kinds of herbs, so you just have to remember that. During the winter I put your tablets to good use and gave them to a couple of friends. Anisi-mov is finishing the rest; he got a bit of scurvy but is better now. See how your tablets helped!

If Lev got sick, he was not likely to recover quickly, if at all, in the infirmary of the wood-combine. There was only one doctor there, hardly any medicine and little food, because supplies for the patients were regularly stolen by the guards.

As the smuggling system developed, Sveta shared more news with Lev as well. On 20 January, she celebrated the eve of Lev's thirtieth birthday by drinking a toast to him with her family and friends. She then went to see Aunt Olga, who had a parcel for Sveta to send to him. 'I made your views known and refused to accept a pillow and a summer uniform,' she explained, aware of Lev's discomfort with people taking any trouble over him. Olga had got herself into a flap about the local soviet moving 'gypsies' into Lev's old room in the communal apartment on Leningrad Prospekt. She had been battling with the authorities to get it back from the 'gypsies', who had packed all of Lev's things into his trunk and thrown it out. Olga was con-cerned that he would be upset by the loss of his belongings, but all Lev really cared about were some photographs that had belonged to his parents. 'The room is no longer mine,' he had written to his aunt,

and there is no need to worry yourself about my property. It's true that I was not stripped of any of my things by my sentence and formally they should belong to you and me, but it's too late to get any of it back now. And I don't need it. If anything remains, don't keep it for me but sell it: you need the money more. Things are so unimportant in the life of a human being: they're not worth any fuss or frayed nerves.

Material conditions were hard for everybody in Moscow. The shops were empty, food was in short supply, and even basic items were rationed. Like many Muscovites, Sveta's family survived by growing potatoes and other vegetables on a suburban allotment that they travelled to on Sundays by metro and train. By the spring of 1947, conditions in Moscow had worsened to the point where people were beginning to worry about going hungry, an anxiety fed by rumours of famine in Ukraine, where several hundred thousand died from starvation in 1946–7. 'As for what is taking place in Ukraine,' Sveta wrote to Lev in a letter so explicit that it would not have been passed by the censors, 'I simply cannot bear to think of it.'

People are crowding on to trains for Siberia or Belarus, but there's nothing other than potatoes there. Trains are being stopped from coming into Moscow, but there are masses of beggars in the city nonetheless. At least half of Moscow's population is now living in worse conditions than even during the war. It is painful to see all this, Levi. Everyone is counting the days until autumn and asking themselves how the harvest will turn out. For the moment, everything is all right at home . . . We have six ration cards for the three of us and can do entirely without going to the private market (the only thing we buy from a private seller is milk every other day) . . . True, we don't see any meat, but there are such things as vegetarians, and it is said that they often live to be a hundred years old. Matters are worse as far as our income is concerned: Papa gets 1,300 roubles, and my salary is 930 roubles, but all this money disappears very quickly.*

* The average monthly wage of a factory worker in Moscow was about 750 roubles.

From the beginning of their correspondence Lev and Sveta had discussed what they had called in code their 'Minimum' and 'Maximum' programmes – the 'minimaxes' for short. The first referred to a request for transfer to a different part of the Gulag, where Lev could do scientific work; the second was more ambitious: an appeal to get Lev's sentence reduced or even to obtain his release. Sveta had been optimistic from the start. 'Both are completely possible,' she had written on 28 August 1946. 'You know about the Stalin Prize winners Tupolev and Ramzin,* but there are many other examples that are not so well known.' It was true that the MVD had a policy of identifying scientists in the labour camps and redirecting them to specialist branches of the Soviet economy, especially to military research institutes under the control of the Gulag. The problem was that the bosses of the camps were usually reluctant to release their scientists, whom they relied on to run power stations, production laboratories, lighting systems and so on. Lev did not think that he could hope to achieve any more than he had done already by getting transferred to the Electrical Group. As for the Maximum, he didn't believe in it at all: 'I don't want you to waste your energy petitioning for the Maximum,' he had written to Sveta. But she continued on both fronts. 'You don't have faith, and I don't have much faith either, probably no more than you do,' she had written in December. 'But, Lev, if there's any kind of chance, isn't it worth a try? I know there'd be more unnecessary pain if nothing comes of it. So we need to be level-headed and not deceive ourselves with hope – but still act. Nothing will happen by itself.'

By February 1947, Lev had concluded that it was too late to think of an appeal of any kind. He thought his scientific research at the Physics Institute was too much 'like student work' to warrant any

---

* Andrei Tupolev (1888–1972), the Soviet aeroplane designer, was arrested in 1937 and worked as a prisoner in a secret NKVD research and development laboratory. He was awarded the Stalin Prize in 1943. Leonid Ramzin (1887–1948) was a Soviet heating engineer imprisoned in the Gulag from 1930 to 1936. He too won the Stalin Prize in 1943.

hope of a transfer, though he promised Sveta that he would find out through Strelkov if anybody from the Gulag's scientific programme was due to visit Pechora; if so, he would ask them. An appeal of his sentence would entail a review of his investigation by the military tribunal in Frankfurt an der Oder. Since he knew that it had all been fixed, he saw no point in reliving the experience, and perhaps making his situation worse. In a long and candid letter of 1 March, Lev tried to rule out any further talk of 'Minimums' and 'Maximums'.

I won't think about the Maximum because witnesses are needed for an appeal to have any chance of success and they're never summoned, and it would be difficult to find them anyway. I'm not even sure that new lies wouldn't crop up between the time of their testimony and . . . the announcement of the verdict. It's true that a person is more experienced the second time around . . . but the chances of success are still slim. Every action can always be attributed to at least two different motives – 'good', which is the natural explanation, and 'evil', which in their conspiratorial way of thinking disguises 'dirty deeds'. The biggest problem is that many of the facts that could stand in my favour have no witnesses, and nobody is going to believe me. The gentlemen professors [procurators] are convinced that anybody brought before them is incapable of possessing sincere motives such as patriotism or adherence to the principles of common decency . . .

With regard to the Minimum, the secret military significance of nuclear and space research rules out any possibility of a person charged under article 58-1b working in these areas, especially someone not particularly distinguished. The fact that a person who has served his time is not allowed to work in a major economic-industrial centre even in remote provincial towns – with the exception of Yakutia, Komi, Kolyma and some others – is a good indication of how the political articles, even the less serious ones, are regarded by the authorities. No testimony on a prisoner's behalf can mitigate these articles. In two months' time someone here is going to be released who was convicted in the 'Tukhachevsky era' [1937]. This person is a former member of the Central Committee of the Communist Youth League, a military pilot and – he's remained so in the camps – a genuine enthusiast. He worked here as a saddler and took on all the problems of the wood-combine as if they were his own . . . More than once, he sold his own bread and denied himself tobacco so that he could buy the leather straps we need in the workshops. And nobody ever thanked him for anything he did or remembered it when deciding where he was allowed to live on his release. You cannot change the terms of your sentence.

Sveta was reluctant to accept Lev's reasoning. She wrote to him on 8 June:

I just don't know what to say. I cannot argue with you, because I know that everything you write is true, and this nasty truth constitutes 99.99 per cent of your situation, and the little that remains is up to chance. Yet it does exist and that, too, is a fact. You should train yourself not to take disappointments to heart too much, but keep trying all the same. I know this is easier said than done. In your place I would not stick my head out either, and that is why I am not urging or insisting now, just trying to persuade you gently. Can putting in applications really make things worse? If not, Lyova, perhaps you would be willing to endure again what you had to go through once?

Sveta's preference was to go on hoping for the 'Maximum' and actively petition for the 'Minimum' – a policy supported by the director of FIAN, who promised he would write on Lev's behalf. 'Perhaps I am wrong,' she wrote to Lev, 'but hasn't it been the case over these five years that it's been easier for you to live with hopes and dreams than without them?'

But Lev had the final word. 'I wrote to you in passing once about a certain Boris German, a chemist from the Kharkov Institute, a galvanizer by profession, who asked to be employed in his speciality,' he wrote on 28 June.

Not long afterwards they called him to the transit camp (not far from us, close to Pechora station). He sat marinating there for several weeks until finally they sent him 'by mistake' to Vorkuta. After several weeks of general work (coal mining in the Arctic Circle) he came back to the transit camp, from which he was once again sent 'by mistake' to Khalmer-Yu (a railway-building camp by the coast [of the Arctic Ocean]), a place where there's no hint of a galvanizer anywhere. On each convoy he was robbed, according to the custom, and the last time he was seen was at the transit camp by an acquaintance, who thought that physically he was half the man he'd been before. No one knows where he is now. He promised to write as soon as he could, but up to now nobody has received anything from him. It seems that a friend of Anisimov, someone called Kuzmich, met a similar fate. He was also called for 'special duty' and vanished. The veterans say that's routine and that the quickest way of 'making it' [to the final stages of exhaustion] is to ask for a transfer to work in your speciality. Hearing this, I tore up the application to the GULAG MVD which I'd written in a fit of optimism . . . Well, let's drop it now.

Resigned to Lev's remaining at the wood-combine, Sveta began to plan for something far more daring than any 'Maximum' or 'Minimum': a secret trip to visit him in Pechora.

6

Sveta had brought up the idea of a meeting in her very first letter. 'I know you will do all you can so that we can meet before another five years pass,' she had written on 12 July 1946. Lev was pessimistic from the start. 'You ask about a meeting . . .' he had replied. 'Svetka, it's almost impossible. 58-1(b) is a terrible figure.'

Lev was right. It was rare indeed for a prisoner to receive permission for a visitor; and if it was given, it was for a family member or a spouse. Meetings were allowed in exceptional circumstances as a reward for 'good, conscientious, and high-tempo work'. The promise of a visit was a powerful incentive for good behaviour by the prisoners. Yet when a meeting did take place, it was often disappointing, limited to a few minutes in the presence of a guard. It was difficult to have an intimate conversation, and physical affection was prohibited. After visits from their wives, prisoners were 'invariably silent and irritable', noted a memoirist of the northern camps.

Visits by a wife or relative were difficult enough, but Sveta was neither of these things. She was just a friend, a class-mate from university, and that was no basis on which to apply for permission to see Lev. But Sveta was determined not to be put off. Encouraged by the news she received from Lev that it was 'possible in principle' for relatives to visit Pechora, she set out 'to find out whether it is personally possible for you and me', as she explained to him. Perhaps the Gulag authorities would agree to count her as a common-law wife. 'Lev,' she had written in the autumn of 1946, when she had been hopeful of making such a trip,

even if it's only a possibility, I beg you to do everything you can to make it happen more quickly. I'm not expecting any leave but I can always get ten days in place of study days or even take an unpaid holiday. Mik. Al. [Tsydzik] will support me.

Not wanting Sveta to take any risks until he found out more about her chances of success, Lev discouraged her from coming that autumn. She would need two weeks to make the journey, he warned her, far too long for her to be away from work without a scheduled holiday, which required organizing months ahead. It had taken Gleb Vasil'ev's mother a fortnight to return to Moscow after seeing her son in August, the only visit Lev knew of, although he must have known that her trip back was exceptionally long (the 2,170 kilometre journey to Moscow normally took two or three days by train). Lev was trying to put Sveta off. Perhaps he was afraid of disappointment, or felt he did not merit so much effort on her part. But there is no doubt that he was afraid of the immense dangers she would face if she went through with her plans to visit him. Sveta was involved in research that had been deemed a 'state secret'; yet here she was, planning to apply to the MVD for permission to travel to a labour camp to visit a convicted 'spy'. Simply by making such an application she ran the risk of expulsion from her institute, or perhaps even worse.

Sveta was not to be dissuaded by estimates of how long it would take her to make the trip or by the dangers that it might involve. Sceptical of the information she received from Lev, she needed to know more. 'I didn't expect a two-week journey,' she wrote on 15 October.

I thought that it was only letters that took that long to travel, what with their not having legs. If it's true (I'll check somehow) then there's no point even talking about my coming in the winter, unless it's during holiday leave. But once again I'm counting my chickens before they've hatched. You've written to me more than once asking if we need special permission or not, and if we do, from whom? I've been told that it depends solely on the authorities at your end (and on how they regard your behaviour), but I've got sufficient grounds not to believe what I'm told. My status doesn't give me any privileges, of course.

The main uncertainty was whether she would be allowed to visit Lev at all, given that she was not yet his wife. Lev could obtain no reliable information. 'They say it's possible to get permission at the Gulag [administration] in Moscow,' he wrote on 9 February 1947.

It seems there is a better chance there than at the North Pechora Railway Labour Camp administration in Abez, where as a rule they grant between 15 minutes and a couple of hours. Apparently, the higher authorities sometimes give authorization to relatives, brothers, wives (both legal and common-law), sisters and cousins for a few hours at a time over the course of several days. Unfortunately, this information isn't from official sources. It's all I was able to find out for the moment.

By 1 March, Lev knew more. It was not encouraging:

As for meetings, Sveta, I don't know how they've been described to you, but in reality they are very difficult and perhaps even humiliating, though not if we sing 'The Slender Rowan Tree'* at

---

* A Russian folk-song ('Ton'kaya riabina'), sad and beautiful, whose words had a special resonance for Lev and Sveta:

> Why do you stand swaying,
> Slender rowan tree,
> With your head bowed
> Down to your very roots?
>
> While across the road,
> Over the broad river,
> Also alone,
> An oak tree stands tall.
>
> How can I, as the rowan tree,
> Get closer to the oak?
> If I could I would not
> Stoop and sway.

such moments, my glorious Sveta. More often than not people are allowed only a few minutes in the guard-house by the gates in the presence of a guard . . . Sometimes – and this happened recently with Boris German and his mother – the guard may decide at the last moment to deny a meeting already sanctioned by the authorities . . . It's true that occasionally meetings of several hours over consecutive days have been allowed within the industrial zone, and some of these have been practically unmonitored (which is what happened with Gleb [Vasil'ev] and his mother) but these are rare and as a rule aren't granted to 58-1 (b) political prisoners. A positive testimonial from the camp administration's cultural and educational department may help, although it's not easy to get one. However, that's not the main problem . . . When I think about the likely nature of our meeting, should such a thing ever take place, I immediately wonder whether it will bring you satisfaction or just reawaken the unbearable pain that has eased off a little as we've got used to the new but already well-established conditions of our current relationship. Won't it make you feel even more acutely the impossible distance separating us? Won't it make it even harder for you to be happy there, where others are happy?

Sveta would not be deterred. Whatever the risks or consequences for herself, she was determined to travel to Pechora and see Lev, even if for only a few minutes. If the Gulag authorities in Moscow would not let her visit him, she would apply directly to the camp authorities in Pechora. And should they refuse, she would look for

With my slender branches
I would nestle into the oak
And with its leaves
I would whisper day and night.

But the rowan-tree can never
Get across to that big oak.
It's condemned forever
To bend and sway alone!

other ways to get into the labour camp, perhaps with the assistance of the free workers who had been helping Lev. If letters could be smuggled in to him, why couldn't she? It was an extraordinarily bold and daring plan. Nobody had ever thought to break into a labour camp before.

For the moment there was time to plan and to collect more information. It was not safe to travel to Pechora during the winter, which in the Arctic might last until May, because of the long hours of darkness and the possibility of trains breaking down in freezing temperatures. Lev was working the night shift at the power station. At the end of March, he detected signs of the coming spring. Struck though he was by the beauty of the early-morning light, he was characteristically wary of hopes and illusions:

When I leave the station in the mornings it's no longer in the twilight shadows that I disliked so much but in the brilliance of the rising, warming sun, which is turning the edges of the snowdrifts into half-melted sugar cubes. It's strange that there are things that don't have anything objectively bad about them but for some reason you have an aversion towards them. That's how I feel about false dawns . . . Once at daybreak I was walking home from work and the moon was already low. I was suddenly dumbfounded by the beauty of the unusual light. The snow's even surface was light-blue from the early sun and densely grey in the shadows, while the slopes of the snowdrifts were still illuminated by the reflection of the fading moonlight. And the morning sky, lifting up through the delicate silhouettes of the pines, changed from gloomy grey and dark blue-green to a tender rose colour . . . At the moment the days are spring-like and wonderful, spring is showing itself in every dirty stain in the slowly melting snow, and the sun is sparing no effort. You look at everything in a better light. You want to talk a little (which I rarely feel like) – to speak of some fine person or . . . just talk nonsense for a while.

With the return of warmer weather there was renewed talk of a visit. During June, Nikolai Litvinenko's parents came from Kiev to see him. 'The meeting was not a cheerful one,' Lev wrote as a warning to Sveta. The North Pechora Railway Labour Camp administration in Abez, to which the Litvinenkos had applied, had given them permission for three visits of two hours each; but the administration of the wood-combine allowed only one such meeting, in the presence of a guard in the guard-house. 'That is the most that we could get,' Lev wrote to Sveta. 'My article would not warrant any more. Nikolai is here under Article 58-1(a).'* The Litvinenkos had not been able to get more time 'despite the abundance of lubrication', by which Lev meant bribes: 'it cost them a huge amount'. Lev had nothing positive to draw from the Litvinenko visit for Sveta:

> Everything was very expensive for them, especially accommodation. At least they have a lot of money, so it wasn't such a burden. I saw them when I was walking to the guard-house pretending to be on business. His mother is quite young but thin, although she said that there aren't a lot of people in Kiev who are as plump as she is, that plumpness is a rare sight there [a reference to the famine]. It's sad to watch such meetings as an outsider, Sveta. It's understandable why Anton Frantsevich† told his wife last year that if she came in spite of his requests to stay away, he wouldn't even see her. Well, God be with them; let's drop the subject until better times.

Lev was so despondent, so discouraging of Sveta's plan to visit him, that it almost seemed he was afraid of seeing her. Perhaps he had been voicing his own fears when he had asked her earlier if a meeting, instead of bringing her satisfaction, might only make the pain of separation worse.

If Lev was depressed by the Litvinenkos' experience, Sveta was encouraged by another visitor to Pechora. Gleb Vasil'ev's mother,

---

* Article 58-1(a) was treason against the motherland – a sentence similar to Lev's Article 58-1(b) (treason against the motherland by military personnel).
† Anton Frantsevich Gavlovskii, a prisoner in Pechora since 1938, worked as an assistant in Strelkov's laboratory.

Natalia Arkadevna, was to make a second visit to Pechora in mid-June to see her son. On her earlier trip, in 1946, she had managed to spend several unmonitored hours with her son, Lev told Sveta in his letter of 1 March. Natalia Arkadevna was confident of repeating her success. Before she left for Pechora, she went to see Lev's aunt Olga, who had been thinking of travelling with her, until, much to Lev's relief, she was dissuaded by her doctor (a fact she did not want Sveta to communicate to Lev). For several weeks, Olga had been telling Sveta about the plans for the trip. Sveta agreed with Lev that it was crazy for Olga to think she could manage the journey – this was a woman who got into a fuss about crossing Moscow by metro – though she thought she had been wise to attach herself to an 'experienced traveller' like Natalia Arkadevna. By the time Gleb's mother was ready to set out, Sveta had been told so much about the proposed trip by Olga that she had worked herself up into a heightened state of excitement: somebody she knew – if only indirectly – would soon be seeing Lev.

Sveta longed for Lev. On the weekend of 7–8 June, she wrote him a letter that Gleb's mother would put into his hand. She started it on the Saturday:

Levi, Gleb's mother visited O. B. [Aunt Olga] and said she would leave [for Pechora] on Wednesday. So here I am, not even knowing what I should write to you. That I miss you? But you know that. I feel I am living outside time, that I'm waiting for my life to start, as if this were an intermission. Whatever I do, it seems like I'm just killing time. I know this is not good. Wasting time deliberately or carelessly is unworthy of a strong person. It is also a fatal mistake, because you can never bring back lost time. I must live, not simply wait. Otherwise, when the waiting is over I may well find myself incapable of building our life together.

I have always had this fear, the fear that love is not enough. One must be able to love yet also to live together and to live in this world, which will probably always remain cruel. Yet it seems to me that, despite time passing, I have become neither stronger nor more intelligent. I do at least get less worked up about such things as my own stupidity or about being true to the people I love, however far away they are from me, which in the past caused me to torment myself and others (you, too, had to suffer on this account). I've lost a lot of H_2O over silly issues such as these. It seems to me that I'm not strong when I have to wait or when I'm angry. That's why I don't now feel that I'm standing firmly on my feet. I need you to lean on – in sorrow and in joy. We have to get through this together, walking arm in arm as we used to do – though I think then I didn't lean on you. I was not heavy on your arm. Am I right? It is not kind of me to write like this, to ask for something you can't give, which can only bring you pain. But I am tired, not just today but in general. I need 'support', even if only through these letters (which are a conversation between us). But, Levi, you must not get upset. In the end, you and I are happier than many – happier than those who do not know love at all and than those who do not know how to find it. I hope this makes sense.

When I am tired, I become prickly, 'unshaved inside', as Irina [Krauze] puts it, and then I don't know how to find support from people who are close to me. I don't know what I want from them. It is not that I expect them to understand or do anything but that I don't know myself what to ask. I remain silent, but actively silent, meaning I withdraw into myself. Even Shurka [Aleksandra Chernomordik] I visit only twice a week these days, and I've offended Irina by failing to go and see her this Sunday (she forgave me as I said I was exhausted). The day before yesterday it was even worse, when she asked me about you and I only shook my head. It was no better yesterday, after the concert, when I ran away from everyone. You see, I can also be thoughtless and vicious, and even though I understand and regret this, I don't know how to make amends for it. That is why I am afraid that one day, if I feel bad (even if only out of tiredness), I won't tell you but only snap and then withdraw. If that happens, Lyovka, you must know that I am not angry with you. Do not lose heart and torture yourself, just wait till I have had a proper rest. Will you promise me that?

What I've written here doesn't seem particularly clever, but then I don't want you to have an exaggeratedly good opinion of me (a bit is all right). For now, Levi, I shall go to bed before I write any more nonsense. The good thing is that, having cried a little before writing, I'm now finishing this letter, I swear, with a smile on my face, my darling, sweet Levi.

This was the first time Sveta had really touched on the subject of her depression, though she did not identify it as such. She could describe her symptoms accurately enough, her tendency to 'snap and then withdraw', but could not put a name to them. There was no public recognition or discussion of depression in the Soviet Union, the 'happiest country in the world'.

The next morning she continued the letter:

About my coming to see you, Levi. I am very worried about my ignorance of where I should go and whom I should apply to. Would you tell Gleb to ask his mother to get in touch with me when she gets back? (That is, get in touch with me first rather than with O. B. [Aunt Olga], whom she is bound to call on anyway.) She's meant to return at some point in early or mid-July, and I could then, if need be, even go out of town to see her, although I have no right to leave at the moment. I don't want to ask for a holiday in July (the first half at any rate), since I need to prepare myself both emotionally and financially for the trip, and I'd like to try to get permission here. Although Gleb's mother says it isn't necessary, it really would set my mind at rest, and in any case it can't do any harm. As for how much time it would take, that I don't know. If I am held up here, Mikhail Aleksandrovich [Tsydzik, Sveta's boss] may well want to go on leave himself. I would then have to wait until he returns before I go. So don't count on my coming soon. In the sense of taking a break, I would even prefer it to be later (in that respect I am unlike everyone else), since an early holiday is soon forgotten and it's as if one hadn't had a rest at all. However, Mikhail Aleksandrovich also likes taking his holidays late, for the same reasons . . . O. B. is here now, so I'll have to stop . . .

We have asked Gleb's mother to take with her the treats that have been trying to reach you since April: sweets from O. B., chocolate from Irina, naturally, and sugar from me, also naturally, because Irina can't stand sugar, whereas I am indifferent to sweets. Since who knows what can happen, I am also sending you (and don't get angry, or you'll burst your liver) some money. That's always useful to have, if not to buy something for yourself, then for your comrades. Another thing I have asked Gleb's mother to take with her is a pair of spectacles for you. It's a second pair which Shurka was able to get (a 3.5 prescription exactly). Papa has got his pair back now. And that's all for now. Take care, my darling. I kiss you very, very warmly.

Gleb's mother was more successful than the Litvinenkos. Once again, she managed to see her son for several hours over consecutive days, this time monitored by the guards but in the smaller guard-house between the industrial zone and the 2nd Colony barracks rather than in the bigger and busier one at the main gate. Lev warned Sveta not to attach too much importance to Natalia Arkadevna's success. Gleb's article was less serious than his; and his mother had been fortunate (or just very good at paying bribes). Sveta would be lucky to see Lev 'for a few minutes' and might even be met with a 'blank refusal' from the MVD. But Sveta was buoyed by what she heard from Gleb's mother. 'Natalia Arkadevna came to see me on Monday,' she wrote to Lev on 16 July. 'She spoke in detail about the material-financial side [bribes] and completely calmed my nerves on that matter. She supported my desire to travel. She is a charming person, that's for sure, and I'm very grateful to her.'

What Sveta had learned from Natalia Arkadevna had not only strengthened her determination to travel to Pechora, whatever the cost, but also reinforced her idea that she could find some other means of getting to see Lev if she was refused permission by the Gulag administration. If not through bribery, she would find a way of smuggling herself into the industrial prison zone.

By 16 July, time was running out for Sveta to make the necessary arrangements for a journey to Pechora before the end of the summer. She had to wait for her boss, Tsydzik, to agree when she could take her holiday, not least because she would depend on him to cover for her while she was in Pechora. In the last week of July, Tsydzik went into hospital. On 1 August he had been due to go away on holiday to Kislovodsk in the Caucasus, not returning to Moscow until 12 September at the earliest, but his trip was now delayed. 'Levenka, my darling, once again we will have to summon all our patience and forbearance – my leave has been postponed,' Sveta wrote on 28 July. 'I am meowing. But I would be willing to wait until December, if I knew that virtue will get its reward (in which case it would not be virtue at all?). Again, I am meowing.'

All through August, with much of Moscow away on holiday, Sveta went on working at the institute, where she took over Tsydzik's administrative duties. 'It's 28 degrees here and everything is covered with a smokey haze from all the factory fumes and dust,' she wrote to Lev on 12 August. 'They're hurrying to decorate the city for its 800th anniversary [on 7 September] and half the streets have been blocked off.' While the city prepared for the festivities, Sveta made her own preparations for the journey to Pechora, which she now anticipated would happen at the end of September. She spent a lot of time finding out how best to obtain photographic materials for Lev Izrailevich, who would put her up in Kozhva and help her get into the wood-combine. 'I asked about the photographic equipment,' Sveta wrote on 12 August. 'There's no shortage at the moment, and it should be easy for anyone to purchase in a shop . . . I'll get hold of everything and, if the trip goes wrong, it will still be possible to send it in a parcel to his address – yes? There'd be one for two – film for him and books for you.'

By this time, Sveta knew that she would be travelling illegally. She had given up on getting permission from the MVD in Moscow and, without that, she had no business going to Pechora, a secret Gulag settlement unmarked on the map. If and when she got there, Sveta planned to enter the wood-combine with Lev Izrailevich and hide in the house of one of the free workers inside the industrial zone. Lev would be able to see her there during his shift at the power station, if he managed to get past the guards at the entrance to the settlement. It was a rash and dangerous plan, involving enormous risks for Sveta. Entering a labour camp without the approval of the MVD was a serious crime against the state. Because her research had military significance, she would be sent to a labour camp herself if she was caught trying to contact a convicted 'spy'. Anyone who helped her would be in trouble too.

To conceal the true purpose of her journey, Sveta planned to make it at the end of a work trip to Kirov near the Urals to inspect a tyre factory connected to her institute. Tsydzik would do the necessary paper work to cover her tracks when, as planned, Sveta sent a telegram from Kirov informing him that she would be delayed on her return to Moscow. From Kirov it would take her only a night and a day by train to travel via Kotlas to Kozhva, where she would be met by Lev Izrailevich. On 20 August she wrote to Lev:

Since there are local trains from Kirov and they're completely accessible, I'll be able to kill two birds with one stone. If Mik. Al. [Tsydzik] returns on the 12th, then by the 15th I'll formalize my working trip to the factory for about 10 days. From there I'll go on, as if still on the work trip, only without a ticket but plenty of vitamin D [bribe money]. I'll save on the cost of the ticket, but the most important thing is that the days spent travelling to Kirov and back won't be included in my holiday leave, so it will be even better for me. I have about 2 to 3 days work in Kirov (I'll need to have a look at the factory, write a report, and give some sort of advice to them). I must confess that I feel a little nervous about the journey. I'll send a telegraph to your namesake (or somebody else?) as soon as I've set out from Moscow, and then again from Kirov – it will all happen in just a month. I don't think I'll get rid of the extra luggage, Levi. Some of the books (the ones difficult to get, like the latest English textbook and nuclear-related books) P. has promised to find for me. Nat[alia] Ark[adevna] is definitely going to send something, some sort of clothing, bread for the journey and so on. As I think I have said already, I want to send a parcel to your namesake, but at the moment I still haven't got any photo equipment . . . O. B. [Aunt Olga] doesn't understand why I don't send the books to you, as I did the suit, but, Levi, I am scared of you. You would be cross with me. I swear on my father's beard that after this I won't poke my nose into a bookshop before the 30th anniversary of the October Revolution [7 November 1947] . . . This letter won't reach you until around about the 5th [of September]. So if you need to tell me something urgently, ask Lev Izrailevich to send a telegram, bearing in mind that my return letter won't arrive in time. Also, you can send a letter to the Kirov poste restante. To be on the safe side, I'll check in at the post office and the telegraph office while I'm in Kirov.

Ten days later, Sveta wrote again to confirm her travel plans:

All my plans remain in place, that is, on the 15th to travel to Kirov, and on the 21st to be with you. If there is an emergency, write on carbon paper to both M[oscow] and the Kirov poste restante or ask the namesake to send a telegram.

Meanwhile the summer was coming to an end in Pechora. 'Autumn has drawn near,' Lev wrote to Sveta on 4 September.

The day before yesterday was the first early-morning frost, which froze all the potatoes in the local vegetable patches except for ours, because half of it was covered at night and the other half escaped because it's near the dryers where there is no frost. All the same, they'll be of little use. Summer was really too short. The nights have already become quite real, there's darkness from 9 till 2.30.

Lev received Sveta's letter of 20 August on 5 September, just as she had predicted. Now that he knew that she was definitely coming, he needed to make plans for her to be received and smuggled in and out of the wood-combine. By 7 September, he had made sufficient progress to write to her:

Svet, your letter, as you supposed, arrived on 5 September . . . but I didn't reply straight away because I needed to clarify something here about your plan. This letter might not get to you before you leave. I'm still unable to write anything concrete, at least not before this evening, but I need to write now to have any chance of reaching you. You will get the exact address of your cousin* – whom you'll be able to stay with for a couple of days – in a telegram in Kirov (at the telegraph office, poste restante). Send a telegram with the details of your departure to my namesake. You will need to go to his house to get further directions and leave surplus baggage. Keep that in mind as your basic objective. We'll worry about what happens next nearer the time. I'm angry with myself about the books. I fear that I've created extra difficulties for you – it would be best to send them to me in a parcel or, if he'll accept it, to my namesake, as you had originally wanted, together with the photography materials.

The day he wrote that letter, 7 September, Sveta was at home as Moscow celebrated its 800th anniversary. She wrote to Lev from her room:

The salute has just taken place. Mama has gone out to have a walk around town but Papa and I already took a long walk yesterday. We can see everything really well from our windows – there are two large, radiant portraits [of Stalin and Lenin] suspended from balloons over Red Square, the sky over the whole city is full of bright red flags (also suspended from balloons), there are floodlights along the A. and B. rings [the Boulevard and Garden ring roads], and giant nets in shades of blue and lilac are moving through the sky (more balloons) with colourful explosions of fireworks from them. I adore the salute . . . The bridges have all been outlined in white lights and covered with lanterns and colourful garlands. The entire river flotilla . . . has been decorated. The Moscow power station is completely illuminated . . . Yesterday Papa and I

---

* Code for the free worker who had agreed to hide her in the industrial zone.

went out at 10 o'clock . . . We had to fight our way through the
packed crowd in the centre. There are orchestras in all the squares
on open-air concert platforms, 120 portable searchlights, markets
with gingerbread houses everywhere . . . I don't think anyone has
ever seen anything like it anywhere . . . The whole of Moscow was
on the streets.

Three days later, on 10 September, it was Sveta's thirtieth birthday.
Lev had no more news. He was worried about her impending trip
and felt confused and frustrated, powerless to help her meet the
many dangers on her way. He hardly dared to hope that she would
come at all.

Nothing ever turns out quite as you expect. I won't be able to find out anything for a while yet. I haven't even managed to see I[zrailevich]. I'll send a telegram when I do – in about two days. Today is your birthday. On this day, I always like to spend some time by myself, so at the moment I'm sitting on my own at work . . . And I think of you. My thoughts are not always clear or happy, sometimes they are confusing – well, as they should be, I suppose. Only one thing is clear – that these thoughts are all that matters in my life, and it's bad that I can't make them lead to anything useful or put them into action.

Sveta had a good birthday, as she wrote to tell him on 12 September:

At the institute they gave me two enormous bouquets of flowers (gladioli, dahlias and asters) and Mama gave me a third one (carnations). They say that flowers are a good omen. I left some of the asters in a flask at the laboratory for myself and some in a beaker for Mikh[ail] Al[eksandrovich]. The rest are at home. Irina and Shura gave me a special article of clothing I had requested for the northern expedition. Shura wasn't there on my birthday . . . but Irina was and Lida from the institute . . . Mama baked a divine cabbage pie and we had two cakes (obtained with ration coupons in place of sugar).

The bad news was that Sveta would not be ready to leave for Kirov on the 15th, as she had told Lev she would be. There were delays at the institute. 'I have the details of the work trip in my briefcase but the payroll office is empty and they're not promising any money before the 20th,' Sveta wrote to Lev. Friends and relatives began collecting money and raised about 1,000 roubles for Sveta, more than her monthly salary. Meanwhile Sveta received 'another 300 or 400 roubles' from her institute (money owed to her for taking charge of the laboratory during Tsydzik's absence) by writing a report 'about wages and discrepancies in the rates of pay' and putting it into a pile of papers which the director signed without checking properly. If she had asked for the money herself, she would have been refused (the institute was short of cash and always looking for excuses not to pay its staff) and possibly accused of lacking the requisite public spirit of a research team leader. There might even have been some awkward questions about why she suddenly needed the money. Sveta was uncomfortable about tricking the director in this way: it added to her general anxiety about the greater risks she would have to take on her journey. 'I'm very nervous about the preparations,' she wrote to Lev. 'It's all down to the same superstitious feeling that if I get everything ready then I won't end up going (or I will, but something bad will happen).'

Lev had still not been in touch with his namesake to finalize the plans for Sveta's arrival. He had heard nothing from Lev Izrailevich since 5 September and had not even seen him then, he explained to Sveta, 'so I wasn't able to let him know what your letter said, give him advance notice, or ask him anything.' There were still important preparations to be made for her visit, which he now planned to communicate by sending a telegram to her in Kirov once he had made contact with Izrailevich. 'All in all,' he wrote to Sveta on 17 Steptember, 'nothing's really gone that well in the last ten days or so.' A major complication that had recently arisen was that Lev was being confined more frequently to the barracks – there had been a security alert in the 2nd Colony – making it harder for him to meet Sveta in the industrial zone.

Five days later, on 22 September, Lev still had not heard from his namesake. He thought Izrailevich must be ill. Nor had he had a letter from Sveta since the 5th. Presuming she had left Moscow already, one of the free workers sent a telegram to the Kirov poste restante on Lev's behalf with the address of Lev Izrailevich in Kozhva where she should go when she arrived to wait for further instructions.

The details of Sveta's journey are not entirely clear; she became confused about them in later years. It seems that she set off from Moscow some time shortly after 20 September. Her father and brother took her to the Yaroslavl station and put her on a train to Kirov, where she must have spent at least three days carrying out her duties at the tyre factory. As planned, Sveta sent a telegram from Kirov to Tsydzik (who was in on the plot) to let him know that she would be 'delayed for a few days'. She then took a train to Kozhva, using a ticket bought illegally by her father from a military officer who agreed to take her with him as his 'personal assistant' on condition that she give it back to him on her arrival in Kozhva. Sveta had the upper berth in a sleeping carriage, an 'unheard-of luxury' for her, as she recalled.

What did Sveta feel as she travelled north, changing trains at Kotlas to continue on her journey to Kozhva? Was she afraid when she saw the first watch-towers and barbed-wire fences alongside the railway track? Did she even think about the risks she was taking by venturing illegally into the Gulag zone? Reflecting on the journey a few months afterwards, in April 1948, Sveta thought she had not been afraid, because she was 'prepared for an unsuccessful outcome, and I was a bit emotionless'. Half expecting failure, she had not invested her emotions in the promise of success, and this had helped her keep her nerve. But as time passed she looked back on her journey with ever more amazement at her own audacity. Sitting in her kitchen more than seventy years later, Sveta would recall that at the time it had seemed 'natural' for her to make the trip. But then she added: 'How could I have gone there without even thinking of the dangers involved? I don't know. It was a foolish thing to do. A devil must have got into my head!'

For the illegal part of the journey, when she was in danger of arrest, Sveta had been given a dress to wear by her friend Shura, who had made it from the khaki wool material of her old army uniform. 'The dress saved me,' Sveta later wrote.

I was trying to avoid the inspectors, who were coming through the carriage checking everybody's tickets and documents, and had managed to keep my head down and put on the uniform, all the while trying not to catch their eye. But one of them came up to me and said there was something wrong with my ticket, it wasn't legal, and he wanted to remove me from the train and take me off for

questioning. How would I explain the false ticket? I had no idea whom it belonged to – a man's name was probably on it, but I was a woman and I did not even know where I was supposedly travelling. Nor could I afford to say where I was actually going. Moreover, I was meant to give the ticket back to the army officer. But then the other passengers, who were all without exception military types and saw me as one of them, came to my defence and started arguing in a friendly manner with the inspector: if there is something wrong, it's not her fault, they said! And the inspector let me stay.

Sveta travelled as far as Kozhva, a few kilometres from Pechora, where she found the house of Lev Izrailevich, a dug-out in the ground, in which he occupied a 'tiny room'. His father, from Leningrad, was staying with him – probably the reason he had not been to see Lev at the wood-combine – so sleeping arrangements were cramped. The next day, Izrailevich and Sveta went together to the wood-combine. From the station at Pechora they walked the length

The station at Kozhva, late 1940s.

of Soviet Street, a dirt-track avenue flanked on either side by eight-apartment wooden houses and 'sidewalks' made of planks laid on the ground. They turned into Moscow Street, passing a large white neo-classical structure, the first stone building in the town, which had just been erected for the administration of the North Pechora Railway Labour Camp, recently relocated from Abez. There were guards outside the building but none stopped Sveta or asked to see her papers, even though she must have stuck out as a stranger. From Moscow Street, Izrailevich and Sveta walked past the barracks of the 1st Colony and the motor garage on Garazhnaia (Garage) Street on their way to the main gate of the wood-combine, where they planned to tell the guards that Sveta was the wife of a voluntary worker living in the settlement.

Security at the wood-combine was in a chaotic state. There were about a hundred guards to patrol the prison zone. Most of them were peasants who, having served in the army, had signed up as guards to avoid going home to their collective farms at the end of the war. Many were illiterate, most were heavy drinkers, and they nearly all took bribes or stole from the prisoners. They also robbed the stores of the wood-combine, especially the stables in the industrial zone and the windmill outside it near the 1st Colony, where at least a dozen guards were involved in a major racket to steal oats and turn them into vodka for sale to the prisoners and free workers. Several tons of oats went missing this way during 1946.

Almost constant drunkenness was the main problem with the guards. The Party archives of the wood-combine are filled with the reports of disciplinary hearings in which guards are reprimanded for 'being drunk in working hours', 'passing out from drunkenness while on duty in the guard-house', 'getting drunk and vanishing from work for several days' and so on. Party leaders all agreed that drunkenness among the guards was the biggest danger to security. Prisoners had walked out of the camp while drunken guards slept in the main guard-house. Others had bribed the guards to let them visit women in the town, offering further bribes to be let back into the barracks zone and counted 'present' at lights out. The remote-

Guards at the wood-combine, late 1940s.

ness of Pechora – a thousand kilometres from anywhere but other labour camps – was a prison in itself.

There were also cases of guards taking bribes to let outsiders into the prison zone. A Party meeting at the wood-combine in 1947 reported on several incidents of 'strangers' being allowed in without a pass to visit the free workers in the settlement. Once inside the industrial zone, the intruders could escape detection: what little street lighting there was – some seven electric lamps – was meant for production purposes rather than security. There were eight watch-towers with searchlights located around the barbed-wire perimeter fences but three of them were missing bulbs.

Lev Izrailevich and Sveta reached the main gate of the wood-combine without interference. It was a ramshackle affair, barely more secure than the wood and barbed-wire fence on either side of it, with a square frame of plywood boards covered with propaganda slogans and topped by the sign of the labour camp, a hammer and sickle. On the right of the gateway was the guard-house, where everybody entering or leaving the wood-combine was meant to show their pass to the armed guard on duty. Convoys of prisoners were counted in and out.

When Sveta told the guard that she was the wife of a voluntary worker living in the settlement, he refused to let her in, declaring that her husband had to come for her. Izrailevich, who had a pass, said he would find her 'husband' in the zone and bring him to the guard-house. He was gone for a long time. The guard began to talk rudely to Sveta, cursing 'northern wives' (women with husbands who were prisoners in the Gulag) in a way that suggested he had guessed her subterfuge. Finally, Izrailevich appeared with the 'husband' – dripping wet and clearly drunk – a free worker from the settlement who had been cast in the role of Sveta's spouse but, when the moment came for his walk-on, had fallen into a drunken sleep and had to be refreshed with a bucket of cold water by Izrailevich. 'The man looked embarrassed,' recalled Sveta. 'To avoid kissing him, I threw myself at him and started cursing: "I wrote to you! And you didn't even bother to meet me!" And, acting ashamed, he just said: "Let's go, let's go!" ' Before the guard had time to question them, Sveta and her 'husband' had passed into the prison zone.

They got to the house where the 'husband' lived. It turned out he had a wife, who had not been told about his promise to let Lev meet Sveta there. There was a furious scene as the wife shouted at her man, whose breath smelt heavily of alcohol. 'It was not jealousy,' recalled Sveta, 'but fear that they might be found out and put into prison' for aiding and abetting Lev and Sveta's crime. Lev had arrived at the house earlier and hidden outside, waiting for Sveta to arrive. He now appeared in the middle of this scene, anxious to protect Sveta from the angry wife. This cannot have been how they imagined their reunion – in this squalid house with a shouting woman and a drunken man – but that is how it had turned out. For six years they had longed for this moment, yet it was so different from the way they must have pictured it, the two of them together without anything to disturb them. It was a tense and dangerous situation – the wife was so frightened and irate that she might call the guards in an attempt to prove her own innocence – and for the moment they could only exchange looks across the room. 'We had to restrain our feelings,' Lev recalled. 'It was not the sort of situation where we could throw ourselves at each other. What we were doing was highly illegal and we had to be on guard.'

The couple lived in two rooms on the upper floor of one of the wooden houses in the settlement: one room was furnished, the other completely bare. 'They brought two chairs for us,' recalled Sveta, 'and we sat together in the empty room while friends of Lev went off in search of another place for us to hide.' Eventually a message came that they could stay at the Aleksandrovskys'.

The Aleksandrovskys lived in a nearby house in the settlement, but Maria, the telephonist, was living on her own there with her two small sons. Her husband, Aleksandr, was in the Pechora jail (he had got into a fight with somebody who had tried to steal from him in the railway station cafeteria and he had been charged with 'hooliganism'). Maria was due to work the night shift at the telephone exchange on Soviet Street. In the afternoon she was expecting a visit from a guard and his wife, but once they had gone, Maria would turn off all the lights to signal that it was safe for Lev and Sveta to come to her house.

As soon as darkness fell, Lev and Sveta crept outside and moved as quickly as they could towards Maria's house. Hiding behind a pile of logs opposite her windows, they waited for the guard to leave. While they were hiding, another guard came up to where they were. They thought he had discovered them, and feared the worst: Sveta would be arrested and charged with a crime against the state; Lev would be given extra years and sent north on a convoy. But then they heard the sound of the guard urinating on the other side of the log-pile. When he had finished he went away.

Eventually, Maria's visitors departed. The lights went out in her house. Lev and Sveta emerged from their hiding place and made their way inside. There were only two small rooms, a single bed in one, where Maria normally slept, and a table, chairs, and bedding on the floor for her sons in the other. When Lev and Sveta came, the two boys were sleeping in Maria's room, so Lev and Sveta took the other. 'That night we did not sleep at all,' Sveta remembered. Lev added: 'It was only when we were left on our own, the two of us together, when we had nothing more to fear and the two boys were asleep that we could act more freely, kiss and hug each other as much as we liked, and so on. But . . . more than that I will not say.' What Lev would not disclose was later revealed by Sveta: 'I asked him: "Do you want to?" And he thought and answered: "But what would happen afterwards?"'

Lev and Sveta spent two nights together in Maria's house. During the day, while he was working at the power station, she stayed indoors and played with Maria's boys. On the second evening, Lev and Sveta ventured out to see Strelkov in his laboratory. Several of Lev's friends came to say hello – they were full of admiration for this young woman who had risked so much to visit them. They all gave her letters to take away and send for them.

The next day, someone came to smuggle Sveta out; she did not remember who. She walked on her own to the railway station and waited in the hall by the ticket office, which only opened shortly before the arrival of a train. Sitting on her suitcase with her head in her hands, she fell asleep from exhaustion, waking after the train had pulled in and everyone else had boarded. Grabbing her things, she bought a ticket and ran towards the train. The passenger carriage for which she had a ticket was already full, but she was allowed to go into 'some sort of sanitary wagon that was completely empty'. She lay down on a bench and went back to sleep.

At Kozhva she awoke. It was late at night. She went to Lev Izrailevich's house, and slept there until morning. Before she left, Lev Izrailevich took two photographs of her as a souvenir for Lev – one of her sitting in a wicker chair against a blanket hung up as a screen, as in a studio photograph, the other of her with her coat and bags departing from his house.

From Kozhva Sveta posted this for Lev:

My darling Lev, I'm still at Kozhva. There was no direct train last night, but today I'll try to get a ticket for one. L. Ia. [Izrailevich] will tell you tomorrow about my departure. It was absolutely fine . . . I slept at the station [at Pechora] and on the journey [to Kozhva]. I got to I[zrailevich]'s at midnight and shook him awake ever so gently. And then I slept again until the morning and didn't wake up once.

For the time being I'm fine, I'm not shedding any water through the little holes I look through. Maybe because everything is still like a dream. Levenka, I forgot to tell G. Ia. [Strelkov] yesterday that I didn't find A[leksandov]skaya [Maria] at home – don't forget to tell him . . . Lev, thank everyone again for me. I'm unable to express myself in words, but maybe they will understand me all the same.

All the best, my darling. I'm kissing you farewell one more time.

L. Ia. [Izrailevich] is preparing a surprise for you – it's a secret for the time being.

Lev wrote to Sveta the same day:

My own sweet Sveta, even the weather is upset today. The wind is fierce and there was hail this morning; everything is so gloomy and miserable. I'm waiting for my namesake to come – maybe he'll come tomorrow. And I'm worried, of course . . . This morning I chatted a little with Gleb [Vasil'ev] until 9 o'clock. We drank tea. Everyone was at Strelkov's and when he left I mounted *Autumn Day** under some glass and hung it over Strelkov's bed and then sat under it for 'good luck' . . . Nikolai [Lileev] wanted to come this evening, Oleg [Popov] will probably drop by a little later, but I want to be alone.

Lev was eager to hear that Sveta had got back safely. There was considerable risk of her being caught on her way out. 'My own sweet, glorious Sveta,' he wrote two days later, 'up to today, 3 October, I

---

* A reproduction of a famous landscape painting by Isaac Levitan which Sveta had brought as a gift.

still haven't heard anything from you. It's awful. And I just can't think about anything else.'

At last the letter sent from Kotlas came with the two photographs of Sveta – the 'surprise' prepared by Lev Izrailevich:

My sweet, my lovely Sveta . . . finally! Thank goodness everything is all right. My sincerest thanks to absolutely everyone. When I read your note I guessed straight away exactly what surprise you were talking about, but it didn't seem any less unexpected or joyful when it came. You will be just the same in 10 years' time (in an armchair) as you are now. But you are always lovely in every way . . .

My truly incredibly lovely Sveta, everyone sends you their greetings but I don't know what to send. I only want to think of you, to write about you. I'm avoiding any conversations except for a few

with Liubka [Terletsky]; and reading doesn't interest me . . . I look at *Autumn Day* constantly and can't tear myself away . . . My sweet and gentle one, I'm squeezing your paws.

By 5 October, Sveta was back in Moscow. She did not send a telegram to Lev Izrailevich, as had been planned, because an earlier one had been intercepted by someone in the post office in Kozhva and 'immediately became the property of all the natives' (meaning that its content may have been communicated to the MVD). But two days later, she wrote to Lev with an account of her journey home:

For 250 roubles I was able to get a seat on a direct train. Your namesake got me the ticket and put me on the train. I took [a photograph] of your namesake's little house, where I spent three nights, as a keepsake. At first the conductor put me in a practically empty compartment but I had barely fallen asleep when he suggested I change places with a man who had ended up in female company, and I willingly agreed. There were three sweet girls, photo technicians for

an air cartography expedition. They had travelled from the end [Vorkuta] and were going all the way to Moscow. There was absolutely nothing to do – I hadn't thought to bring a book for the return journey – and so I slept the whole way . . . I didn't even wake up when the train arrived.

I got home on the morning of the 5th (at 4.30), had a little nap, and played with Alik for a while. Then I went to the banya and cooked lunch. Mama's temperature was 39 again that day . . .

Moscow met me gloomily – cold and rainy (but not hopeless) and the daily worries over bread are now over potatoes, which are hard to find in the shops and at the market already cost 7 roubles (they used to be 3). Everyone is stocking up . . . Sugar has vanished along with pastries and bread rolls. It's depressing. The trees have almost shed their leaves now and there are no flowers at the market stalls. Well, Levi, my dear, I'll say goodbye for the time being. Much, much love. Everyone I've had time to visit here sends you their regards. Sveta.

Send my regards and thanks to everybody there.

7

Shortly after Sveta's departure, winter came to Pechora. To Lev the two events seemed connected. 'The first snow fell tonight,' he wrote to Sveta on 13 October.

> The ground has been frozen for two days and everything has suddenly become wintry. I haven't been able to write . . . It's not winter itself that's to blame, of course, but the absence of Svet ['light'] which comes with the winter. Winter numbs the emotions. Thoughts lose their agility; restlessness and motivation ebb away. Time itself seems to slow down and freeze in the white expanse.

Lev's spirit had soared with Sveta's visit. But her departure had left him sadder than before. It underlined what he had been missing for so long – what he would now have to live without. 'Svetinka,' he wrote six days after she left, 'the more I think about you, the more I forget your face. I cannot picture you in my imagination any more – I see only little bits of you. I think I want to weep.' Self-pity was alien to Lev but he was clearly suffering. 'Well, that's enough,' he went on. 'I'm going to stop whimpering now, although in truth all I want to do is write your name, Sveta, in all its grammatical variations, formal and familiar. I'll pull myself through somehow.'

Three weeks later, Lev was still accepting of his fate, having given up all hope of his release:

> You once asked whether it's easier to live with or without hope. I can't summon any kind of hope, but I feel calm without it. A little bit of logic and observation do not leave room for fantasy. I don't know why I just wrote that but, since I did, I'll leave it. It's not exactly what and not exactly how I'm feeling, but I can't convey anything in

its entirety at the moment – for that it's necessary to think, and it's much better not to think.

But then he sent another letter with some thoughts on happiness, a feeling he had rediscovered when Sveta was with him. His reflections were prompted by the news that Uncle Nikita and his wife Elizaveta had been disappointed by a visit from their son Andrei on military leave:

> It's a truism that people are rarely able to make use of what they have and even more rarely able to notice their own happiness. It's sometimes necessary to look at yourself from the outside and report to yourself – consciously, not intuitively – on what's what. To say, what I have is happiness – more than I've ever had, so that any change will probably be for the worse . . . I'm grateful to fate and to nature, to you and to myself, for the happiness I was granted, that I was able to see it, at the time and not just when it had passed.

Lev settled back into the daily routines of the labour camp. In early December, there was a change of personnel at the power station. The old station chief, Vladimir Aleksandrovich, a former prisoner, was transferred to the central power station in the town. His replacement was Boris Arvanitopulo, another former prisoner. Lev got on well with both men. An electrical engineer with a promising career before his arrest in 1938, Aleksandrovich was a heavy-drinking, sentimental type, mournful over the death of a daughter and inclined to self-pity on account of the loss of his career, but 'good-natured' and 'cultured', in Lev's opinion. Aleksandrovich lived with his wife, Tamara, in the settlement inside the industrial zone. He was one of the free workers who smuggled letters in and out for Lev. Sometimes he would give Lev money in exchange for clothes and other household items that Sveta would send from Moscow. When Aleksandrovich moved to the power station in the town, he tried to persuade Lev to join him there, but Lev rejected the offer, because 'it is safer for me here', as he explained to

Sveta. He liked the new boss, Arvanitopulo, whom he found 'intelligent, nice, not over-educated and sensible'. The Gulag authorities were sending prisoners to the remote 4th Colony newly opened in the forests to the north. The last thing Lev wanted was to be selected for one of these convoys, and he was less likely to be transferred if he stayed in his present job.

'There have been some changes at the plant,' he wrote to Sveta. 'They're choosing people to send to the 4th Colony to do logging and construction on the road to it (15 km), and women are arriving here in ever-growing numbers to replace them. They're being put into the 3rd Colony. Some of them are already working in the workshops.' It had been a long time since he had seen such a large number of women – the camps he had been in during the war had contained separate female zones – and the sight of their being forced to do manual labour made a 'disturbing impression' on him. His views on women were still tinted by pre-war attitudes of veneration and romantic chivalry. Talking to these women troubled him even more. 'Many of the women who have arrived here talk fearfully about the places they came from [other labour camps and colonies of exile],' Lev reported to Sveta. 'The minority who are able to recall these places without fear are themselves capable of arousing in the observer, if not fear, then a distinct feeling of uneasiness. It's all so painful to see.'

Sveta felt deflated after her return from Pechora. Perhaps she was feeling the emotional effects of seeing Lev – the consequences he had warned about when he had wondered whether a meeting wouldn't 'make it even harder for you to be happy there, where others are happy'.

Her way of coping with their separation was to keep busy. She threw herself into her work, even though her heart was not in it. She inspected factories in Tblisi and Erevan; campaigned for district elections to the Moscow soviet; delivered speeches at trade union meetings; edited the wall-newspaper at the institute; took on the training of new researchers; wrote her dissertation; translated articles; went to French and English lessons; sang in a choir; practised the piano; and organized a Mathematics Club. Lev found it hard to picture her in these new settings. 'When I think of you,' he wrote on 3 February 1948, 'and I think of you every minute I am free, I can see you clearly only in certain situations.'

> How, after pondering something, you look up suddenly to answer. How you sit when you're talking to somebody. How you sleep (that's something you're unable to imagine, even approximately!). How you quickly braid your hair (a skill that is unfathomable to me). But I can barely remember your voice – only your laughter occasionally and certain phrases and your tone. Fear prevents my imagination from picturing you in unfamiliar surroundings, fear that something will not be quite right, not how it is in reality but worse.

Sveta had a lot of news for Lev. In December, the government had devalued the rouble by nine-tenths and abolished rationing. There was a rush to purchase goods with the old cash, resulting in long queues at all the shops, but gradually the situation settled down. For relatively well-off families like the Ivanovs the new consumer opportunities were exciting. 'Life without the rationing system has its negative side – a mass of temptations with no restraint,' Sveta wrote to Lev on 24 January.

> At first people squander everything, then they realize that they need to be more careful, but after a new pay packet it all begins again. People have completely stopped eating black bread (we've had 1 kg for three days and it looks likely to last several more), and the hunt is on for white baguettes (4 roubles each – they used to be 1 rouble 40 kopeks) . . . At first it was impossible to get hold of pastries – but now our hunger for these has been satisfied . . . The late-night shops in our area are a godsend. There's a grocery store in our building, a delicatessen by Kursk station, a Tsentrosoyuz [Central Cooperative store] by the Pokrovsky Gates. There's never anybody there after 10 o'clock and it's easy to buy tea, sugar and butter etc. Bread and potatoes are also available for sale in institutions' cafeterias. Mama goes out early for meat (but that's because she likes quality at bargain

prices). There are queues for flour and more queues for milk, because in comparison with everything else it's cheap – 4 roubles a litre . . . One more thing I can report is that since the New Year my pay has been rounded up to 1,000 [roubles] . . . Domestic life – light, gas, heating – is absolutely fine, the trams etc. have improved. There are new carriages on the Metro fitted out with what looks like redwood; there's also lighting over the seating as well as in the middle and large windows . . . And on that note this bulletin comes to an end.

Sveta wanted to share this new bounty with Lev and his fellow prisoners by sending them parcels more regularly. She refused to listen to any more of his protests. 'So, my darling, foolish Lev,' she wrote on 30 March, 'how can you say you don't need anything until next year? Just the same dry crusts . . . Do you really think that I can sit here drinking delicious tea with jam, or nibbling on a biscuit with some milk, and not think about sending you anything?'

Lev continued to object to her sending food but he did ask for medicines for sick friends and other prisoners. Strelkov still suffered from stomach pains, which Lev described in great detail so that Sveta could get a diagnosis from her doctor friend Shura and send the appropriate medicines.

The patient is 49 years old, has a generally cheerful disposition and looks youthful . . . Since 1938, he's suffered from a hernia (the size of a goose egg). In 1920, he was shot in the chest: you can still see the 5 cm scar of the entrance wound underneath his right nipple, and the 4 cm scar of the exit wound near his spine between the same ribs. In October 1947, he began to suffer from periodic attacks of acute pain in and around his stomach – a band the width of 2–3 fingers on a level with his 7th–8th rib, starting on the right-hand side about a palm's width from the middle and moving to the left, a distance of 2–3 fingers from the middle . . . The pain is very intense, sharp and nagging, lasting for 8–14 hours without any real let-up. If he lies down on his back during an attack, the pain intensifies; if he clasps his knees to his chest, it lessens. His usual diet (for the past several years) has consisted of: fresh black bread; thin soup made from fine-ground barley, pearl barley or oatmeal and salt, with water; watery kasha with exactly the same 'ingredients' but much less concentrated; tea and coffee substitute either with sugar or without. Of these foods only fresh bread leads to an attack . . . There is little chance of a change in his diet.

Sveta wrote back with a diagnosis from Shura, who had consulted doctors at the First Moscow Medical Institute and agreed with them that the most likely explanation was a problem with his liver. She sent a range of medicines, some probes to take a sample of his bile, and advice on what to eat, promising to send him dried white bread.

Liubomir Terletsky, Lev's bunk-mate, was also ill. He suffered from scurvy, the result of eight years in the labour camp, and was broken psychologically. 'Liubka is gloomy and barely talks,' Lev wrote to Sveta. 'He is afraid of beauty and does not want to see it in nature or in books, because it reminds him of home.' To fight the scurvy Sveta started sending sachets of vitamin C powder, and gradually Terletsky recovered his strength. But the crippling psychological effects of camp life were still marked. 'My Liubka is very slowly returning to civilization,' Lev reported to Sveta.

Today I asked him why he pulls such terrible faces when he shakes hands with people and why he greets them so awkwardly. Looking somewhat embarrassed, he replied that over the last 8 years he'd got used to the fact that people never say hello or goodbye, just mutter swear-words at one another, and only use their hands to hit somebody – and so he's never sure if people are sincere when they extend their hand for him to shake. He offers his handshake as though he's performing a medieval show of deference. 'But,' he says, 'I catch myself doing it and sometimes manage not to appear so timid.' With luck, in another year he'll once again be greeting people normally.

In May 1948, Aleksandovich's wife Tamara, who was also ill, came to Moscow to see a doctor. Sveta helped her in the capital, and, on her return to Pechora, gave her a box of medicines she had collected for Lev's friends.

Sveta was herself unwell. She was losing weight, sleeping badly, feeling irritable and tearful – all clear signs of depression, though no one talked about such things in the Soviet Union, where optimism was compulsory and people who had problems were expected to pull their socks up and get on with it. The Ivanov family had many friends who were doctors, and Sveta went to see a lot of them. They all assumed that the problem was physical. They took blood tests, thought they had detected an inflammation of the thyroid and sent her to endocrinologists, who gave her iodine and Barbiphen (phenobarbital), but no one asked her how she felt emotionally. Sveta did not know what to make of what the doctors said. She was unsure whether there was anything wrong with her physically. All she knew was that she felt and looked unwell. She wrote to Lev:

The endocrinologist said she has no doubt there's an increase in thyroid activity (headaches, temperature, cardiodynia, weight loss, nervousness, etc., etc., including some kind of peculiar shine to my eyes – in my opinion that's just because of the temperature). I would be happy with such a diagnosis – I really hate uncertainty. She has prescribed pure iodine tablets, to be taken together with iodine potassium, Barbiphen, bromine, camphor and valerian extract. I have to take them all for 20 days, then stop for 10 days, then take them for another 20 days and go back to see her. Everything's fine apart from the fact that there's currently no valerian, so it's not possible to start the treatment. I went to see our doctor again today to give him the test results and tell him about my visit to the endocrinologist. He was really surprised at my sed rate.* He probably thought that all my ailments were caused by nerves, but nervousness alone doesn't increase the sed rate. He referred to the endocrinologist's prescriptions quite condescendingly: 'It will do you good to take them, but in my opinion it's not the most important thing.' (He didn't say what is.) 'My advice

---

* The sedimentation rate of red blood cells.

is to be sure to take cod-liver oil until the summer.' (And if it doesn't help?) I can't find any scales to weigh myself on, so I can't ascertain objectively whether I've actually lost weight or whether my weight loss is all in the subjective opinion of others. It seems to me that I'm not any thinner than I've been, and I was thinner last summer, but it's true my face is looking pinched, which really doesn't suit me and is making everyone sigh and exclaim: 'What's the matter with you?' Both to my face and behind my back they talk about how I was when I went to Khromnik* ('a captivating girl') and how I am now (obviously implying that I'm old and ragged, that I've become a hag).

Lev was the only person she could talk to about how she felt. In February 1948, a few weeks after her return from Pechora, she wrote to him:

My darling Levi, I want to be with you so much but I haven't even had any letters. I'm trying to break through to the surface and stop being angry. The word 'can't' has reappeared in my vocabulary. I can't bear seeing people who aren't happy when objectively they have everything they need to be happy. I can't sympathize with them; I can't stop being sharp or impatient. Irina rang on Saturday and invited me to go to Losinka for the day but I turned her down. I can't accept the comfort friends offer. I need all or nothing. Once again everything is black and white. But all the 'can'ts' can be explained by just one 'want'. Everything inside me is becoming harder and there's no way I can stop it. That's why I respond harshly to Irina, hang up the receiver, and then start to cry.

Writing to Lev was an outlet for her depression. He understood her moods. 'N. A. [Gleb's mother] rang the other day and asked me if I was all right, and, hiding my sadness, I said that I was fine,' she wrote to Lev on 2 March,

* The institute near Sverdlovsk where Sveta had worked in 1943.

but the truth is that even I don't know what to do with myself in this despondent mood. Levi, my darling, if I sometimes write nasty letters, I know I don't have the right, but who else can I cry with except you? When I write to you, I become less tense. So, again, Levi, don't get angry if you get such a letter. Anyway, by the time you receive it, my mood will probably have passed and I'll be jumping for joy. All right, my darling? I never write to make you angry or increase your pain. I've been weeping for several days in a row now, not just when I go to sleep but as soon as I wake up, early in the mornings, before lunch and afterwards. The most important thing, Levi, the most important thing, well, you know yourself what it is . . .

Levi, I hope that we will never feel guilty towards each other and will forgive each other for anything important, and if it's unimportant we'll try not to be angry (although it's usually those who are closest who bear the brunt).

Sveta did not want to burden Lev with the idea that her depression had anything to do with his imprisonment. He had enough to cope with as it was. And she knew she had to remain strong to help him through the coming years. In many of her letters she talked of other reasons for her low morale. 'A depression has come over me and I'm waiting for it to end,' she wrote to him. 'I don't know why January is so difficult. Maybe because at one time it was the happiest month, what with Mama's birthday, Christmas and New Year. Maybe it's because I've felt unwell since before the New Year. I get irritated, and I'm really tired all the time.' But Sveta's depression had nothing to do with her mother's birthday and everything to do with the fact that she and Lev were separated, as she sometimes revealed between the lines:

Having swallowed all kinds of pills (in a real, not a figurative, sense) I've forgotten how to cry (so if I need to swallow something in the figurative sense, I'm prepared). I've been sleeping badly recently, maybe because our room is so airless – it's been cold outside at night and Papa is scared of draughts so he keeps the windows closed. My little window doesn't open wide enough in any case. I've seen you in my dreams at least five times. Maybe it's because the end of your sentence is becoming more real or closer. It's probably superstition that I'm not going to see you now but for some reason will have to wait until the autumn, which may be better anyway.

Skiing and skating lifted her mood. 'At the moment,' she wrote to Lev on 10 March, 'skiing is the one thing I enjoy without reservation – better than literature, concerts, even people.'

It's so beautiful in the forest when the sun is peeping through, so pure (in all senses of the word) that you catch yourself thinking (and then accidentally saying aloud) that it's good to be alive. I don't know why it is, but it is not so painful. Some kind of physiology of happiness.

Sveta wanted to spend more time doing winter sports, although her mother tried to keep her in, feeling she was physically unwell. Only Lev encouraged her to get out more, to beat back the depression by living her life. 'Go somewhere,' he wrote on 15 April. 'Besides your physical well-being, there's the matter of your inner state, which has just as much effect on your psyche as external factors and sometimes may be the original cause.' Worried about Sveta's health, he wrote to his Uncle Nikita, hoping that he would keep an eye on her. 'It is very hard for her,' he wrote to him that April, 'hard in every way, although she does not say so directly.'

Sveta had a small circle of girlfriends in whom she could confide. Apart from Irina Krauze and Aleksandra Chernomordik there were three other women in particular with whom she spent a lot of time. Each had lost a husband and a child, yet each had found a way of living with her suffering that called forth Sveta's sympathy and led her to identify with them. First there was a woman from her institute called Lydia Arkadevna, a keen sportswoman and mountaineer, who fostered Sveta's enthusiasm for skiing and skating. 'So why have I turned to Lydia?' Sveta wrote to Lev on 25 February.

Because she's smart, quick-witted, lively, strong, interested in a lot of things, etc. etc. She is a marvellous skier and she goes skating often, and she does all that even though she's nearly 10 years older than me, her husband perished during the war, she lost her 14-year-old son a year ago (in a terrible street accident)* and she remains alone in the world. I watch and learn.

There was also a younger woman, called Klara, a technical assistant at one of the institutes, whose family had been repressed before the war. Klara herself had been expelled from the Kharkov Chemical-Technological Institute during her first year of studies, after which she had spent some years in exile, judging from Sveta's comment in one of her letters that an 'over-acquaintance with geography' was the root of Klara's problems. There had been several attempts to force her out of the institute, but she clung to her position, badly paid though it was. Klara had also lost a child. Her husband was a prisoner in Pechora, and she had travelled there on more than one occasion to see him, staying with Tamara Aleksandrovich. Lev thought well of Klara and defended her against Vladimir Aleksandrovich's claim that she was waiting for her husband only because he came from a well-to-do family. Lev's personal impressions of her, though, were 'too superficial' for him to be sure ('nice-looking, almost bland, with a vampirish manicure and rings . . . she seems moderately intelligent, hardly capable of such low calculation'). Sveta's comments about Klara were typically blunt and self-revealing:

I can imagine that Tamara likes Klara more, because of her greater femininity, her love of order, of comfort, clothes, etc. They're probably also close because they're both mothers and they've both lost children, whereas I'm just a grass bride.† That's probably the real difference,

* His stomach was ripped open by a piece of iron protruding from the side of a passing lorry.
† A bride who has lost her groom (*solomennaia nevesta*). In Russian folklore grass was used as a symbolic payment on the agreement of a contract.

but I find it difficult to decide which is worse. Also, Klara is affectionate, and I'm not. Klara, of course, has cried on her shoulder, whereas I have not.

Finally there was Nina Semashko, Lev and Sveta's friend from the Physics Faculty, who had lost her husband, Andrei, in the war, and then her baby son. Writing to Lev about the death of Nina's child, Sveta touched on her own suffering:

It's always difficult to bury someone but somebody small and young is a different thing entirely. An outsider perceives a child only in the present, but for the mother the present stretches back into the past and envelops everything in the future. There's not just the 9 months of waiting and the 11 months of feeding but, long before that, the desire or reluctance (or anxiety about whether it's even possible). I don't know if I'm being clear, but this future is everything, all plans and dreams, right up to and including the desire to have grandchildren. And so [the death of a child] rips out such a chunk of this everything that it seems there's nothing left to fill it with. Fortunately the world is such that the pain dulls over time . . . Nina is still young enough – and she has the freedom – to decide that another child may fill that void, but now is not the time to talk to her about it. At the moment she just says that if a person is unlucky, there's no point in striving for anything or searching for happiness.

Sveta longed to have a child. She was thirty years old. She knew that she would have to wait eight more years, at least, for Lev to be released and that he might not return at all. Perhaps that was what she meant when she wrote that she was waiting for her 'life to start'. After her trip to Pechora, Sveta was certain that her future – her 'everything' – was tied to Lev. But they had decided not to have a child as long as he remained a prisoner. Lev reflected on their decision years later:

I didn't want to compromise her future with my present or future. I did not want her, out of love for me, to sacrifice herself, to tie herself to my fate. That's why I didn't want us to be bound by children. No one knew what would happen as long as Stalin was alive. I could expect nothing good. To burden Sveta with a child in such a situation – in which I could not help her and might subject her and the child to a terrible existence – was not something I could do. In Stalin's time, prisoners released from the labour camps, 'enemies of the people' like myself, could not live normal lives. They were often rearrested or sent into exile . . . I couldn't burden Sveta and her family with the terrible difficulties, the unhappiness, they were certain to suffer if we had a child. But Sveta wanted one.

Sveta invested all her maternal affection in Alik, Yara's son. Her letters contained regular reports on her nephew, whom she obviously adored. 'Leva', she wrote, 'Alik is turning seven, not eight, and we celebrated his birthday on Sunday.'

Today Lena [Alik's mother] brought him with us to see Obraztsov's *Puss in Boots*. He said he liked that it was so short, and although he understands that the animals aren't real (he's a good enough actor himself to know that) he nevertheless thought that people climb into (put on) the puppets – which means he didn't notice that they were too small. He's already been to real theatres – he went to *Tales* at the Children's Theatre. Do you remember *Terem-Teremok* and *About the Goat*?* I think you and I saw them the last time we were together, not counting our final trip to the cinema – I can't remember what the film was. Alik has grown a lot, so he's got thinner, but he's not skinny at all. His physical courage and self-possession are improving slowly . . . [He] gets As in Russian and arithmetic, but Bs in physical education. I told you already that he understands that $1/7$ is less than $1/5$, and Lera [from his school] has taught him how to subtract fractions (not too difficult ones) from whole numbers. Now he's become interested in engineering – he's always trying to take

* Shows at the Central Children's Theatre based on tales by the Soviet children's poet Samuil Marshak.

something apart and climb inside and put it back together in reverse. He's not noted for his tidiness. But I don't have any idea how to 'educate' a child.

In fact, Sveta's mother, Anastasia, had suggested that she consider working as a teacher at a nursery. Sveta doubted her own abilities as a scientist, and her mother thought she might be happier if she spent more time with small children. Lev encouraged the idea. But Sveta decided against it in the end, on the grounds that she lacked experience of mothering and did 'not know how children grow'. Meanwhile she loved it when Alik came to stay with her. His naughtiness reminded Sveta of her own childhood:

Alik is capable of waking me up at 6 o'clock (after he himself has already had a good night's sleep, of course). He loves to make noise, forgets to wash his hands, plays happily with a bicycle that spends most of its time upside-down, and climbs fully dressed into a wash tub full of soap suds. I don't know whether I'd be upset and angry if I'd been a goody two-shoes myself, but I remember all too well how we made the apartment ours, turning all the chairs over, crawling under the beds and tables. And nobody yelled at me, even when I was jumping around and broke my tooth on the headboard or cut my head against the radiator (maybe Yara was told off, but I wasn't). You see, I'm quite a poor mentor and childminder, since I rely on heredity and the natural course of things in the belief that it's simply not possible for anything truly bad to grow out of something so small and glorious. But the worst thing is that I'm a 'theoretician-childminder', far removed from practical experience.

By coincidence, Lev was also playing the role of 'mentor and childminder'. On 5 October, the day Sveta arrived back in Moscow from Pechora, Lev had received a visitor:

A young girl came to the power station and I said, 'Are you coming to see us?' 'Yes.' 'Well, come on then.' Looking suspiciously at

Nikolai Bogdanov [a mechanic at the power station], she asked me: 'Why aren't you dirty, mister?' And, taking hold of my belt, she led me around the generator room and began to ask whether the machines were resting and why there were so many clocks everywhere and whether there would be light if the furnaces weren't stoked. We quickly became friends and I learned that her name is Tamara Kovalenko, she comes from the Vinnytsa region, and her father works at the stables.

Tamara was eleven years old. She had an older sister called Lida and a younger brother, Tolik (Anatoly). They were ragged, shoeless children neglected by their mother, who worked as a laundress, and always hungry, because their father spent most of the household income on vodka. The Kovalenkos were among the 500 'special exiles' in the wood-combine, many of them living in the barracks of the 1st Colony, just outside the prison zone, but children like Tamara were free to roam around the labour camp. They were never stopped or searched by any of the guards, so they could run errands for the prisoners, who gave them sweets and money or made them wooden toys in the workshops. The town children would search for toys near the prison-zone perimeter, where prisoners sometimes threw them over the fence. These anonymous gifts were found in many homes around the labour camp, where they served as a reminder of the prisoners' longing for their own children, winning human sympathy for them.

Tamara started coming every day to visit Lev. He became fond of her, giving her food and beginning to teach her how to read and do arithmetic. 'I was enlisted as a father again today,' Lev wrote to Sveta on 25 October.

I arrived for my shift and suddenly Tamara appeared with her sister and little brother. I wrote to you about Tamara – she's 11 years old and infinitely sincere and affectionate. Anyway, having spotted me, she abandoned her little family (her sister is 14 and her little brother is 6), telling them to go home without her, and ran to me. She threw her arms around me – I don't know how she managed it – and announced that she had missed me very much, that she had come twice before but hadn't been able to wait for me, and that she was going to stay with me until the whistle blew (at the end of my shift at 5). She told me that she's going to school now, she's in the second class, so it seems her parents have seen reason. She pulled out an old red silk ribbon to tie a bow and with regret said that she had only one. Sveta, if you can, slip a few more ribbons into a parcel of books – and some kind of children's book.

It was not long before Lida came as well. 'She is older and . . . acts more grown-up. They've become the daughters of three electricians and one machine-operator, but it seems they think of me as their main "papa".' Thanks to Lev's tutoring, the girls' grades improved at school. Then Tamara stole some trinkets from one of the prisoners. Lida returned the missing things, but Lev was disillusioned. 'I have lost faith in myself,' he wrote to Sveta. 'There's no need for more ribbon. Tamara won't be coming to the station any more.'

Lev was studying hard, reading up on electrical engineering in any books that he could find, in an effort to improve the functioning of the power station, whose poor capacity was holding up production at the wood-combine. Without enough electricity the workshops were often forced to shut down (in May 1948, it was calculated that the machines were idle for almost a quarter of the working time). The prisoners sat around all day, smoking, playing cards, until the power was turned on again; then they had to work around the clock to meet the production plan. 'There is no rhythm in our work,' complained one of the Party leaders of the wood-combine at a meeting on 12 May. 'We reel from one frenzied burst to the next, trying to fulfil the plan.'

Lev was highly critical of the erratic work culture of the wood-combine. He thought the place was run by 'idiots' and often wrote of the 'stupidities' committed by the bosses whose determination to increase output at all costs frequently led to mechanical breakdowns, accidents, fires and general chaos – all of which made it even harder to fulfil the plan. On 12 May, for example, Lev described the ongoing repairs at the power station:

There's such a dreadful shambles over making the new concrete floors. We've had to do a lot of the dirty work – replacing the wiring of the motor pump which the electrical department had done abominably, installing new circuit breakers and so on. The reason the floor job is being done so sloppily is that none of the bosses overseeing it care one bit; they won't be punished if it's done badly. Enormous amounts of labour, materials, time and energy are just wasted here – nothing is done responsibly. Things that took 10 years to make are abandoned after a year; installations meant to be temporary are refitted to last for years and only made to look as if they meet the plan. Everything is done haphazardly – unless it's overseen by someone like Strelkov, who worries about every detail, but he's one in a thousand and even he's not always in a position to do anything about the stupidity and stagnation that are so much part of the system.

Lev's efforts to improve the working of the power plant were completely voluntary. His motivation was not political, as it was for Strelkov, an old Bolshevik who believed in the system and tried to make it work. But, like him, Lev was conscientious by nature and took pride and interest in his work. 'I'm unable to sit calmly in a room if there's something wrong with the ticking of its clock,' he wrote to Sveta. 'I cannot relax if the timing between its 'tick-tock' and 'tock-tick' is uneven. When I see our electricians, even our best ones, at work, I think, what a torture it would be for them if I were their manager.' And those electricians would agree:

Yesterday one of our operators remarked that I'm always finding something to do. 'Lev,' he said, 'you without work is like a fool without a smack' (a smack around the head, that is). It's a crude but vivid comparison: one man walks about looking for something constructive to get on with and is at peace when he finds it; another hangs around, poking his nose where he shouldn't and disturbing everyone, eventually gets smacked on the head for it, and, having learned his lesson, does nothing.

But there was more than conscientiousness in Lev's efforts at the plant. There was self-esteem, the desire to accomplish something positive while he was a prisoner, perhaps the recognition that he needed at least to learn some new skills in these years, if they were not to be wasted altogether and he was to come out of the camp in the right frame of mind to rebuild his life (looking back on his prison years, Lev was always proud of what he had achieved by improving the capacity of the power station so that it could fuel the wood-combine). He also needed to distract himself, to block out negative and self-destructive thoughts and lose himself in work to help the days pass by – a method of survival adopted by many prisoners.*

Self-protection also played a part. By making himself useful at the power station, he was able to keep his privileged position and reduce the danger of being sent away on a convoy – his greatest fear – or put back into a hauling team. He hoped also to reduce his sentence. On 1 May 1948, a new credit system was introduced for the 'auxiliary operations' (including the power station) at the wood-combine: days in which a prisoner fulfilled between 100 and 150 per cent of his production quota were henceforth to be counted as 1.25 days; between 150 and 200 per cent as 1.5 days; between 200 and 275 per cent as 2 days; and higher than 275 per cent as 3 days. 'So,' Lev wrote to Sveta, 'we may be due a quarter of a day, which means 6.5 days a month, or 2½ months a year, and there's also the possibility of additional credits in the event of a particularly excellent appraisal by the head of the facility, or the complete loss of credits in the event of a poor one . . . It's all a bit of a lottery.'

The risk of being put on a convoy was a real one in 1948, when the 4th Colony was being developed and prisoners from the wood-combine were being sent to it. Skilled prisoners were also being

---

* This is one of the main themes of Aleksandr Solzhenitsyn's novel *One Day in the Life of Ivan Denisovich*.

transferred to the 3rd Colony – made up mainly of criminals and workers who had broken camp rules – where labour discipline had completely collapsed, barely one-third of production targets were being met, and there were riots in protest against the poor living conditions. During the summer of 1948, a number of individual escapes and even mass break-outs from the 3rd Colony encouraged prisoners in the 2nd Colony to plot their escape. They were not discouraged by the news that several escapees from the 3rd had been shot in the forest, while others had returned because they could not bear the mosquitoes.*

There were rumours of a 'large contingent of prisoners' being transferred to the camps of north Siberia as a way of dealing with the unrest, Lev wrote to Sveta on 24 June. He warned her not to send any parcels until he was able to clarify the situation, as he was expecting the politicals, including himself, to be selected first for the convoy, possibly 'within the next few days'. On 25 June, he wrote again, this time advising her not to plan another trip to Pechora and asking her to write to him through Aleksandrovich, in case he was sent away:

> Well, Svetishche, some instructions for you in view of coming events: don't spend your holiday leave undertaking a journey. Think of coming here only if a work trip won't require any particular effort, if there is one at all, that is. The chances of success are going to be reduced to practically nothing as of the day after tomorrow. It

---

* In *White Nights*, his account of his imprisonment in the Pechora Gulag from 1940 to 1942, Menachem Begin, later to become Prime Minister of Israel, quotes a fellow prisoner, who claimed the 'north-flies' of Pechora were even worse than ordinary mosquitoes: 'They guard the prisoners better than all the *strelki* [sentries] with their rifles. How? Once a prisoner got out of the camp and ran away. A *strelki* fired after him, chased him, hunted for him with bloodhounds, in vain. The prisoner had vanished . . . Three days later the escapee returned of his own accord . . . He was unrecognisable. They took him to "solitary". But he swore he would never again try to escape. The north-flies had taught him a lesson.' (Begin, *White Nights*, pp. 160–61).

seems that all who have the most serious article [58] are going to be dismissed from their jobs – except for those doing 'general' work – and resettled in the 3rd Colony (by the river), which is being redefined as a 'reinforced regime'.* It will be completely impossible for you to stay, even for a short time, in the industrial zone (where we're working at the moment). The only way it could happen is if there is an individual exception. But I'll say it again, the likelihood of that is practically zero – this time it's going to be a lot tougher . . . The best thing would be for you not to attempt a visit at all. Are you listening, Svet? Do as I tell you. Accept this as my final decision . . . Agreed, Svet? That's how it is. As to the future, we'll discuss it later, because at this point we can only guess at what's going to happen . . . In case you need it I'll send a new address in a few days time when 'Zh[aba]' [Aleksandrovich] gets a new job. But don't use it too often. It will work for the time being. One more thing, Svetishche. You must not keep this letter – that's why it doesn't have a number. And write to let me know you received it – just say the one dated the 25th arrived.

Sveta did not do as Lev asked. His letters were precious – she kept them all. Nor did she abandon her plan to visit him.

Lev and Sveta had been discussing a second trip since April. This time she was far more apprehensive than before. The original plan was to go in the summer. Tsydzik, Sveta's boss, encouraged the idea, advising her to take more time than she had done the previous year. 'Yesterday, M. A. [Tsydzik] asked when I was planning to go to Kirov,' Sveta had written to Lev on 16 April.

---

* Lev was probably thinking of the 'special regime' camps (*osobye lageria*), of which ten were established in the spring of 1948 to isolate the 'most dangerous' political prisoners ('spies, diversionists, terrorists, Trotskyists, right-wingers, Mensheviks, Socialist Revolutionaries, Anarchists, nationalists, White emigrants and participants in other anti-Soviet organizations'). The 'special regime' camps were located in the harshest regions of the country, including several near or above the Arctic Circle (Inta, Vorkuta, Noril'sk and Kolyma). Prisoners had numbers branded on their skin, wore striped uniforms, and were allowed only 'minimal contact with the outside world' (Applebaum, *Gulag*, p. 419).

I told him I had applied for holiday leave in August and had also put my name down for a scheduled inspection of the tyre factory in Kirov that month. But he said: 'Go in July, when it's warmer, and "sit"* there for a while so that you won't have to do everything the same way as last year.' So there we are. But this time I'm frightened, much more so than before. Somehow I was more prepared then for an unsuccessful outcome, and I was a bit emotionless. But now I cannot even think.

At the end of May, Sveta's plans to travel north at the end of a work trip to Kirov were jeopardized. The institute was threatening to postpone factory inspections by scientists because payments due from partner organizations had not yet come in. 'If the work trips fall through for the whole summer,' Sveta wrote to Lev, 'I'll take my holiday in July and that will be that. It's not what I want. I'm too conspicuous at the institute for my absence not to be noticed, so people will start asking where I've been and what I saw.' Lev disagreed. He felt that Sveta should heed Tsydzik's advice, since she was relying on his help to conceal her journey. He also feared that travelling later than July 'might turn out to be difficult'. On 8 June, he had written to Sveta to say that she should write with the details of her journey to Tamara Aleksandrovich, who had offered to meet her when she came to Pechora.

But now came those rumours of a convoy to Siberia, and Lev, thinking he was about to be transferred to the 3rd Colony, sent word to Sveta on 25 June to abort all plans. As it turned out, the day after he sent that message, on 27 June, the situation changed again. 'The latest decision by those fickle local (or not so local) powers that be is for everything to remain as it was, or almost as it was, for the next month at least, because the fulfilment of the plan could seriously suffer if the proposed reform (remember my letter of 25 June?) is put into effect,' Lev wrote. A convoy of prisoners had just arrived in the 2nd Colony from Siberia, 'the place where they had planned to move us after the

---

* Russians spoke of people 'sitting' in prison.

3rd Colony', Lev explained, and he thought this gave 'some credibility' to the decision to delay sending prisoners away. 'It's possible,' thought Lev, 'that they will make this the place to concentrate the "unreliables" with the most serious articles. Sveta, the advice in my letter of the 25th holds. This piece of paper is only for immediate reading. I'll write again soon, but I have to send this off at once.'

On 1 July, Lev confirmed that the 2nd Colony was going to become a 'reinforced regime' for the politicals, and that those with lighter sentences, the so-called 'common articles' (theft, murder, hooliganism, labour desertion and so on) were going to be kept in the 3rd Colony, where conditions would be easier. 'Apparently, it's not going to add any particular restrictions for us [the politicals in the 2nd Colony],' Lev added, 'but the free workers who are currently living inside the industrial zone are going to be removed, along with the small production units where free workers and the special exiles are employed.' The departure of the free workers from the industrial zone would rule out a repeat of the previous year's arrangements, when Sveta had met Lev at the Aleksandrovskys.

Lev was right about the tightening of security inside the industrial zone, though rumours about the imminent removal of the free workers were not entirely accurate. The Gulag bosses of the wood-combine had indeed resolved to be more vigilant in stamping out contact between the free workers and the prisoners. At a closed Party meeting on 12 May they had agreed that such contact was to blame for many breaches of security, including the smuggling of letters, the black market in vodka and the illegal entry of unauthorized visitors into the prison camp. They had considered moving the free workers out of the industrial zone, but in the end dropped that option as impractical, because it would require building new housing outside the zone. Instead the bosses decided to increase the separation between the settlement where the free workers lived and the rest of the industrial zone by putting up a new barbed-wire fence with a guard-house.

Sveta was proceeding with her plans to travel to Pechora that summer. 'The matter is resolved,' she wrote to Lev on 25 June, just as he was writing to her not to come. 'I will go to Kirov and then immediately, as last year, I'll extend my leave and spend as long as possible where I really want to be.' Four days later, the chief account-ant of the institute informed her that there was no money for work trips until the end of August at the earliest, so she applied to change the dates of her holiday to July; she would travel to Pechora then. She expected to leave by 10 July and had already written to Lev Izrai-levich to warn him of her arrival. Tsydzik consented to the holiday but advised Sveta to go to Kirov anyway – advice she agreed with – as a way to conceal her actual plans.

On 8 July, Sveta received Lev's letters about the tightening of security and the inadvisability of her coming. She said she would do nothing until she had further news from him. Someone needed to remain in charge of the laboratory during the summer months, so she would stay in Moscow through August, while Tsydzik went on holiday, and in September she would leave, either for Pechora or, if that was still not possible, for Pereslavl'-Zalessky, 100 kilometres north-east of Moscow, where she would stay with her brother, Yaroslav, in his rented dacha for a week or two.

By this time, Lev was feeling the effects of the tightening of secu-rity. 'Slowly they are introducing all sorts of strict new rules here,' he wrote to Sveta on 7 July, 'though so far they have not brought any serious unpleasantness.' He had not received any letters from Sveta for ten days and did not know whether this was a result of the new regime. 'Everything is changeable, one shake and the colours change, like a kaleidoscope.'

The next day, Lev made contact with Lev Izrailevich. He phoned him from the power station, where there was a telephone in case of fires at the plant, and found out from him that Sveta was still plan-ning on a trip. The security measures were proceeding apace. In mid-July the 'special exiles' were moved out of the industrial zone in preparation for the arrival of a new convoy of political pris-oners, reinforcing Lev's belief that the wood-combine would become a special regime camp. On 21 July he again warned Sveta that it was too difficult to plan a meeting for that summer. 'Maybe 1949 will be a better year,' he wrote. 'It seems that the so-called reinforced regime is going to come into effect here no later than next week.'

Despite her decision to put off her holiday, Sveta was persuaded by her mother to take a break and join her brother's family in Pereslavl'-Zalessky from mid-July. Their wooden summer-house had an orchard garden and overlooked a peaceful lake surrounded by pine forest. It was beautiful and quiet. They went boating on the lake and hunted for mushrooms. She slept a lot. But without Lev she felt she could find no spiritual rest. 'My darling Lev,' she wrote on 23 July,

> a week has already passed and I haven't written anything. I caught up on sleep, sunbathed; everybody says I've lightened up a little. I'm behaving myself, sensibly, I'm not crying. I'm trying not to think about you, but I have dreams where I see you in a haze. I'm keeping myself on a tight leash so that I don't think about your letters, about what's in them, about what's possible and what's impossible. I'm not doing too badly here, but that's my head speaking, not my heart. I'm unable to enjoy the lake, the forest, or the air with the whole of my being. My body is relaxing but not my soul.

On 31 July, Sveta's mother arrived from Moscow, bringing three letters. Sveta could hardly contain her excitement as she opened them. But hope turned to disappointment when she read the short last letter of the three, the one in which Lev ruled out any meeting for that year and observed sensibly but almost casually that 'Maybe 1949 will be a better year'. Sveta was furious – with everything and everyone – and she took it out on Lev. She could not understand how he could be so willing to wait a whole year when she was so desperate to visit him. In despair, she scolded him for thinking that she could be kept on hold without any certainty of seeing him. 'I'm interested, Levi,' she wrote on 2 August, 'how do you see it? That it would be better for me if there hadn't been so many "if onlys". You can't answer that – it's not a question but a reprimand.' Not until 9 August could she write to Lev in more collected terms:

I haven't written for a week because my soul hasn't had (and still doesn't have) any peace and quiet. When Mama came to see us in Pereslavl' and brought your letters I fell apart again, completely. (This is not to say that you shouldn't have written.) I got angry at all those sensible adult people who discouraged me from going to Pechora earlier, and at Mama, who forced me to take holiday leave (although she was completely right), but most of all at myself, of course, because at 30 years of age I should be deciding things for myself. I was angry that I hadn't hurried to see you earlier, that I hadn't immediately rushed home and gone to the institute to formalize my work trip when it was still possible to do so. Now it's too late. And I'm seething and don't know what to do.

Worried that her earlier 'reprimand' might be seen as cruel, she made her meaning clearer now: 'In my last letter I scolded you so that you would never think my life could be better without you. I'm repeating it to be on the safe side, in case you didn't get that letter.'

Sveta was desperate to visit Lev. If she heeded his advice, yet another year would pass before she saw him again. She would be thirty-two in 1949. How much longer could she wait for her life to start? How long could it be before she had a child? She knew the cost of being tied to Lev (he had warned her of it many times): the growing possibility that she would never have a child. And at times she found it hard to bear.

In both her letters of 'reprimand' Sveta raised the issue of having children. She wrote to Lev about a conversation she had had with Uncle Nikita in which he insisted that no one had 'the right to give life', and that 'people had children for egotistical reasons, thinking only about themselves'. Sveta had replied that 'new life brought the possibility of more goodness in a world that needed it'. She thought that Nikita was bitter because 'he feels guilty towards his son for having given birth to him if he could not ensure that he had an easier and more joyful life.' The answer was to have more than one child, Sveta concluded. If Nikita had had another child, a younger one, or even better, an older one so that by now he would already have some grandchildren to look after and give meaning to his life, then such thoughts would never have entered his head. Maybe gender makes a difference here. For a woman life has already been fulfilled if she has loved and had children. For any (or almost any) woman, that is the central focus of her life, however many different interests she may have in public life, work, etc.

Back in Moscow, Sveta once again decided to travel to Pechora – and before the summer ended. Natalia Arkadevna was leaving for Pechora on 18 August to see her son Gleb. It was agreed that Sveta would find a way to persuade her institute to release the funds to send her on an inspection trip to Kirov shortly after that. Natalia would send a telegram to the post office in Kirov letting Sveta know if it was feasible for her to attempt a second visit to the labour camp. Time was running out but the risks involved in going without enough preparation were high. 'On the one hand, chances diminish every day,' Sveta wrote to Lev on 13 August, 'but on the other, it's impossible to travel without having made the necessary arrangements – and making the arrangements is very difficult.'

So it seems the wisest option is to wait until N. A. arrives – then she can send me a telegram . . . She's going to leave on the 18th so it's unlikely she'll be able to send it any earlier than the 19th, which means that I need to be in Kirov until the 20th. I'm scared of waiting any longer. I can't find a happy medium. Maybe it would be better to travel with her, but then there might be a problem getting the tickets. If I don't hear from her, I'll just risk it on my own, in which case I'll arrive on the 22nd or the 23rd. I'll send a telegram from Kirov, of course, but that may not get to you in time. It would be nice one day to see each other again without all these plans. According to the new timetable (for this year), trains arrive no longer at night but between 10 and 11 in the morning (according to I[van Lileev – Nikolai's father]) – but maybe that won't be too difficult. If there's no one to meet me, I will look for them at work (with light luggage and no obvious signs of having just arrived) rather than go directly to their apartment.* I think that would be best – I'm so nervous about making a wrong move. My stupid head managed to forget his [Arvanitopulo's] name and patronymic during the holiday (although I can remember the initials) and I can't work out the necessary information from the letters either, because I have lost them. I remember I put the letter with the most important details aside somewhere so that it would be to hand, but where is that 'somewhere'? I'm going to have to look through all the letters yet again. I'm still pinning some hopes on the namesake [Lev Izrailevich]. I've also written to him to make sure he doesn't go anywhere on those days and at those times. He knows how little I know my way around, after all. I'm so afraid that fate will turn against me that I'm not telling anyone about my travel dates and time in case I tempt it. I'm hoping to deceive it and sneak by, despite its being a leap year. Because of that fear I'm absolutely not planning to bring anything with me . . . I have three requests: 1. send me a telegram immediately, 2. understand mine, 3. meet.

Five days later, Sveta had not yet left Moscow. There were difficulties getting train tickets (not uncommon in the Soviet Union, where people queued for days at ticket-offices). 'Goodness knows when I'm going to depart,' she wrote on 18 August:

There hasn't been a separate booking office for people travelling on work trips for three months. If you're lucky you can get a ticket in a day at the advance booking office, or in a couple of days, because they note down who's in the queue so that it can start again unchanged the following day . . . But through my own stupidity we've already flushed two days down the drain for nothing. I took my place in the queue, then left for work with Yara and then Mama

---

* Sveta is talking about making contact with the unnamed voluntary workers who will put her up in the settlement inside the industrial zone, Boris Arvanitopulo (the head of the electric power station in the wood-combine) and his wife Vera.

taking over for me, but the tickets ran out before Mama got to the window, and, not realizing that she had to secure her place in the queue, she went home. She was angry with herself and the following morning she went early to stand in the queue, but when I arrived to replace her it turned out she'd trusted some policeman who had told her that all the tickets for trains in the direction of Gorky were at a different window. To cut it short, she wasn't standing in the queue I had been in, and I didn't have time to start all over again since I really had to be at the institute . . .

In the end, despite more confusion, Sveta's mother managed to get her a one-way ticket for the 21st. The ticket was valid for only six days, just enough time for Sveta to do her work at the factory in Kirov and travel to Pechora, though it would be touch and go. She had to make up her mind whether to go to Kirov on her way there or on her return. She decided to stop there first. That would allow her to check at the post office for any telegrams from Natalia Arkadevna and to send a message to Tsydzik postponing her return. It would also mean that she could buy a direct ticket home. 'It's a pity to stop in Kirov,' she wrote to Lev, 'but I'll be less anxious when it's done.'

Sveta left Moscow on 21 August. When she got to Kirov she sent a telegram, which Lev received the next day. But, contrary to her instructions, he did not reply, thinking it was too late to reach her. Instead he waited to see if she would come. His friend and boss, Boris Arvanitopulo, who had agreed to meet Sveta and put her up, went to the station on the 23rd. He watched the train pull in and looked for a thin young woman with plaits and a rucksack among the passengers who made their way past him towards the station-hall. Sveta was not among them. On the 24th he returned to the station, but she was not on that day's train either. Each time Boris came back to the camp without Sveta, and each time Lev was driven mad with worry. 'So, my darling Sveta,' he wrote on the 24th, 'I sit here and think, will you come or not? And if not, then it will be all my fault for listening to N. A.* and not sending a telegram to K[irov]. I can't think about anything else. Perhaps something has happened to you.'

Sveta had indeed run into trouble. On the stretch between Kirov and Kotlas, some of the carriages at the back of the train had been decoupled after the inspectors found a fault with their wheels. There was a mad rush by the passengers to find places in the forward carriages. Sveta grabbed her things and just managed to make it to the front end of the train before it departed; what happened to the other passengers, who were not as quick, she did not know. Greater danger was to come. At Kotlas she was sitting on her rucksack in the station yard, waiting for the train to Pechora and hoping to avoid attention, when a policeman approached her. As she was in civilian clothes, not in the khaki dress that had helped her on her first journey, she had probably thought it best not to wait inside the station-hall. The policeman could have asked to see her documents and demanded to know where she was travelling, in which case she could have been in serious trouble. But he turned out to be friendly and concerned only for her safety. There were thieves about, he said, and she would be safer if she waited for her train inside the hall.

On the 25th Sveta finally arrived in Pechora. Arvanitopulo met her at the station and took her to his house just outside the perimeter fence of the wood-combine. The Arvanitopulos had a telephone. Boris had constantly to be on call in case of a fire at the power station, where there was also a telephone, which Lev had access to when he was on his shift. Sveta called Lev. Her call was put through at the telephone exchange by Maria Aleksandrovskaya, the woman who had harboured Lev and Sveta in her house the previous year. Lev told Sveta that someone had informed the guards about her plans to enter the labour camp illegally and that 'they were eagerly awaiting the opportunity to arrest her'. Not all the guards were that hostile, however, it would seem, since one of them had warned him of the threat. Lev had transformed one of the storerooms in the

---

* Natalia Arkadevna must have advised Lev not to send a telegram.

basement of the power station into a 'conspiratorial apartment', where she could stay with him if she made it through.

Determined to see Lev but not wanting to risk arrest by entering the camp illegally, Sveta went to the headquarters of the Gulag administration, the large, white classical building she had passed by with Lev Izrailevich on her way to the wood-combine the previous year, to apply for official permission to visit Lev. It was a courageous thing to do, since the MVD administrators almost certainly knew about her illegal entry into the camp in 1947 and may now have ordered her arrest. She climbed the stairs to the second floor, where she found the door to the offices of A. I. Borovitsky, the boss of the labour camp, at the end of a broad corridor with wooden floors and large windows from which she could see the chimney of the power station in the wood-combine. In the large main room of Borovitsky's offices there were plaster bas-reliefs made by prisoners, depicting northern forest scenes, building sites and railways. Borovitsky was not there when she arrived. She waited for him to turn up. She was exhausted after her long journey from Moscow. 'I waited the whole day for the head of the administration to come and was still waiting for him late at night,' she recalled.

Like all the other Gulag bosses, Borovitsky worked at night, as Stalin did. The clocks in every office were set to Moscow time. No boss could afford to be asleep if the MVD in the capital called. Eventually Borovitsky came and received Sveta in his office, where he sat between his desk and a large safe. Polite and courteous, Borovitsky immediately agreed to Sveta's request and signed an order, which he put into her hand as he showed her out. 'I thanked him enthusiastically,' recalled Sveta. But once out on the street, she looked more closely at what was in her hand. 'There was a bright street-lamp there or perhaps a searchlight, and in its light I read the document: "Allow a meeting of 20 minutes in the presence of a military guard."'

The meeting took place the next day in the small guard-house at the entrance to the barracks block for the prisoners of the 2nd Colony. The guard on duty turned out to be kinder than his boss. He allowed Lev and Sveta to meet on their own in a private recess off the main room, where there was a table and a bench. The recess had a door that was kept open but the guard did not come in. On the table was the register in which the guard was meant to keep a log of visitors. Sveta had been given twenty minutes, but the guard did not record the time of her arrival. If anybody asked, he would say that she had just arrived and he had not yet made a note of it in his register. In this way Lev and Sveta were able to be together for several hours that day. Before his shift ended, the guard told them to return the following day at noon, when he would have another shift. Sveta came back at the appointed time. Lev then appeared, and they spent the whole of the afternoon together sitting on the bench in the recess. All that time, just out of view behind the door, prisoners and guards were passing in and out of the guard-house. The time was both more than they could have expected and hopelessly inadequate.

Sveta left Pechora on 30 August. She was taken to the station by Lev's loyal friend Stanislav Yakhovich, who helped her get a ticket and put her on the Moscow train. 'My darling Lev,' she wrote on her way to Kotlas, 'a second day without you has already come and gone.'

My wagon is a combination one (sleeping at the top, sitting at the bottom), which means people come and go more often [than in a sleeping car]. But everyone in my compartment is travelling all the way to Kotlas, where the train is scheduled to stop for 5 hours. Kotlas is a dreadful place – there is nowhere else as filthy along the whole route. I will sleep. It's a cold night but I've got a woollen camisole with me. And I've wrapped myself in a blanket and won't freeze . . . The forests are already not so marshy but beautiful in that autumnal way . . . Below me on the lower berth are some children – a 10-year-old girl, a girl and a boy of 5, and another girl of 3. They belong to three sisters whose husbands have all been killed – and who now live together as a family. The children are lovely. Well, Levi, that's everything for now. Look after yourself and greetings to everyone.

It was not until the evening of 4 September that she arrived home, to find her parents worried sick (they had not received any of the telegrams she had sent, as promised, to let them know she was all right). Sveta wrote to Lev that evening:

My dear, dear Levi, I'm home at last. I had wanted to send you one more letter from Gorky but I didn't have time. I wrote to you twice while travelling – once from some station or other and then from Kirov. The rain made all the side streets in Kirov impassable, but it was just clay-mud, not bogs as in Kotlas. The train from Kirov to Gorky was like something out of the Ark, but my berth was fine and the people were nice, so I arrived in good spirits. On the berth below were a mother and grandmother with a 3-year-old boy who's not yet walking and talking. The doctors say there's no need for treatment and that with peace and quiet, nursing and care he'll be fine by the age of 6. The boy is beautiful to look at – enormous eyes with long, thick, curly eyelashes – and he's so affectionate . . . There was one other woman travelling with me, a Muscovite as well, who had waited ten years for her husband [to return from a labour camp], moved to Kirov to be with him, only to discover he had married someone else. For her, the world became an empty place.

We got into Moscow almost three hours late. I was home by 8 and Mama met me on the stairs . . . Now it's 9 o'clock and pitch dark outside. Well, my darling, I'll say goodbye for now. Remember everything. I hope your soul will be at peace and your heart will not be disturbed by thinking too much. But just in case something foul does get into your head, write to me about it at once and I'll try to find a remedy. All the best and greetings to everyone.

Sveta was always drawn to people who had lost someone, but this was the first time she had met a woman who had lost her husband to another woman in the labour camps. The Muscovite's story was not unusual. Many couples were torn apart by ten-year sentences: wives who renounced or could not wait for husbands in the Gulag, or who thought they were dead, so they started a new life with someone else; husbands who encouraged a divorce to save their wives and children from discrimination as 'relatives of an enemy of the people' or gave up on their wives and married women from the camps who might better understand what they had gone through.

This time, Sveta was lifted by the trip to Pechora. 'I looked at myself in the mirror today,' she wrote to Lev the day after her return. 'I look much better than I did after coming back from Pereslavl'[-Zalessky].' Three days later, she was feeling 'blissfully happy and kind towards everyone.' Even three weeks later she still felt the effects of her trip. 'I am full of happiness,' she wrote. 'Not only am I not crying any more, but the other day I even caught myself smiling on the tram.'

Lev, meanwhile, could think of nothing but Sveta. 'My darling, lovely Sveta,' he wrote on 4 September, when he was still waiting to hear if she had returned home safely. 'I don't know how to describe my condition. "Longing" is not right – there's worry too. All I think about and see is you, not the whole of you, I see only your eyes, your eyebrows, and your grey dress.' Five days later, still not having heard from Sveta, he wrote to wish her a happy birthday on the 10th, but his mood was sad:

> My darling Sveta, tomorrow is your birthday. It's so difficult for me to wish you anything, my darling – there is such an enormous contrast between what I want for you and what is possible now and in the future. So everything I wish for must sound like a madman's ravings, which no one believes. If this letter could get to you by tomorrow I wouldn't write it. I don't want to upset you on this day with pointless reminders of our situation. Sveta, Sveta, if only fate had been more generous, if only it would smile on us . . . I don't know what will happen in the future, how it will be, but I want to believe that we'll have one. Is it really too much to believe? . . . Look after yourself, Svet. Be healthy, Svetinka.

On 22 September, three weeks after Sveta's departure, there was still no word. Other prisoners were receiving letters sent from Moscow only a few days before, but nothing came for Lev. He was beside himself with worry:

My darling Svetinka, no letter has come from you. God knows what I'm thinking about as I write to you now. I'm not embarrassed to be a 32-year-old simpleton who sounds like both a ludicrously sentimental 16-year-old and an anxious old mama, only afraid that I'm pestering you and you'll be annoyed by my lamentations if everything is all right and it's just something to do with the post. Is that the reason?

At last a letter came, on the 23rd.

I was imagining the wildest things and was in the most unbearable state, when suddenly a man arrived whom I don't even really know and handed me a letter, and as soon as I saw your handwriting I forgot to thank him. Svetik, you are mine, my darling, glorious Svetlaninka. The only trouble is that I can't picture you when I read your letters. There are two Svetas – one seen with the eyes, the other who appears in your letters. If I want this other Sveta, I remember phrases you've written, but they come to me without a voice and they aren't associated with your appearance. If I want to see you, then it's easier for me without your letters. Mind you, it doesn't follow from this that life without your letters is easier for me, Sveta, my darling.

Gradually, Lev settled back into a routine. Winter came again. The labour camp was not prepared. There were broken windows, holes in the roofs of many of the buildings and not enough heaters or electric lights for the barracks in the 2nd Colony. The administration talked about rewiring the whole wood-combine, but nothing was done. In November, once the river had frozen, the annual clean-up of the labour camp began, with huge bonfires of wood-waste products on the ice.

Lev was busy with repairs at the power plant. 'The days are passing by very quickly,' he wrote to Sveta, 'and in the evenings I'm ready to sleep because I run around all day doing jobs at the station. Liubka and I together – thank God he hasn't left yet – have finished the installation of one of the panels, and for the first time since the station opened the newly installed equipment is working without a hitch.'

Lev was worried about fresh rumours of a convoy to the north-ernmost 'special regime' camps. When the list of prisoners for that convoy was finally announced, his closest friend and bunk-mate, Liubka Terletsky, was on it. On 2 November, Terletsky was sent to Inta, one of harshest mining camps in the Gulag, 180 kilometres north of Pechora on the railway to Vorkuta. It was a catastrophe for Lev, who loved Liubka like a brother and worried about him because of his youth and physical frailty. 'This evening they sent Liubka away after all. Scoundrels, they're all scoundrels,' he wrote despair-ingly to Sveta late that night. Lev was particularly disappointed that Arvanitopulo had done nothing to help Terletsky, who had worked hard for him at the power station, while the new head of the Electri-cal Group, Aleksandr Semenov, who hardly knew Terletsky, had 'tried to do everything he could' to save him. 'If only he'd had a little more freedom of action,' Lev wrote, 'perhaps he could have worked something out. It all stinks to high heaven.'

Lev was afraid that his friend would not survive the convoy. 'Liubka had become quite ill after all the strenuous work, he was overcome with nerves and had lost weight,' Lev wrote to Sveta on 3 November. 'A journey in the current frost is difficult enough, even for those who are stronger, but in his condition I fear the worst . . . I didn't think I could ever feel so close to somebody. Do you think he will hold out for the next 11 months?'*

Survival in the Gulag was heavily dependent on the support of friends, and Lev thought of Liubka as his only truly close friend in the labour camp, as he explained to Sveta on 9 November:

I was never able to cry on anybody's shoulder, unless it was yours, but with Liubka here I found it easier to bear difficult moments. I never told him anything if the cause of my misery was private, and generally our friendship didn't involve any kind of sentimentality. But even having an argument with him brought some relief, or just talking about random things, trivial things . . . Liubka, Liubka, if

---

* All that remained of Terletsky's ten-year sentence when he was sent to Inta.

only I knew you were still alive, if only you can hold out until the day of your release. Sveta, I told him your address to memorize – you don't mind, do you? Just in case it turns out to be the only contact he has, although he might not even try to write – that would be very much like him.

On 3 December, Lev sat down to write a letter to Liubka:

Well, my friend, don't be angry that I'm writing to you. I don't even know if or when this letter will be sent. It's wretched egoism on my part, of course – I can't overcome the desire to say a couple of words to a living soul, if only by correspondence, since there is no living soul around here. Perhaps it would be better for you not to get letters – I know you – but if you can bear it, then this letter won't cause you any harm.

Liubka, no matter how bad it is there, just think of one thing: it's simply foolishness to hold out for 8½ years just to give up in the 9th, whether things will be better for you after the 9th or not.

Lev wrote in detail about everything that had happened at the power station in the month since Liubka left. The news took up twelve pages. He then signed off:

Liubka, I didn't want to say this to you at all, but really there's no sense in not saying it – namely, that you are missed. S. writes that she would like to shake your hand. Consider this handshake done, together with mine, and remember her address: 8, 17, SAI, Kazarm, M. – keep it in your memory in case of any parcels. And don't be afraid should there be a parcel – I only requested vitamins to help your scurvy, and they cost next to nothing. Well, anyway, stay alive, my man.

The letter was never sent, because Lev did not know how to get it to Terletsky at Inta. He was not even sure if he was there.

8

My darling Sveta, it's already time to wish you a Happy New Year. I thought this year I should wish the simplest things for you, and you should try to wish them for yourself . . . Wishes from people who are close to you don't have to be especially lucky, and, as for happiness, it is incredibly vague, and perhaps it doesn't quite fit into our reality . . . I want you to smile more often, to sing more or hum something to yourself, and for your eyes to squint a little, as they do when you find something funny, or for them to open wide with your eyebrows slightly raised when you see something that makes you happy. I want all of these facial expressions of yours to linger on your face more often . . . And so, Svetin, my darling, my lovely – to continue with these simple things – please don't overlook the upkeep of your plaits, and, in case you chop them off, make sure you look after your dishevelled locks, that is number one. Second, try not to let your Sundays pass without getting away for a while from domestic or official chores, to ski, skate or boat or just to go somewhere . . .

Darling Sveta, be well – in the end there is no other way to tell you what I wish; here there should be some kind of superlative to intensify the verb but not the adjective.

Sveta had a great deal of work and a lot to worry about at the start of 1949. She was up to her eyes in administrative duties at the institute, struggling to deal with building work and renovations in preparation for her laboratory's move to the fourth floor. At the same time she was organizing new research on the compression of rubber, joining the battle for more funds from the ministry and writing up projections for the Five Year Plan. Sveta did not like the work. 'There is no joy in it,' she wrote. Under growing stress, she was afraid of getting into trouble for making a mistake or 'allowing something to be done which is not allowed'.

It was at the height of the Cold War, and Soviet scientists were under growing pressure from the state. Physicists were criticized and removed from their posts for 'bowing to the West' or for holding to the 'idealist' philosophy of quantum mechanics, which once again was attacked, as it had been in the 1930s, as incompatible with dialectical materialism, the 'scientific' basis of Marxism-Leninism. Some were purged for being 'cosmopolitans' (i.e., Jews), an 'anti-patriotic group' accused of undermining Soviet art and science in the ideological struggle against the West. At least two of Sveta's colleagues at the institute (Vitaly Epshtein and Lazar' Vinnitsky) were forced to find work outside Moscow because of the 'anti-cosmopolitan' campaign, which took off from January 1949, and there were dismissals of many other Soviet Jewish scientists in the world of research institutes in which she moved.

Lev was concerned at the toll all this was having on Sveta's health and mood. Sveta was taking cod-liver oil and Barbiphen – 'to calm my nerves,' as she explained to Lev, 'and so that I don't go off the deep end and snarl at everyone'. The barbiturates seemed to have a positive effect. 'These pills are helping me,' she wrote to Lev.

> Firstly I'm holding up somehow, I'm laughing and not crying (maybe I'm laughing so as not to cry), and secondly, although my appetite has not come back, I've stopped losing weight (when I was weighed at the factory I was 56 kg) and everyone agrees that my appearance is starting to improve.

Though Sveta did not pride herself on being attractive, others thought she was. At a party at Nina Semashko's she found herself engaged in a late-night conversation with a small group of friends, including:

> Pavel, an acquaintance (not a very close one) with whom I suddenly found a common language for the first time in 13 years. I have to

admit that I would never have allowed myself if I'd been completely sober – the conversation was about humanity, happiness, work and other lofty matters. I got home at 3 a.m. And this same Pavel (not exactly in a state of sobriety himself) reproached me on the way home for having in the past played it both ways – for knowing I have you but telling him all kinds of things. I swear, I can't remember ever having said more than two words to him. I always thought that he was devoted to Ninka and indifferent to me. If I did ever say anything to him, it was probably just something to avoid the necessity or the possibility of having a serious conversation.

Pavel was not the only man to show an interest in Sveta. At the end of the war there had been an episode that she had told Lev about in 1948. She had only mentioned it in the context of an argument she had had with her friend Irina Krauze about a mutual friend who was having an affair with a married man. Sveta had disapproved of their friend's behaviour on the grounds that it involved a lie, and this had reminded her of a young man who

was planning to get married when I suddenly appeared on the scene and a week before the wedding we had a talk. He told me that he had never met anyone better than me and that his fiancée couldn't stand up to any kind of comparison with me, and he was suffering terribly. I replied that I was waiting for you (this was in 1945) and asked why he was in such a hurry to get married if she wasn't the best person for him. He should wait until he met someone else. He said that it was useless to wait. Whoever you select, there will always be somebody better whom you'll meet one day, and, in order to be moral, once you've made your choice you have to close your eyes and never look at anyone else ever again. And, since he had already promised he would marry her, everything was decided. I said it was disrespectful to her. I just can't accept such blind morality. I don't need the kind of morality that drags you by the tail and uses force. Perhaps that's just my youth and foolishness?

Maybe it was also that she was lucky – in knowing that she had the man she really loved, even if she could not have him yet.

Lev agreed. He did not need to compare Sveta with anybody, because it was her he loved.

As for the 'best' and closing your eyes for the future – of course it's false and impossible to live like that. Objectively, there must be others who are better, the world is bigger than 'her', but that's not what it is about. Which is that for 'me', that is 'him', well, it's easier for me if I philosophize in the first person so I'll use 'I' and 'you'. The point is that you are the best for me – not because you are objectively so but because *for me* you are the best and *I don't need anybody else*, not even the Queen of Sheba, because I love *you*, for all your particular qualities – even your shortcomings are dear to me – while your merits are a source of joy. At the start [of a relationship], of course, feeling comes from pleasing qualities, but then they play a secondary role . . . Disappointment often plays a part, or external circumstances – losing that force of attraction and so on. But when a person has known someone very well for a long time, not just for a month or a year, but over many years, this danger boils down to nothing. That's how it seems to me, in any case. The colour of our blushes or the number of grey hairs become insignificant. Common sense won't help with this at all, especially not mine. I love you, and that is all. And for how long? Well, it seems like it will be for ever, that's how it seems now. It seemed less certain before, when we were apart, but now I believe, I believe, I believe. What else can I say?

Lev thought that a person who could even think in terms of finding 'someone better' had lost the 'capacity for emotion'. When he wrote of 'common sense' he had in mind the 'hollow-hearted reasoning' that could make such calculations, and referred to 'Prelude to a Poem on the Five Year Plan', the last poem of Vladimir Mayakovsky, in which there was a line about 'shameful common sense':

She loves me? She loves me not?
I crack my knuckles, knead my hands, and fling
My broken fingers to the winds.
So wreath of daisies you chance upon in spring
And use to tell your fortune
Are torn and flung away.
Let me discover grey in beard and hair,
Let the silver of advancing years ring out in peals
I hope and trust that I shall never
Come to shameful common sense or reason.

Sveta longed for Lev. 'For some reason, I've been seeing you in my dreams all week,' she wrote to him on 5 March. 'It didn't make me all that happy, because, although I could see you, I wasn't able to touch you (Alik says this about God, whose existence he finds conceivable, apparently), and you were moving away from me the whole time.' Lev too had dreams about her. He could hear her voice but not see her. He could see a letter she had sent but could not touch or open it. He saw her not only in his dreams 'but also in reality, relentlessly, and it's really getting bad'.

Lev was seeing Sveta all the time. When he was on his shift he was often thinking about her and having conversations with her in his head. He was irritated by the attempts of his shift coworkers to talk to him. 'Nikolai [Lileev] has had to switch to the night shift,' Lev wrote to Sveta, 'and I'm feeling liberated from the need to account for my thoughts ("What are you thinking, Lev?" What a stupid question!).'

Lev was busy with repairs at the power station at the start of 1949. The previous autumn he had designed a steam-heater for the engine but when it was delivered after the New Year it turned out they had made it the wrong size, so it had to be sent for repairs to the main workshops. On 18 January, he had his first day off in more than half a year. 'There will be more free days,' he wrote to Sveta, 'although the good they bring me is not much.'

After the departure of Terletsky, Lev found little comfort in his friends. He was becoming more self-sufficient and did not want to became close to anyone. 'I like being on my own at work,' he wrote to Sveta on 19 January. 'People come to talk with me of course, but that doesn't bother me as long as I'm not made to feel awkward out of a sense that I need to repay their friendship or kindness by opening myself up to them, which I absolutely cannot do with Nikolai [Lileev] or anybody else who thinks he is my friend.' Lev was alienated by the banter of the barracks, where without Terletsky he felt more isolated than before. 'Today was an idiotic day,' he wrote on 20 January. 'In the barracks there are so many stupid, wild things done, so many jokes and pranks, that I can't help but get annoyed and wonder how it's possible for someone like A. A. [Semenov],* with a normal mind, to go along with them, especially when these practical jokes are at the expense of someone present at the time.' He felt unable to join in when the other prisoners fooled around. He was irritated by their drinking and singing, even by their noisy games of dominoes in the barracks after work. While Lev would be lying on his bunk, trying to read *Anna Karenina*, his fellow prisoners would be creating havoc around him. Sometimes, however, he too enjoyed the party. 'The people in our barracks are having fun today,' he wrote to Sveta on 25 January. 'There's no particular reason. The floors and windows are all shaking with their dancing and the sounds of their guitars, and surprisingly the best musician turned out to be Aleksandrovich. I take my hat off to him!'

Three weeks later, there was a quieter party, for Strelkov's fiftieth birthday. Lev came with Lileev to drink tea with him in the laboratory. 'It was a sad day,' Lev wrote to Sveta, 'and I could not bring myself to wish him happy birthday. He understood, of course, why we had come but said nothing.' Strelkov continued to be ill, with scurvy and increasingly acute attacks caused by gallstones. Nothing could be done by the doctors in the infirmary, who lacked the

---

* The head of the Electrical Group, Semenov was a political prisoner, sentenced to ten years in 1944.

(*top*) Lev and Svetlana in 1936
(*bottom*) Lev (*third from left*), and Evgenii Bukke (*second from left*) in 1936

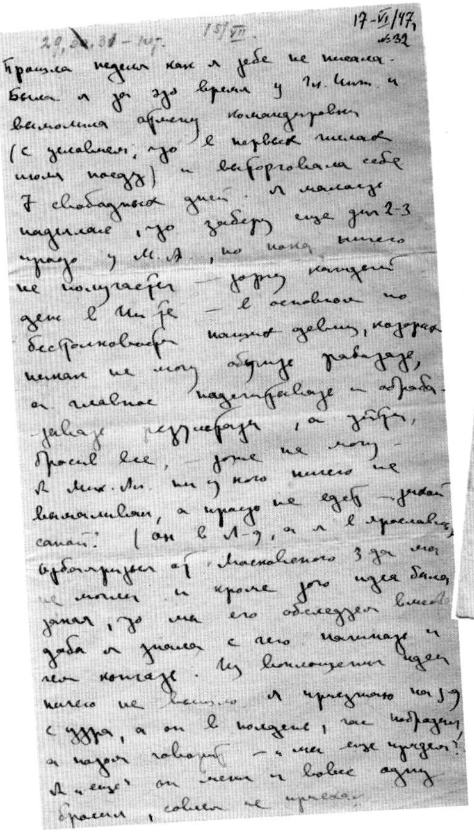

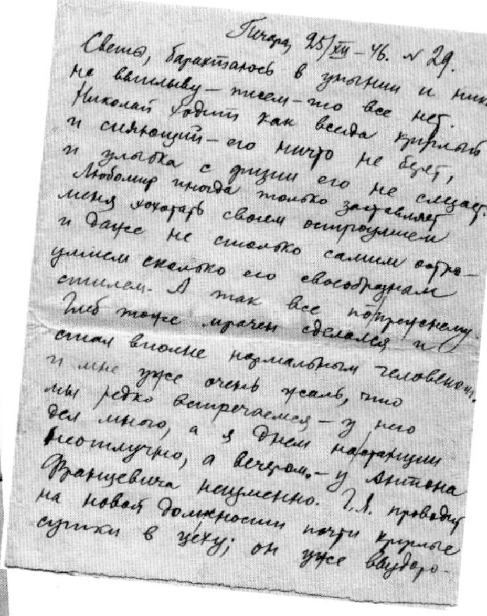

Svetlana's letters on the left,
Lev's on the right

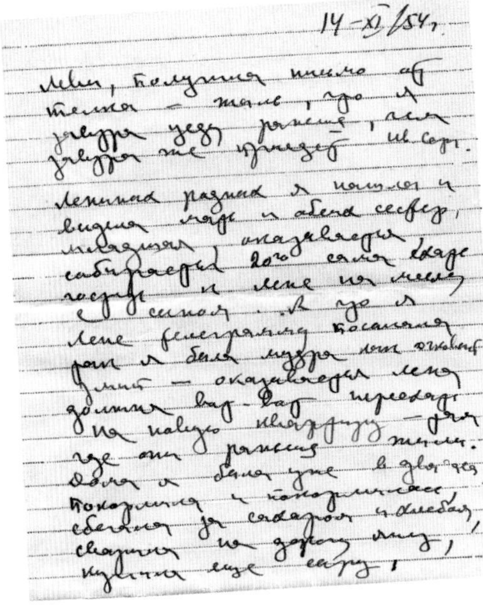

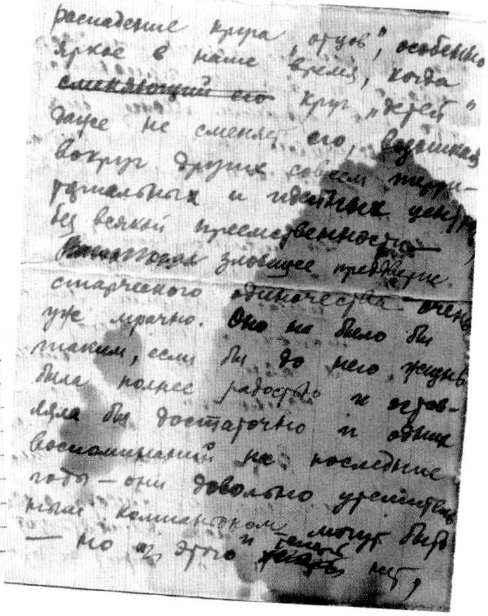

(*top*) The industrial zone of the wood-combine in 1956
(*bottom*) A view of Pechora River from the wood-combine

(*top*) The club house in the wood-combine
(*bottom*) Wood-Combine Street

(*top*) A convoy outside the 1st Colony (drawn from memory by Boris Ivanov)
(*bottom*) The remains of the wood-combine, with watchtower,
    in the 1980s

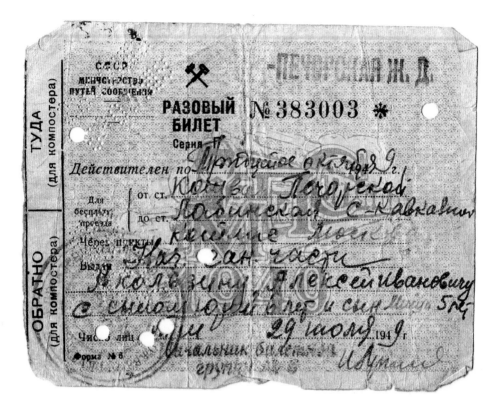

(*top*) A train ticket for the Pechora railway, 1949
(*bottom*) Lev's boots from Pechora and the suitcase he made before
his departure from the labour camp in 1954

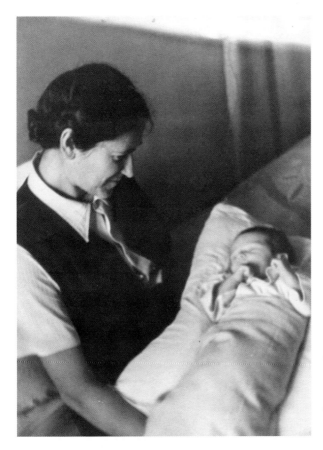

(*left*) Svetlana with her daughter Anastasia in 1956

(*below*) Lev with his children at Nikita's dacha

Svetlana and Lev, Moscow, 2002

expertise to carry out the difficult operation he required. Lev felt sorry for Strelkov, as he explained to Sveta:

Nobody has done as much as him for the production of the wood-combine, and not only has he received no thanks but the people who have benefited from his work are trying to keep quiet about it so as not to reveal that their own work is being done for them by others. The local bosses don't lift a finger to help him beyond his individual ration, which he should get anyway because he's ill.

There were even sadder celebrations on 17 April, the twenty-fifth birthday of Strelkov's daughter, Valya, who lived in Moscow with her husband and her son, whom Strelkov had never seen, and Strelkov's wife.

Only 25! And if G. Y. [Strelkov] lives to see her she'll be 37! – under 40! But will there ever be such a meeting? It's really hard for him and sometimes when I'm leaving him his misfortune and pitiful situation are enough to make me weep . . . It is getting to the point where I want to bang my head against a wall and grind my teeth from impotence and indignation at everything that has been done to him. He's a wonderful person even though we often argue (quite civilly, of course).

Spring came late to Pechora in 1949. There was snow in May, and the first warm days did not arrive until mid-June. The long cold winter put an extra strain on everyone. With the river still frozen, timber could not be brought in to the wood-combine. There were frequent power cuts because the power station relied on burning wood. In the saw-mill and workshops machines could not be powered and lay idle; workers had to resort to hand-tools, and the wood-combine fell far behind its quota so that the Gulag authorities reduced food deliveries. Throughout that winter there were chronic shortages of warm clothes, boots and gloves for the prisoners. Many became ill as they were forced to work for longer hours in freezing temperatures to make up for the shortfall in output. In the 2nd Colony, where Lev was a prisoner, one in ten prisoners was estimated to be sick during the first quarter of 1949, but only 1 per cent were allowed to be ill officially on any day.

Lev was concerned for Konstantin Rykalov, a political prisoner and wood-chopper at the power station, a large man who had been a boxer in his youth but had been worn down by the hardships of the camp, eventually becoming incapacitated with an acute form of TB which made it hard for him to breathe. Lev was fond of Rykalov. He described him to Sveta as 'an educated man, strong, honest to the point of pedantry, and, despite the two years he has spent here, an incorrigible searcher after truth'. Lev went to see Rykalov in the infirmary:

> I found him dressed and relaxing in the corridor, complaining that for exercise he's been chopping wood and quickly getting exhausted. 'But where on earth is your axe?' I ask. And he replies: 'I came across a really bad knot in the wood so I hit it a bit harder and the axe handle broke in half. They're going to make a new one.'

Rykalov was working to regain his strength and hoping to become an electrician at the power plant with the help of Lev and Semenov. He would visit Lev in his lunch breaks:

> Two or three days ago, feeling ashamed by his reproach that I don't go to see him any more, I paid him a visit and we spent the evening drinking tea. I listened to his reminiscences over a packet of photographs and, although it was all a little alien to me, I didn't begrudge spending my time that way – firstly because he's unquestionably a fine fellow with a good heart, who is interesting for his likes and his abilities, and is quiet; and secondly because he's lonely here, and I know that he finds it easy to talk to me, and this brings him some relief, which makes me feel good because I've helped someone. That's me analysing it now, but at the time I was simply having a nice time.

Rykalov became a stoker in the boiler room of the drying unit, but he could not cope with the heavy work and seriously injured his back (the former boxer had overestimated his physical capacities). Refused access to the infirmary, Rykalov was put into a punishment block after he had been caught smoking in an undesignated place. Given only bread and water, he became very ill and had to be released on the request of a doctor. He was taken to a special zone of the infirmary for TB sufferers and given lighter work duties inside the industrial zone.

Visiting Rykalov in the infirmary, Lev was struck by the kindness of one of the nurses there who was, 'it seems, not a native here but who inherited the post or has family'. There were many exiled nurses in the infirmaries of Pechora. On 20 April, Lev wrote to Sveta about a medical assistant in the sick-bay of the transit camp called Nina Grin,

> a woman in her forties who will be in her fifties when she ends her work trip [i.e. sentence] here. But I think her real name ought to be Grinevskaya. When the patients ask for something to read she gives them *Scarlet Sails* or *Gliding on the Waves*.* The patients all love her.

As Lev had evidently guessed, Nina was the widow of the writer Aleksandr Grin (or Grinevsky), whose romantic seafaring fantasies, much read and liked by Lev at just this time, could not have been more removed from the grim realities of the Gulag. After her husband's death in 1932, Nina had qualified as a medical assistant and worked as a nurse in Feodosia in the Crimea. During the war the Germans sent her to a concentration camp near Breslau. For collaborating with the enemy, she was given ten years in Pechora by the Soviets in 1945.

Another nurse in the transit camp was Svetlana Tukhachevskaya, the daughter of Marshal Tukhachevsky, who had been tried in

---

* Novels by the Russian writer Aleksandr Grin (1880–1932), whose real name was Grinevsky.

secret and shot as a spy in 1937. After the arrest of her father, Svetlana was sent with her mother, brothers and sisters to Astrakhan, and then, when her mother was arrested, she was placed in an orphanage, where she stayed until 1941. In the chaos of the first days of the war she ran away from the orphanage but was tracked down by the NKVD and sentenced to five years in Pechora. She was taken off the list of prisoners and hidden in the infirmary by one of the doctors, a repressed German national named Agata Rempel, who saw that Svetlana, a beautiful young woman, then aged twenty-four, and the daughter of a famous Soviet marshal, would not survive if left to fend for herself among the prisoners. Svetlana worked in the infirmary and lived in various houses in the town, where she was taken in by voluntary workers who concealed her whereabouts.

On 2 July 1949, the Party leaders of the wood-combine met to discuss how to carry out an MVD decree (No. 10190) calling for stricter isolation of the prisoners. Nothing had been done to implement the decree since it had been issued in March 1947. There were no systematic searches of the prisoners and their barracks, so all sorts of things were smuggled in and out of the prison zone. There was still no proper segregation between the industrial zone and the settlement of free workers. The guards at the main guard-house were corrupt and took bribes to let goods and people through. Many of the guards were in cahoots with the prisoners in the black market: a prisoner called Liashuk was a skilled tailor who made clothes for many of the guards; another, Kozarinov, was a cook who made them meals. There was even a black market in 'government secrets' (official documents) stolen from the headquarters of the MVD inside the settlement and sold to the prisoners, some of whom got hold of their personal files and forged alterations to the articles of their sentence or even changed the date of their release.

The upshot of the meeting was a new system of passes; stricter controls on visits; more searches of the barracks; the prohibition of military uniforms (which were still worn by some prisoners); the ending of dry rations (which could be used in an escape); the repair of the perimeter barbed-wire fence (which had several holes in it); the clearing of the bushes between the fence and the windmill (where axes, pliers, saws and other tools had been thrown from the bushes into the barracks zone); the increased manning of the watchtowers (three of which had been left unguarded for several months); and finally, after a year of discussion, the construction of a fence and new guard-house between the settlement and the industrial zone.

'How it's going to work out this year with the visit I just don't know,' Lev wrote to Sveta. 'The new procedures offer no comfort.' Once again, Sveta was determined not to be put off from trying to see Lev: 'The decision made little sense last year, but victors are never judged.* I've been coping so far, but fortune might not always smile on the brave.'

This year there were added complications. The institute did not have the funds to send her on a trip just to Kirov, but Tsydzik did not want to lose her for a month by letting her inspect the factories 'along the entire route' – in Omsk and Sverdlovsk and Kirov – which would justify the costs but jeopardize the institute's fulfilment of the plan, because Sveta was needed to direct the latest research projects in the laboratory. By 4 July, Sveta had secured a work trip to Omsk and Sverdlovsk, from where she hoped to travel on to Pechora, but nothing was for sure: a colleague, who had got the Kirov trip, was being slow in going there, and Sveta could not leave until she had returned.

Three weeks later, Sveta's colleague had still not left for Kirov, and she was now resigned to coming out to see him during a week's holiday in the autumn, 'which up to now has been a lucky time'. Lev had warned her that the tighter rules were restricting visits to 'between 30 minutes and two hours with the usual "dressing" [code for: in the presence of a guard]'. Litvinenko's mother had visited in

---

* Sveta is quoting a famous phrase attributed to Catherine the Great ('pobeditelei ne sudiat'), supposedly said by her in 1773 when General Suvorov was brought before a military tribunal after successfully storming a Turkish fortress on the Danube River against the orders of Field Marshal Rumiantsev.

June. Even after paying bribes, she had been given just three meetings of three hours on her own with Nikolai. Lileev's father had been no more successful, receiving only two meetings of the same duration with his son. In a coded letter, in case it fell into the hands of the authorities, Sveta asked Lev to send her more details about the risks and chances of success of bribing guards with vodka ('vitamin C')* or money ('vitamin D') to gain more time or privacy. 'Wives are more interesting to me than mothers,' Sveta wrote, underlining her desire to see Lev in a situation where they might be on their own, 'but then I'm purely interested in the practical issue of where meetings can take place.' In his equally coded reply, Lev warned Sveta not to build up expectations of achieving much by paying bribes:

> You probably already received advice about three days ago from I. S. [Lileev's father] on the various technical matters and have realized that even optimum conditions don't promise much chance of success. Fermentation using preparation D or its organic equivalent [alcohol] helps very little. In any case, it cannot change the details of space and time [how long or where a meeting could take place], and at best can only reduce the number of components [get the guard to leave the room], and even then not always. That's how it is. Statistics show that you're right, wives are less interested in their husbands than mothers are in their sons. According to local data, the ratio of the first to the second is zero, so there's no specific information regarding the first case. But it's unlikely it will be any different from the second.

Sveta was not to be deterred by the difficulties or by the likelihood that she would be able to see Lev for only a few hours, if at all. 'It might be possible to think of a more "interesting" holiday option,' she wrote to Lev, 'but I won't be capable of any kind of "relaxation" if I don't have a meeting with you behind me.'

* The Russian word for vodka starts with the third letter of the alphabet.

I wonder why others are so scared of brevity and prefer nothing to having just a little, whereas it seems to me that 3 hours is better than nothing at all. Maybe it's bitterness? I think I'm able to decide for myself whether something's better for me than nothing. And for you as well. What is easier for you, Levi? After all, we will have a chance to see each other, isn't that right? And to touch – to make sure we exist in reality and not just in letters. That is surely better than nothing. But maybe I am taking on too much in deciding this for you.

Lev replied:

It doesn't matter how long our meeting is, as long as we see each other. That is not in question here. It won't make it any more painful for me to wait for you afterwards. And even if it is painful, it will still be better, better because there will be the certainty that it not only *was* but still *is* and may still be in the future – but at any rate *it is*. And if I never mention this, it is because I think it is selfish, a form of indirect pressure when it shouldn't even be mentioned at all. It's not that I don't believe in you, Sveta, so please don't be angry.

In August, an opportunity arose for Sveta to travel to Ukhta, a Gulag-dominated industrial town near Izhma on the railway between Kotlas and Pechora. The factory had asked the institute to send a specialist to check the work of its laboratory, and Tsydzik had selected Sveta for the job. He had no idea where Ukhta was: when he had informed her that she would have to go there instead of Omsk, he had apologized for having spoilt her plans to travel to Pechora to see Lev. 'I asked Mikhail Aleksandrovich if he knew where Ukhta was,' recalled Sveta, 'that it was barely 250 km from Pechora, and that I could think of nothing more ideal, as long as he didn't worry if I came back two or three days late from my work trip.' Sveta left by train for Ukhta on 30 August, and spent at least a week there, staying in a village near the factory. When she had done her work, the factory officials suggested that she fly back to

Moscow – there was a flight about to leave from the airport at Ukhta – but Sveta said she would prefer to go by train. 'They took me by car to the station [at Izhma],' recalled Sveta, 'and I tried my hardest to persuade them that there was no need for them to wait for me to get on to the train. Luckily the train for Moscow and the one from Moscow going to Pechora arrived in Izhma almost simultaneously.' Once her hosts had disappeared, Sveta bought a ticket for the northbound train and climbed on board.

In Pechora, Sveta stayed with Boris Arvanitopulo and his wife, Vera, with whom she had stayed the year before. She was in Pechora from 9 to 12 September but this time she had far less time with Lev – probably no more than a couple of hours, and in the presence of a guard, either in the main guard-house or in the smaller one where they had met the previous year. As Lev had warned, the tightening of security had made it practically impossible to get more time, even with a bribe. But both of them were heartened by the brief meeting – it made the separation of the coming months less difficult to bear – and that made her trip worthwhile. To be with Lev for this short time she had made a round trip of 4,340 kilometres.

Sveta left the Arvanitopulos in the early morning of 12 September. That evening she posted a letter from the station at Tobys', just south of Ukhta:

> My darling Lev, the journey is fine.
>
> Give my thanks to Zhaba [Aleksandrovich].* I didn't go anywhere yesterday evening, I just got changed, collected my things and went to bed at 10 o'clock. Vera woke me up at 4 – it was already getting light. There was nobody at the ticket window and I managed to get a ticket only when a delayed northern train pulled in and pandemonium broke out – everyone had to buy a ticket or get one stamped at Pechora. I gave Boris 125 for the transfer and Vera 50. She refused, of course, but then she took it readily. I promised to send her a pattern for a fashionable flared skirt and she is still planning to send

---

* He must have helped Sveta in some way during her visit.

money for a fur coat. I tried to convince her to buy it herself when she is on holiday. But my chief hope is that she's not able to save the money up . . .

I saw Lev Yak. [Izrailevich] in Kozhva . . . I think he looks just the same . . .

Passing Ukhta and Izhma, I felt almost as if I were passing through my own home town, it looked so familiar. The village was mostly visible from the train but not the factory – it's behind the hill. The sun is already setting and they're promising a 30-minute stop, so I'll be able to send you this letter.

Look after yourself, my darling.

It seems a strangely routine letter for her to have written after such an intense meeting with the man she loved – as if she needed to control her feelings on the long journey home. 'We made it to Kotlas,' she wrote in her 'second letter from the road' on 14 September. 'The night went well . . . They're not really bothering to check passengers systematically but they're going up and down the carriages carrying out selective checks.'

Lev, by contrast, was far more lyrical. 'My darling Sveta,' he wrote on 16 September,

you are still everywhere with me. If something lovely comes to mind – a melody, or a piece of Pushkin or Burns or a painting – I think of you and see you, your face and eyes, and I feel easier remembering your smile. I don't know whether it's good that I write to you about this – I would write it for myself and not for you, but I can't not write. Sveta, my Svet, my dear Sveta. When I hear a melody I know you like, it seems I'm listening to it with you and I grow calmer, more able to bear things. I become kinder to people. My Sveta, how wonderful it is that *there is you*, that always and in everything – in poetry or prose, in music, or even in my circuit diagrams – I see only you.

Twelve days after her departure, Lev started seeing Sveta in his dreams again, 'only now I see you without any features or a face at all, but somehow I know it's you'. For several nights he had nightmares, but then, for three nights in a row, he had the same extremely vivid dream that he had dreamed in the SMERSH prison in Weimar in 1945, the dream of Sveta in a white dress.

A few weeks later, Lev read Turgenev's *Home of the Gentry*, a novel about love denied by circumstance and the fleeting nature, if not unattainability, of happiness. Lev read until late into the night and then wrote to Sveta with his thoughts:

I understood that the most terrible thing in life is complete hopelessness . . . To cross out all the 'maybes' and give up the fight when you still have strength for it is the most terrible form of suicide. It's almost unbearable to watch it happening in others. Unjustified hope – salvation for the weak in spirit and intellect – irritates me. But the loss of hope is the paralysis, even the death, of the soul. Sveta, let us hope, while we still have strength to hope.

9

'1950. Half a century is coming to an end,' Lev wrote to Sveta on 8 January. With the start of a new year, he was counting time. In two weeks he would be 33.

> I feel like I am halfway through my life – which is fine so long as it is only halfway. How many of the remaining years will I have to cross off for old age? These calculations have meaning only if there are no 'ifs' – any one of which could put a stop to my personal calendar in an instant.

For the moment, Lev's priority was to survive the freezing temperatures: 'Biting frosts are setting in. It was minus 47 yesterday, and the day before it was minus 49. Today it has "thawed" a bit to minus 36, but the temperature is dropping again now.'

The population of the Gulag reached its peak in the early 1950s. According to official statistics, the labour camps and colonies of the Gulag system then contained 2,561,351 prisoners, a million more than in 1945. Although this was only 2 per cent of the country's total labour force, the Gulag's actual contribution to the Soviet economy was far more significant. Gulag labour was especially important in the mining of precious metals in cold and remote regions, where free workers were very expensive, if not impossible, to employ. It also played a major role in the so-called Great Construction Projects of the late 1940s and early 1950s that came – officially at least – to symbolize the post-war achievements of the Soviet system: the Volga–Don canal; the Kuibyshev hydroelectrical station; the Baikal–Amur and Transpolar railways; the extensions to the Moscow Metro; and the vast new complex of Moscow University on the Lenin Hills, one of seven wedding-cake-like structures

('Stalin's cathedrals') in the ostentatious 'Soviet empire' style that shot up around the capital in those years.

Sveta was impressed by the new university, whose main building, by far the tallest in the city, could be seen from almost everywhere in the centre of Moscow. 'It's like an entire town lit up at night and the contours of the main building are illuminated really beautifully,' she wrote to Lev. Whether Sveta knew that the new complex had been built by Gulag labour is doubtful. She would express the same naive enthusiasm for many of the other Great Construction Projects of Communism that, unbeknown to her, were built by Gulag prisoners. Lev, too, was impressed by the propaganda image of these vast building sites. In the club-house of the wood-combine, where they sometimes showed films, he saw a documentary about the Volga–Don canal, and 'for the whole hour,' as he later wrote to Sveta,

> I had no other thoughts or feelings but a sense of pride and admiration for the power of the human mind and the systematic and harmonious transformation of thousands of ideas into a tangible marvel. The film had a lot of shortcomings, of course, a certain haste and patched-together quality in particular, but even so it made an enormous impression.

How could Lev be so impressed? He knew that Gulag labour was being used on the Volga–Don canal, if only because one of his fellow prisoners, Aleksandr Semenov, the head of the Electrical Group, had applied successfully to be transferred to its building site as an engineer. Lev's political views had surely changed since his arrest by SMERSH in 1945. He had no more illusions about Communism or Soviet justice. Yet he still believed with pride in the progressive force of Soviet science and technology, even within the Gulag. His own conscientious efforts to improve the working of the power station were a mark of this belief.

The Gulag was a vast archipelago of labour camps and construction sites, mines and railway-building sites, a slave economy that cast a shadow over the entire Soviet Union, yet few people were even aware of its presence in their midst. The post-war years saw a gradual merging of the Gulag and civilian economies. Every year about half a million Gulag labourers were contracted out to the civilian sector, mostly in construction, or wherever the civilian ministries complained of labour shortages; about the same number of free labourers were paid to work in Gulag industries. The Gulag system was increasingly compelled to resort to material incentives to motivate even its forced labourers. The population of the camps had become more unruly and difficult to control with the post-war influx of Red Army servicemen, foreign POWs and Ukrainian and Baltic 'nationalists' hostile to the Soviet regime. These prisoners were not afraid of violence. Unless they were rewarded, they were likely to refuse to meet their targets.

In 1950, the North Pechora Railway Labour Camp was reorganized as Pechorlag (Pechora Labour Camp) and charged with constructing a second railway track between Kotlas and Vorkuta. The temporary single track that had been built in such a hurry during the war years was unable to cope with the massive increase of coal production in the Vorkuta basin or with the needs of Pechora, which had become a major industrial centre thanks to the production of the wood-combine.

The building of a second track was a challenge for Pechorlag's bosses. Heavy manual work would be required to clear the forest, dig the embankments, prepare and lay the sleepers and the tracks. Thousands of new prisoners would be needed for the labour camps and colonies along the line. Productivity at the wood-combine would have to be ramped up to meet the increased demand for sleepers, barracks and other building components. The Gulag bosses were under intense pressure to complete the railway within a year. Without new incentives, they had no chance of getting it done in less than two or even three years. The prisoners were simply too demoralized.

At a series of meetings in January 1950 to discuss the failure of the wood-combine to fulfil the plan in the previous year, all the usual reasons were given: shortages of raw materials and energy, poor organization, lack of expertise among the prisoners, etc. But the bosses noted in particular an 'alarming increase in prisoners failing to meet their norms' and 'increasing refusals by the prisoners to work'.

To speed up the building of the railway the Gulag authorities put in place a new system of material incentives, including the payment of wages. The idea of paying prisoners had been introduced by a government decree in November 1948. The decree allowed a few selected camps to pay money 'bonuses' of up to 30 per cent of what workers in corresponding civilian sectors received. From the spring of 1950, these bonuses were extended throughout the Gulag (except for the special regime camps).

The wage system was instituted at the wood-combine on 1 May. General labourers were paid 90 roubles a month, skilled workers double that amount.* Under the new system, the wood-combine would have to make a profit to keep receiving money and supplies from the Gulag administration in Moscow. Nobody was sure whether the projected rise in productivity would be sufficient to cover both the wages of the prisoners and the costs of their food minimum, which continued to be guaranteed. Even the leaders of the wood-combine had their doubts, despite the billboards they plastered everywhere – in the club-house, the workshops and the barracks – to advertise the scheme. In the 11th Colony, one of the remote forest camps where the wage system had been tried out earlier, there had been a rise in productivity, but not enough to compensate for the expenditure, since many prisoners were still not working any harder than before. For the prisoners there were two main problems with the money system: it was difficult to stop the guards from stealing their wages or taking their money in bribes; and there was nothing much to buy. The kiosk in the remote colony had a few tins of sausage meat, some boiled sweets and little else,

---

* By comparison, voluntary workers in the wood-combine earned on average about 800 roubles a month, and administrative personnel around 1,200 roubles per month in 1950 (GU RK NARK, f. 173, op. 1, d. 1, l. 2).

though vodka and tobacco could be purchased easily on the black market.

Still, Lev was pleased to be earning money. It allowed him to repay what he saw as his debts to his aunts, Uncle Nikita and other relatives who had sent him parcels and so to feel less like the helpless 'child whom people spoonfeed' when, in his view, it was his job 'to care for them', as he had explained in his early letters to Sveta. In July, Lev sent some money to Aunt Olga. 'They are threatening to turn us into capitalists by moving to a system of cash accounting,' he reported happily to Sveta. Later in the year, he sent Sveta 200 roubles he had saved so that she could give them to Aunt Katya for a short stay in a sanatorium.

Another concession to the prisoners was a resolution passed by the leaders of the wood-combine in the spring of 1950 allowing them to grow their own vegetables on allotments. Lev and his friends in the Electrical Group organized a 'collective farm', where they grew lettuces, radishes, peas, beets and blackberries, all rich vitamin sources. Strelkov, the 'chairman' of the farm, took a 'fatherly pleasure in it', Lev wrote to Sveta, 'and enjoyed listening to us praise the vegetable garden and his cooking'. He even rigged up lights to guard the crops when it got dark, though Lev was sceptical of this effort, and thought that thefts would be reduced by only '1 per cent at best'. Strelkov and his 'farm-hands' also grew nasturtiums and asters under glass and bred rabbits in the basement of the power station (they made electric heaters for the pens), allowing them to cook up delicious rabbit stews. 'We've belatedly started doing some work in the vegetable garden,' Lev wrote to Sveta in mid-October.

The harvest is small and not very profitable but it's gratifying, especially for G. Y. [Strelkov]. He still has some tomatoes ripening on his window sill and, apart from those, we've got nothing left in store but potatoes (of which, by the way, there's no shortage at the moment). All the other fruits of the earth have been eaten. There was even rhubarb and spinach – like Western Europe on Komi soil. Nikolka [Litvinenko] gets great comfort from it all. He's currently switched over to rabbit breeding – there's no regulation against it yet – so there's a group of six long-eared souls living in the station's basement which N. is intending to put into a stew . . . I'm not a part of that enterprise, just observing the creatures with great pleasure. The object of our attentions at the moment is our cat Mitka (not the one that lives with G. Y. but the one in our barrack), who has picked up some kind of illness which mostly affects his eyes – they're watering . . . For want of a vet, we're treating him ourselves, giving him vitamin C to drink and washing his eyes with boric acid. He deserves good care: he's a consummate mouser, his behaviour is beyond reproach, and he has a wonderful nature.

There were other small improvements at the wood-combine. Bigger barracks were built for the prisoners. There was a new club-

Strelkov and Lev (back row) with Lileev (left) and Litvinenko outside the laboratory.

house in the settlement, now accessible to all the prisoners, with a library, a radio tuned to national stations, a ping-pong table, and a place for playing cards and dominoes. A post office and small shop were opened near the guard-house, where prisoners could buy bread and sometimes even butter, sausage, sugar, vodka, tobacco and fabric for clothes, though deliveries were unreliable (the shop had 600 metres of towelling but nothing warmer to sell to the prisoners). 'Why send me sugar, when I can buy it here. And toothpaste and soap – there is everything here now,' Lev wrote to Sveta. With the help of the voluntary workers, he could also buy things from the growing number of small shops in the main town, where there was a slightly wider range of food in tins, dried fish and occasionally vegetables, tea and coffee cubes.*

Pechora itself was rapidly developing, offering new working opportunities and even entertainment for the prisoners. In 1949, a

Five prisoners of the Pechorlag football team.

Palace of Culture was opened in the town centre. Built entirely by the prisoners, the classical colonnaded building contained an auditorium in which all the furniture was made by the carpenters of the wood-combine. Films shown in the auditorium had separate

---

* Small cubes of instant coffee pre-mixed with dried milk and sugar.

screenings for the voluntary workers and for the prisoners (marched to the palace under armed guard). There was a resident orchestra and, from 1951, a resident theatre company made up of prisoners. Gulag bosses derived prestige from these 'serf theatres' and 'serf orchestras', and they bargained with one another for the best musicians and actors. There were also football teams composed of prisoners and voluntary workers from the different sectors of the town (a railway-workers team, one for the shipbuilders and another for the wood-combine). These teams played matches at the new stadium near the Palace of Culture. When bigger matches were held between a team from Pechora and one visiting from another Gulag town, prisoners were marched to the stadium to cheer on their team.

At the heart of these developments was the notion that the Gulag should function as a parallel civilization to Soviet society, that it should re-educate the prisoners, 'reforge' them as Soviet citizens by means of propaganda and cultural activities. The idea of reforming prisoners through work had been central to the founding ideology of the Gulag in the early 1930s. Later in that decade it was largely forgotten, as the focus of the camps became the maximum exploitation and punishment of 'enemies of the people'. But from the end of the 1940s, as the Gulag bosses looked for ways to motivate the prisoners, they returned to the original idea. In the wood-combine the Party leaders introduced a scheme for teaching prisoners industrial skills. In 1950, they organized a 'training complex' on the site of the recently decommissioned 1st Colony on 8 March Street where 'deserving' prisoners were trained in geodesy, topography, railway construction and engineering during working hours. The teachers were all former prisoners.

Lev was not chosen for the training, but he had started giving informal lessons to a small group of workers at the power station, including a twenty-three-year-old stoker who came to him for maths and a thirty-year-old fitter, whom he taught a sort of engineering course. The role of teacher suited him. He was kind, approachable and generally liked, so people often came to him for practical advice. And helping others satisfied his need to find a higher purpose in the camp.

Lev was acutely aware of his privileged position in the camp and felt strongly that he ought to use it to help prisoners worse off than himself. For eighteen months he had written to the MVD authorities asking for an address for his poor friend Terletsky. Finally, in

Terletsky in exile in Siberia with Irina Evgenevna Preobrazhenskaya, daughter of the Bolshevik economist Evgenii Preobrazhensky.

July, he learned that Terletsky had been released from the Inta special regime camp and was living in exile in a small village in the Krasnoyarsk region of Siberia. Lev wrote to him and sent him money by transfer, but the money came back with a short note stating that 'financial aid is not needed'. Lev saw this refusal to accept his help as typical of Terletsky's pride. 'So he's undoubtedly still alive, probably healthy and as obstinate as ever,' he wrote to Sveta. 'I feel really sorry for him and don't resent at all that he does not reply. If I could be certain that my letters wouldn't cause him pain, I would continue writing without his replies. Ah, Liubka, you foolish man! Despite his outstanding intellect he acts like a child sometimes.'

Lev was equally concerned about Oleg Popov, the young half-Latvian in the Electrical Group. In February 1948, Popov had been moved to the 3rd Colony, returning two months later clearly traumatized by his experience in the harsh regime of the penal colony, where he had worked in a hauling team. 'His hands are covered in frostbite, he has lost a lot of weight, and his eyes have a strange look,' Lev remarked. He was disturbed by the change in his friend's appearance. 'After Oleg came to see me, I could think of nothing else,' he wrote to Sveta. 'My conscience has been troubled for two reasons: that somehow I may have been partly to blame for his fate,* and because my own position is incomparably better than his.'

In April 1948, Oleg was sent to a nearby transit camp, where prisoners were being collected for a convoy. Before it left, Lev wrote to him and gave him Sveta's address. For ten months they heard nothing, but then Oleg wrote to Sveta. He was in a special regime camp in Kos'iu, 100 kilometres north-east of Pechora on the railway line to Vorkuta, breaking stones in a quarry. Conditions in the camp were very bad, he had hurt his hand, but he wanted her to send him books. Worried about him, Lev began to collect money from the other prisoners and sent parcels to Oleg. Sveta also sent him things. Then she started getting letters with requests for the same items she had already sent; some were written in a strange English with mistakes in her address. It turned out that the other prisoners were forcing him to write to her with requests for parcels they would

---

* Lev had no reason to think this but he felt guilty because he had not been sent to the 3rd Colony.

keep. He had been trying to prevent the fraud by muddling the address.

As soon as Lev began to earn his own money, he saved as much as he could for Oleg. In February, he sent 150 roubles, which Oleg 'spent on bread'. Sveta was troubled by the news: it was possible, though odd, she thought, that 'he was allowed to spend such a lot on bread'. Suspecting that he was still being bullied by the other prisoners, she held off on parcels and sent him only small sums of money for the next few months. But Lev found out from another prisoner who had seen Oleg that he was in fact obsessed by bread: having fallen ill from hunger and exhaustion at the quarry, he was spending every rouble that he could on food from the kiosk at Kos'iu. On learning this, Sveta began to send him parcels again, as well as money to buy bread. 'I received three letters from Oleg,' she wrote to Lev on 19 July.

He's feeling a bit more cheerful and has got my parcel, though he's not allowed to receive any money until the kiosk is restocked – it's empty at the moment . . . I can see I've planned his parcels badly. Following the path of least resistance, I sent him kasha (he asked for either black bread crusts or the cheapest kasha), but it's not remotely clear how he'll cook it. I should have dried some crusts. I sent him another parcel on Sunday with fine-ground barley as well as noodles and cornflakes. I also put a note in the parcel along with 25 roubles. I never thought that was possible but those who send parcels regularly say it is (up to almost 100 roubles) and Oleg wrote that it's a more reliable method.

Lev continued to worry about Rykalov, still in the infirmary for TB sufferers. 'It's not good,' he told Sveta. 'He's feeling dispirited . . . and is weak. It's very difficult to get into the infirmary at the moment but I'm going to try to visit him. One more case and I'll become a fatalist – it's simply amazing how all the people I like are so unfortunate.' In 1949, after a number of escapes, the infirmary had been enclosed by a barbed-wire fence, and access was restricted.

Lev told the guards that he needed to check the electrical wiring in the ward – a lie that would have landed him in serious trouble if it had been exposed – and in this way he was able to visit Rykalov on several occasions. The former boxer was extremely ill. 'I thought it was the end,' he later wrote to Lev, 'the illness had broken me and I thought that no one needed me.' But Lev's visits lifted his spirits.

Lev contacted Rykalov's sister in Moscow, and she sent parcels of fresh food and medicine, which Lev brought to him in the infirmary. Rykalov had become so despondent that he thought his nine-year-old son would not want to see him any more. His face had turned yellow from jaundice and he was afraid to return home looking so weak. But Lev persuaded him not to think like that. 'I've stubbornly been making him – and have made him – realize that his son needs him no matter what condition he's in,' he explained to Sveta. 'This means that he must hold out at whatever cost. (Incidentally, I would never be able to convince myself of the same thing.)'

Lev was also doing all he could to help Strelkov. In January, Strelkov suddenly took a turn for the worse, with 'sharp pains in his bladder', as Lev explained to Sveta in a letter that revealed much about the treatment of the sick in the Gulag:

His condition is really quite bad. It's practically impossible to get any kind of effective help here under the current system of medical care. 'Surgery' hours, available to everyone, are as a rule handled by somebody who has been educated to a level no higher than that of a feldsher [rural doctor's assistant] – his methods and treatments are on a par with those in Chekhov's stories. The so-called medical board – which carries out 'general supervision' – is a joke. A couple of doctors see about 200 people an hour on a first-come, first-served basis, assessing them mostly by how they look; the board has no incentive to do anything different and most of the locals have probably never experienced anything else . . . People are saved only by their body's defence mechanisms. One detail of G. Y. [Strelkov]'s 'examination' shows how attentive the general board is: after he complained of heart problems, a woman began to 'listen' to his heart, having forgotten to ask him not to breathe, while she carried on a conversation with a colleague; after 15 seconds of this she suddenly remembered something and suggested that he get dressed and leave.

In principle, specialists (urologists, neuropathologists, etc.) are supposed to see patients at the clinic from time to time, but people here have been waiting to see them for years and are referred to the clinic only in exceptional circumstances. One of our operators has been complaining of stomach pains for more than a year but was prescribed a 'treats everything' hot brick until a month ago, when we had to take him to the infirmary, where he's currently waiting to see whether he'll die before or after an operation for advanced cancer . . .

Treatment at the infirmary is useful only in that it allows for a brief rest – as the doctors are well aware – or for isolating infection. The infirmary limits itself to these two functions except when surgery is required. Then patients are sent to the surgical hospital. It is better than the clinic and staffed with experienced personnel. But its benefits are bestowed only after the physical integrity of the body has already been violated.

G. Y.'s best option might be to get sent to this hospital . . . But it's almost impossible to get there from here without being referred for an operation. G. Y. doesn't have much 'influence' among the medical people, despite the enormous services he has rendered to them (from providing their pharmacy with distilled water, which otherwise they would have had to travel 5 km to get, to making speculums). But like any decent person, he's no good at reminding them about these services, and they easily forget, especially as they don't worry themselves over other people's misfortunes.

It's really distressing to look at G. Y. He has aged a lot over the past year. If he receives no treatment this year, and if you see Valya [Strelkov's daughter], advise her to be more resolute in her intention [to visit him] this summer. Otherwise she may not get a chance to see her father again. And tell her not to pay any attention to his objections (if he makes any). Even though he never mentions it, I know he's still secretly hoping that she'll come, and, if she doesn't, he'll be really upset. So try to talk to her about it, Svetka.

Sveta called on Valya to persuade her to visit her father, but Strelkov's wife and the rest of her family were opposed to the idea. '[Valya's mother] arrived as I was already getting ready to leave,' Sveta wrote to Lev.

Her face showed no emotion, she didn't ask a single question, and she replied vaguely to my hello. I think she is hostile towards me because I'm leading Valya astray by advising her not to wait another 12 years [to visit Strelkov] on top of the 13 that have already been lost. G. Y. didn't agree before, but he should be persuaded that it's for the best that she visit soon. However, even if G. Y. were to give his consent, and Valya wanted to go, all her relatives are against it (except for some aunt who lives in Siberia).

Valya did not go to Pechora. Without medicines or proper treatment for his gallstones, Strelkov became very sick. The only pain relief came from a blue spectrum therapeutic light (the Minin reflector, widely used in the Soviet Union), though Lev himself was doubtful that it did much good.

Sveta was helping Lev to deal with all this suffering. She was sending money, food and medicines. Perhaps as a consequence of these efforts to help people worse off than herself, she was better able to keep things in perspective in her own life. 'I'm not crying any more,' she wrote to Lev on 25 March. 'I'm not avoiding people and they don't irritate me as they used to do.'

She was annoyed, however, when she was called by Aunt Olga, who claimed to be gravely ill. When Sveta arrived at Olga's communal apartment, she found her 'walking round her room – which means she's not dying yet'. Perhaps it was the contrast with the genuine suffering of Strelkov and Rykalov that irritated Sveta. 'I am no Christian,' she later wrote to Lev, 'and I can't bear theatrics in real life.'

I poured it all out to Mama. She understood my irritation but said that Olga's theatrics are a human weakness. What can I do if I'm such a harsh person? I promised to go to see Olga during the holidays. Then at 6 in the morning, when I was up to my elbows in washing, tidying up and general housework, Serg. Nik. ['Uncle Seryozha'] arrived suddenly – it turns out that some neighbour [of Olga] had called him. I didn't rush over there this time but waited till after lunch. It seems that she'd felt quite well the day before and had decided to do a little ironing and sewing, as a result of which she'd started having heart trouble again. But when I got there, I found her quite cheerful (to judge by her talkativeness). At this point I snapped at her a little – if she's so ill she should lie down and not do things that are unnecessary. And she shouldn't complain so much and should remember that hers is not the most terrible and awful illness, that thousands die from cancer and goodness knows what other ailments, with far more suffering.

Knowing a little about material conditions in the Gulag and a lot about the sacrifices people made for love, Sveta was also exasperated by some of her friends, who had everything they wanted but still could not find happiness or even recognize their good fortune. One day in mid-May she went to see her old friend Nina Semashko, who had just moved into a new house with her husband Oleg. Three years before, they had lost their baby son, but now their lives were starting to improve, at least in material terms:

I expected to see 4 walls, so to speak, several people I knew, and a few familiar objects (old bits of furniture), but I found a room full of newly bought items: a wardrobe, a bookcase, a china closet, two fold-out dining tables, a writing desk, a dressing table with a marble surface and five mirrors, a kitchen table, two settees, and I forgot the wooden double bed. It's good, and I should be glad that people's lives are beginning to improve, but the idea that all of this is necessary for life and for happiness made me heavy-hearted. People who used to drink tea from a pan have bought a teapot – it's a small thing but something to be happy about. Here, though, they've bought a whole house, and yet they're anything but happy. It's true, it's all bought on credit, which dampens the joy somewhat, but all the same. I arrived at half past nine. Nina was finishing tidying up and suggested that I take advantage of the bathroom (done up very pleasantly with a shower). I agreed. Oleg arrived at 10, when I was drying my hair and Nina had climbed into the bath. And all evening long, he kept up a stream of caustic remarks. Nina would ask him to do something (take the rubbish out, for example) and Oleg would reply with 'Tomorrow' or 'What do I have a wife for?' That kind of thing. It made me sad.

Sveta's own new acquisition was a camera. She bought it so she could send photographs to Lev. 'Thanks to them,' he wrote to her, 'I feel I am almost by your side.' Lev enjoyed receiving pictures of Sveta, but he was also interested in the technical aspects of her camera:

Sveta with Lev's aunts. Olga (left) and Katya (right).

Yesterday I got a few letters and a photograph. The photograph is technically poor, so it's possible to blame the camera, but, all the same, you still look really lovely, Sveta, and I like it very much. So on the basis of this opinion and your mother's (but not yours, naturally!) you can hold your head up high (according to some people here, you look much older [in the photograph] than you do in real life). It's clear from the photograph that Aunt O. is well enough to cope with her legal worries over the dacha. She looked significantly worse in the last one you sent. The opposite needs to be said about Aunt Katya – in the photograph taken the month before last she looked livelier and younger and the expression on her face was more natural. It's a shame if this photograph is more true to life. It's really good that you've got your own camera now. What is its aperture, lens and depth of field?

There was reason to hope the intimacy of the photographs might soon become more real. One of the improvements at the wood-combine in 1950 was the construction of a 'House of Meetings' (*Dom svidanii*), where, on the granting of official permission, prisoners could spend time privately with visitors. Located next to the guard-house at the entrance to the 2nd Colony, the house was really no more than a log cabin consisting of a room in which there was a bed, a table, some chairs and a small kitchen. But it was a private place: a prisoner could meet his wife there without the presence of a guard; he could spend a night with her.

At the end of June, a decree was posted in the wood-combine announcing the rules for the house: a prisoner could meet there with any visitor, it did not have to be a wife or a relative. On application to the main administration of the labour camp, every visitor would be granted a discretionary length of time, depending on the status and the conduct of the prisoner.

Sveta was determined not to miss this opportunity, even if it meant she had to travel the breadth of the Soviet Union. At the end of August, she was due to go on a holiday to the Caucasus. She had planned to travel to Erevan, Tblisi and Batumi and then spend some time in the mountains. But she now decided to make her trip there shorter so she could visit Lev before she returned to work. 'My holiday leave finishes on the 23rd [of September],' she wrote to him on 13 August,

> the 24th is a free day, and then I need to find another six by any means I can (without pay for 'family reasons', 'sabbatical leave' or whatever); the 1st is a Sunday again, and on the 2nd I'll be back at work. I decided that I'll come to you no matter what (unless something extraordinary happens), and if there is any problem I will deal with it on the way. I'd prefer that to wasting any more time in the Caucasus, which could put my trip to you at risk. Do you understand, Levi? I'm still afraid of procrastination and delays.

Sveta left Moscow on 26 August. As agreed with Tsydzik beforehand, she sent a telegram from Batumi advising him that she needed to postpone her return to Moscow by six days. From Batumi she bought a train ticket directly to Pechora. Travelling first to Moscow, where she stopped at home to collect some warmer clothes, a woollen blanket and a bedsheet, she then took the northbound train to Pechora. From Batumi she had travelled 4,200 kilometres by train to be with Lev.

Sveta had permission to spend three days with him in the House of Meetings, a stretch of time that must have seemed a luxury. From the station Sveta walked directly to the main administration of Pechorlag, the same white building where she had been the year before, to get the necessary document. It seems she arrived on 26 September, because on that day Lev wrote to Nikita that he had 'met S.' The sheet and blanket she had brought from Moscow were evidently for the bed in the House of Meetings. Sveta recalled that Lev remained at her side for the whole time. He did not have to leave for his work shifts, as prisoners with visitors would normally have done, because the officials, with whom he got on well, allowed him to stay with her. These were blissful days for them. For the first time they enjoyed the ordinary happiness – which for so long had seemed impossible – of living together as man and wife.

Sveta left on the evening of 28 September. She wrote to Lev, probably while waiting for her train at the Pechora station. As usual, she filled her letter with mundane details, as if to distract herself from the terrible emotions she must have felt on leaving him.

> Farewell, Levi.
>
> I managed to get a ticket easily, but only for a sleeper in a combination carriage.
>
> I was at the girls' house – I saw Lida and Nelly [Kovalenko]. It turns out they've already got dark-blue ribbons, but they were very pleased with the red ones. To be on the safe side, I made a note that neither Nelly nor Tolya [Tolik] has any exercise books. And Lida isn't studying at the moment, she's looking after somebody else's child. She's planning to travel to Dnepropetrovsk with her sister, Tamara, to study at a technical school. I approved of the plan and gave them my address.
>
> I'll send you a description of my journey. But for now I've run out of energy and so I'm going to stop writing.
>
> Somehow, Levi, look after yourself. And greetings to everyone.

She was back in Moscow early in the morning of Sunday, 1 October, and returned to work the following day. No one asked her where she'd been.

Lev wrote to her on 29 September. He wanted her to know that she had made a big impression on his friends, who had come to see her in the House of Meetings, some to thank her for the parcels and medicines that she had sent:

> My darling Sveta, all the warmth has left with you – the air yesterday evening was already quite autumnal, and it snowed in the night, though it turned into slush by the morning.
>
> I received many compliments intended for you. One of them went like this: 'How that girl can talk! She could talk with the dead!' (in the sense of being able to bring the dead back to life – not to be confused with 'talking to the dead'). I. Z. [Bashun, a senior mechanic at the power station] doesn't really get into conversations with strangers but he says he found it easy to talk to you.

And N. L[itvinenko] showed up slightly stunned a couple of evenings ago. He said that he expected to meet an imposing woman, 'at
any rate, much more imposing than you' (me, that is), but it turns
out (and both God and you forgive me for my bravery in telling
this), 'she's just a slip of a girl'. There you go – take it as you wish. I
was, of course, very pleased! Thank you, all you intelligent people!

Over the next weeks, as Lev and Sveta settled back into their
routines, they began a conversation about how they would spend
the four years until his release. Sveta started it, outlining her 'ideal
life' for the coming winter, which entailed a lot of skating, skiing,
swimming and music. 'I can't decide,' she wrote on 14 October, 'if
it's bad to think of things that are purely for pleasure, to dream of
spending time with no purpose.'

Because right now what I really want more than anything is to be
healthy for our life in the future. Conditions are hardly going to be
easy and I'll need to be strong and resilient. Maybe that's just an
excuse for laziness. I usually prefer outings that have a purpose
(picking mushrooms and berries or reaching a specific destination)
to aimless wanderings. But now I have only one goal: to wait for
you. The word 'wait' is too passive: heartache drains my energy and
stops me from getting on with life. Something you once said just
popped into my head: 'I wouldn't go anywhere without you.' That's
true, Levi. But I want the world to be good and interesting for you,
even without me in it. That will be a real victory for me because
then I will stop worrying about you. It's not good to count on only
one person (the same as having just one child).

Lev replied with one of his most passionate letters. It was written
in the first three days of November.

I agree with you that the world is a good and interesting place no
matter who is in it, but only in the most general sense. For none of
it is true insofar as it relates to you, Sveta. Svet, the world is unques-

tionably good, but it's so much more beautiful when it is lit up by you that I wouldn't want – and would never want – to look at it without the illumination you bring to it.* Do you really want me to enjoy the world in the dark, or at best in the half-light after you have gone away? 'Not to count on only one person'? Sveta, Sveta, if it hadn't been you writing that, if it weren't just your endless selflessness (there's no other word for it), if I'd received your letter from anybody else, I would have stopped writing. While I agree with the general theory, it's an example of faulty reasoning.

'That will be a real victory for me because then I will stop worrying about you.' If only you'd written it in the conditional, Sveta.

It cannot happen, and it cannot happen because it would mean the end of everything that's still human inside me. It would be moral suicide, not victory. Whose victory, and over whom? Yours, over yourself? In this sense, to claim a victory over yourself is nonsensical, and for somebody or something to vanquish you inside me is impossible – because of age, temperament and our shared and ill-fated past. And why would you try to argue me into such a hollow 'victory'? It's cruel, not kind. Has there really been so little spoken, written and sung over the last thousand years by human beings who have a heart and soul? Svetlye, I don't need these false consolations; you would be better off, seriously, simply spending the winter skiing, at the swimming pool, and in the country, taking care of yourself.

Sveta replied:

My darling Lev, I received your letter of 1–3 November yesterday. Levi, I didn't manage to express myself correctly and I don't even now know the best way to say what I mean – only God forbid that I should want somebody (or something) to vanquish me inside you. When I wrote about victory, I meant our victory. Not victory over us but victory over everything cruel that we've had to face, over the burdens that have made us stumble and caused us pain. I don't want

* Once again, Lev is linking Sveta with the Russian word for 'light' (*svet*).

the pain to make you forget even for a moment all the good in the world – the earth and the sun and the water and, most importantly, people and relationships. I don't want this joy to subside, and I want us to be young for a long time. Reasoning – any reasoning – doesn't come into it. Levi, if the world is lit up already, then I hope it stays as bright, despite the laws of physics and regardless of the distance from the source of light. And in reality there is no distance, since the source is your attitude towards others, which means it's always within you . . . Nevertheless, I'm right about not counting on just one person, Levi. Life should be taken on so firmly that not even the greatest sorrow can change this attitude, as long as it's not a small-minded attitude from below but a wise, almost Tolstoyan, attitude from above. In that case it's far from the destruction of what's human; on the contrary, it's what makes us human. I'm frustrated that I can't express myself better; you might as well tear this letter up. I feel compassion for someone who loses his zest for life on impact with it (maybe love as well as compassion), but I have the greatest respect for those who remain on their feet (if they do so not out of flippant bravado, but through willpower, intelligence and character) . . . I come across more bravely in company than I truly am, but I try to keep going and I think that's how it should be. Oh, I give up; I can't do it. I wanted to write a nice, humorous, cheerful letter and tell you that your letter was like a song to my ears, but instead of that I've got angry with myself almost to the point of tears for my inarticulate mumblings. Well, what's there to say about the weather? Only that it's horrible.

10

'My darling Sveta, the New Year has started as a continuation of the old,' Lev wrote on 4 January 1951. 'We spent New Year's Eve quietly and modestly in the barrack, where thanks to Lyosha [Anisimov] there was a bushy Christmas tree, which was decorated fairly respectably by a collective effort.' As they counted 1950 out, Lev was thinking there was one year less until the date of his release.

For the moment, as he struggled with the minus-40 temperatures of January, Lev could think of little else except Sveta. 'My darling,' he wrote on the 13th,

> I still haven't sent you the letter from yesterday but once again I'm drawn towards paper – for no particular reason, just to find a place to write your name: there's no room left for it inside my head, where I've been repeating it incessantly in every intonation and in every permissible and impermissible grammatical form . . . I've tried to busy myself more with work so as not to think so much about Your Ladyship, and I've managed fairly well – so there you go.

There was a lot of work for Lev to do at the power station. Two German 'reparation generators'* had turned up in Pechora unexpectedly, 'probably en route for somewhere else', Lev supposed, and he was involved in fitting one of them to supplement the output of the power station at the wood-combine. The second generator was being fitted at the power station in the town. The rapidly developing industries of Pechora urgently required more electricity.

---

* Part of the seizure of industrial goods by the Soviet occupation force in Germany and agreed to by the Allies at the Yalta Conference in February 1945 as reparation for the damage caused by the German occupation of the Soviet Union.

Before 1951, the wood-combine had provided much of the town's needs, even though it was itself buying in supplies of electricity from Cheliabinsk, because the power station in Pechora was too small to meet demand. There were frequent struggles over energy between the town (where the Gulag bosses wanted constant heat and light for the comfort of their homes) and the wood-combine (where fuel was needed to fulfil the production plan). The arrival of the German generators would relieve the wood-combine 'of the need to feed the town,' as Lev explained to Sveta on 7 April, 'so there will be fewer conflicts, because without the new engines power-cuts would become unavoidable'.

Meanwhile the power station was closed down for three weeks of repairs following an accident in January. The wood-combine fell behind the plan for the first quarter of the year. In heated arguments the bosses of the labour camp sought to blame one another for the failures, which could bring the wrath of the MVD in Moscow down upon them all. When energy supplies were finally restored, production was ramped up in a desperate attempt to make up for lost time, but this only led to further accidents and stoppages. On 9 May, the 'safety officer' of the wood-combine reported no fewer than twenty-nine 'serious accidents' – with thirty-six fatalities – since the beginning of the year: safety regulations were ignored and there was 'chaos' everywhere, he said. A dozen men were killed in the 5th Colony when a lorry carrying seventy men to work skidded on ice and overturned. Two men in the 3rd were crushed to death by timbers falling from a railway truck. 'We're living and functioning just the same as always,' Lev wrote sarcastically on 10 June.

> For many of our uncles [MVD bosses], the construction project is a kind of game. The managers energe from their offices once a week or so and arrive in their cars (a journey of 1 km), have a walk around and shout: why the hell is it going so slowly?! Nothing is getting done! – something along those lines but in more pungent language. Nobody gives any practical instructions, such as how exactly to

speed things up. The uncles of a slightly lower rank stand around looking interested, now and then making helpful comments that are too imprecise to apply and so are pointless. None of the engineering managers take the trouble to think about the cause of the problems (the main one – unfortunately unfixable – being that they didn't think the project through when they should have), and all of them apparently consider that the very fact of their visit has given us the necessary supervision and assistance. Ah, those good-for-nothings!

Seven of these 'good-for-nothings' were sacked in April and later arrested after being found guilty of mass theft and fraud by a special MVD inquiry. They had stolen and sold off privately 8,000 metres of rigging gear, 200 kilograms of tomatoes, seven boxes of butter, six of sausage and fifty-seven mattresses. Responding to the scandal, the Party leaders of the wood-combine resolved to be more vigilant.

One of the first victims of the new campaign was Boris Arvanitopulo, the head of the power station, with whom Sveta had stayed on her visits in 1948 and 1949. Arvanitopulo had a history of trouble with the authorities. In March 1950, he had been hauled before the Party leaders of the wood-combine and given a 'severe reprimand' (*strogii vygovor*) for 'distancing himself from the responsibilities of management', that is, for fraternizing with the prisoners and sometimes getting drunk with them. Arvanitopulo was reprimanded six more times the next year, once for 'accommodating unauthorized persons' in his home (possibly a reference to Sveta), and in January 1951 he was blamed for the accident at the power station. Now he was charged with the 'theft of socialist property'. He had paid for a wardrobe to be made for his wife, Vera, in the furniture workshop and had tried to smuggle it out of the industrial zone by bribing one of the guards with 300 roubles. There were calls for him to be sacked and sent before the People's Court. The Party chairman and deputy director of the wood-combine, Zotikov Serditov, wrote a formal denunciation to the MVD in Moscow, and Arvanitopulo was dismissed. He continued to live with his family in Pechora but went in search of work in other towns, where he was unwanted, because of the black mark against his name. Lev felt bad about it all. 'It is a catastrophe,' he wrote to Sveta. 'Vera cannot feed and bring up their two children as she should. It's true she has a trade – she is a cook – but how she is to manage is not clear (though it is too early to talk about that yet) . . . Boris is holding up but Vera (whose greed caused all this) cries all the time.'

Arvanitopulo was not the only member of the administration to have close associations with the prisoners. Vladimir Novikov, the

The administration of the wood-combine, 1950. Novikov (second from right) Serpunin (second from left) and the MVD director of the wood-combine, Boris Popov (third from left), are in the middle row. The three men on the right of the front row and the six in the centre of the back row are all prisoners.

head of production, was often seen playing dominoes in the barracks, and Ivan Serpunin, the chief economist, counted many prisoners among his friends. A group photograph of the administration's members at around this time shows a combination of MVD and Party officials, voluntary workers and prisoners. The striking thing about the photograph is how relaxed everyone looks. Despite their different ranks in the Gulag system, there is no real hierarchy in their seating arrangement and little sign of tension among them. The MVD director of the wood-combine appears at ease in the centre of the group with prisoners sitting at his feet and standing in a cluster behind his back.

From 1951, the camp's security began to fall apart. Whether it was because of the growing intermingling between officials and prisoners, the greater opportunities for bribery or the massive increase in the supply of vodka is hard to tell. No doubt all these factors played a role. At a Party meeting on 6 June 1951, the commander of the guards, Ivan Koval'chuk, revealed that there had been twenty-seven individual and group escapes by prisoners in the previous three months. There were even cases where the guards – bribed with a litre of vodka for each man – had helped prisoners to escape. Some prisoners got out by jumping on to railway wagons leaving the industrial zone; others simply walked out the gates while the guards were drunk or got past them by threatening them with knives, saws and blades.

Security was particularly bad in the 2nd Colony, where Lev was a prisoner. Koval'chuk had uncovered a conspiracy of forty prisoners planning a group escape. Although the guards had known about the plan, they had done nothing to punish the conspirators. To complicate matters, a large contingent of the prisoners was on strike. They would not turn out for roll call but stayed in their barracks playing cards. They were not intimidated by the guards, who were mostly peasant boys, lamented Koval'chuk, 'many of them hostile to the MVD themselves'. If not sympathetic to the prisoners, the guards were nevertheless unopposed to their offers of cash, a drink of vodka or a sexual favour from a female prisoner.

On 25 April, the Party leaders of the wood-combine discussed a planned uprising that had been discovered in the 2nd Colony. A group of prisoners intended to start a fire in the workshops on 1 May to facilitate a mass escape, on the assumption that the guards would all be drunk on the May Day holiday. The Party leaders took charge of security. They told themselves that the uprising was polit-ical, linked to the Cold War. 'Our enemies in the camp are expecting a new war,' one of them declared. 'They are following international events and rejoice that they have allies abroad.' On 1 May, the entire membership of the Party in the camp (twenty-five full members and twenty members of the Komsomol) was mobilized; given guns, they were posted in the workshops inside the industrial zone. For the prisoners, 1 May was a normal working day, and it passed with-out incident. They must have been aware of the tightening of security and decided to abort the uprising. But, as they had expected, many of the guards got drunk. In the evening there was a brawl among the guards in the club-house.

Sveta spent May Day marching to Red Square with her colleagues from the institute. 'We had a lot of fun,' she wrote to Lev. It had poured and they all 'got drenched'.

> People were singing: 'Pour cold water over yourself if you want to be healthy' and 'Become as hard as steel'.* I passed through Red Square at 2.30 but there was such a downpour at 2.45, when I was on Maroseika, that the demonstration had to be brought to an end. I walked home in water up to my ankles (my shoes are still not com-pletely dry). People were laughing that the toe holes in their sandals were designed to let the water out. A hailstorm broke over part of the city. Large hailstones covered the ground by the institute and stayed there for 3 or 4 hours.

What was Sveta thinking as she marched past Stalin on Red Square that afternoon? Did she even look towards the Soviet leaders on top of the Lenin Mausoleum waving to the masses marching past? Did she ever think about Stalin? Or about the system that had taken Lev from her? There is very little about politics in Sveta's letters. It is clear that she does not like bureaucracy or its jargonistic prose. She is scornful about 'Diamat' (Dialectical Materialism), which she is

---

* Both lyrics from songs in popular Soviet films of the 1940s.

forced to study at the institute; is troubled by the purges in the scientific world and the 'anti-cosmopolitan' campaign against the Jews; and is very wary of the MVD, whose agents bother her from time to time with questions about Lev (having intercepted at least one of Sveta's telegrams from her trips to Pechora, they were surely watching her). Yet she takes an active part in politics and public life. She volunteers for election work in the district soviet. She represents her institute at trade union conferences. She is a member of the Communist Party and writes reports for Party meetings in the institute. For someone in her senior position – engaged in a research project with military significance – it was, of course, expected that she demonstrate her loyalty through such political activities. Not to do so would have drawn attention to herself. But, judging from her letters, Sveta carried out these duties to the Party in the same conscientious manner as she did her research work: there was no divorce between them in her professional identity. Despite all her doubts, she believed in the socialist ideal of progress through science and technology, including the propaganda message of the Great Construction Projects of Communism built by Gulag labourers.

Like millions of other Soviet citizens, Sveta lived in a dual world of belief and doubt. In her public life she was a functionary of the Soviet system; her research on tyre production was important to the military-industrial complex, which also rested on the exploitation of prisoners like Lev. But in her private life, emotionally, she identified completely with these prisoners, and tried to ease their suffering by sending money, food and medicines. The tension between these two modes of consciousness must have caused her some anxiety. A week or so before she took part in the May Day celebrations on Red Square, Sveta had dreamed about Lev. The dream disturbed her because it was so exact a picture of his circumstances in the labour camp – conditions that she knew were terrible. 'Levi,' she wrote on 23 April, 'conscience and grief are gnawing away at me.'

Whether it was because I was tired yesterday or I slept on the wrong side I don't know, but right up until morning I dreamed that I had gone to see you, in conditions as they are now, and in my dream everything was so very real – all the people, gestures, words. They were not just familiar, but exactly as I had seen them. I woke up with a terrible longing.

Sveta's anxiety may have been connected to the fact that at this point she had shelved her plans to visit Lev that year. On 2 April Lev had written to warn her that he had decided to apply for a transfer to the Volga–Don canal to work as an electrician on the nearly finished building site:

I'd like to follow in the footsteps of the beard [Aleksandr Semenov, who had successfully applied for a transfer to the Volga–Don]. Pros: 1. It will earn a reduction of a year. 2. The work will be more interesting, and my brain needs that. 3. It's in the south. Cons: 1. There's not much time left on the building phase. 2. What would happen to me then? Where would I be sent? 3. The journey. Overall it can't be worse there for my health than it is here. But issues of a different order are worrying me more – whether we'll be able to see each other this year and my reluctance to leave G. Ya. [Strelkov] here all by himself.

Lev wanted Sveta to approve his plan for a transfer. 'The final word is yours,' he wrote three days later. He was 'very pleased' when she gave it the 'go-ahead'. But that jeopardized their summer plans for a meeting. On 25 April, Lev told Sveta that she should give up any plans of 'special expeditions' to the North until he had heard from the authorities. 'Decisions like this can drag on for months,' he wrote, 'so there's no point waiting to hear anything.'

If anything does happen, I'll let you know by telegram – or rather somebody will let you know, since I won't have the time, it's usually a matter of hours rather than days from notification to departure. Because of your stubbornness [over sending parcels] . . . I've accumulated some dead weight – a wardrobe of clothes – which I'll give to Ant. Mikh. [Iushkevich, a fellow prisoner and invalid], or try to send back to you beforehand, either through the Litvinenkos or by some other means. Perhaps – and at your discretion – it would be best to 're-supply' them to Oleg. I will try to take some books with me, if it looks like that's possible. And I'll ask if the rest (not all of them of course, but only the most important ones) can be forwarded to me – either directly or through you. Don't organize any special expeditions, Svet, just do whatever is convenient for you, because it's really difficult to guess what will happen. Let's hope for the best.

With Lev hoping for a transfer south, Sveta planned to join a touring group on a camping holiday in Tuva, Siberia, during the summer. She was looking forward to a holiday but worried that she would not have the time to visit him. 'My conscience has been troubling me,' she confessed on 22 June. 'Why am I itching to go to Tuva when I need to be with you?' The Siberian trip would take a month, her entire holiday, whereas a vacation in the Caucasus, where she had gone the previous year, would give her time to travel to Pechora at the end. A week later the camping trip fell through, leaving Sveta free to visit Lev, who by this time had learned that there was 'no need for labour on the Volga–Don [canal]', nor on any of the other building sites, such as the Khakovka hydroelectric power station in Ukraine, where he would have liked to be transferred. Sveta shared his disappointment, but she was pleased that she could come to see him now. She wrote on the evening of 29 June:

Levi, I really want to go to sleep, but even more than that I want to tell you right away that my fate has been decided, though not as you proposed – that option never even entered my head. So as not to hold things up, I'm not going to go to Tuva, it's settled, and I'm relieved because I'll be nearer to you.

Lev was genuinely disappointed that she was giving up a vacation. 'Don't think I'm glad you're not going to Tuva,' he replied on 7 July.

There might have been one evening, when I'd just found out your plans for Tuva, when I was a little bit low – I'll admit to that. But then afterwards it was quite the reverse – I always wanted you to have the holiday and was ashamed that I could have thought about it any other way.

Sveta now proceeded with her plans for Pechora. She would come in August, following a trip to the Caucasus, when again, as in 1950, she got a four-day extension to her holiday allowing her to travel to Pechora before her return to work. 'My darling Lev,' she wrote on 15 July,

> I received permission from the director yesterday for the four extra days, so if nothing goes wrong, everything will work out fine. The travel voucher is for seven days. I'll be home on the 9th–10th, which means I'll be with you on the 13th or 14th, and be back at work on the 20th.

Sveta arrived in Pechora on 15 August and stayed, it seems, with the Arvanitopulos, where she received this note from Lev:

> Welcome, Sveta. While we congratulate ourselves, this time may be less joyful than the last. First of all, for almost a month now they've been allowing meetings only in the central guard-house and not in the guard-house of the colony, that is not 'at ours', like last year and not the way it was for I. S. [Lileev, Nikolai's father] and Litv[inenko]. So it's unlikely we'll be able to say everything we'd like, what with the compulsory attendance of one of them [a guard]. All the more reason, therefore, not to ask for more than one meeting, especially since your time is so limited and you have to be back by the 20th, as you warned. Do you really have to go tomorrow if there has been no change to the dates of your leave? Maybe take B. G. [Arvanitop-ulo] with you; he might be of help in getting the meeting moved to our guard-house, and since there's only going to be one, perhaps getting it extended to more than 2 hours. But I'm not very hopeful about it. Restrictions have now been tightened here, generally

speaking. And you won't recognize a single person charged with carrying them out. So, Svete, be prepared for the worst and try not to get upset in front of them. Take no notice of them. In any event you'll be able to tell me about your trip and also about my aunts, Uncle N., E. A. [Aunt Katya] and A[leksandr Ivanov], and all the others, including Alik . . .

Lev had made toys for Sveta to take back for the children of family and friends before the start of the school year on 1 September:

Incidentally, about the three trinkets – you might want to give them to Alka for the beginning of the school year (or whenever's best), to Alenka [Semashko, Nina's eleven-year-old daughter] for her birthday, and the third as you see fit (or in case you lose one along the way). I'm afraid they only look well-made, and in truth I feel self-conscious about their being shown to someone who can tell. Although you won't notice anything without my explanations, there are enough flaws in each one that they'd never be accepted by the Quality Control Department. They're suitable as toys for children, however – only you have to give them with the condition that they won't cry if they lose them.

Sveta must have succeeded in getting to see Lev more than once, because she was still in Pechora (though no longer with the Arvanitopulos, it appears) when she received this on the 17th:

Good morning, Svetlye.

Don't forget to drop in on B. G. [Arvanitopulo] while he's at home – a courtesy visit, among other things. I forgot to pass on K. S.'s* request yesterday, if there's any condensed milk in the local

---

* Konon Sidorovich Tkachenko, one of Lev's fellow prisoners, an engineer and laboratory assistant to Strelkov, who was responsible for maintaining the correct chemical composition of the water in the boiler system of the electric power station.

shops and you have the time to drop in, would you buy about 4 tins and bring them with you when you come to see me? I'm asking because it's difficult for him to pass on the message any other way. Maybe you could even ask Viktor to buy them and then you'll just need to bring them with you.

But it doesn't matter if you're not able to.

Well, Sveta, that's all for now. L.

Later that day a note came by hand with confirmation of a meeting arranged for that evening: 'Well, all right, Sveta – after seven. (They do a check at 7.) It's possible to arrive at 7 and wait. I hope everything is going to be all right.'

Sveta left the next morning. Lev had given her a bunch of flowers grown on the allotment to take home. She was back in Moscow three days later:

So I'm home, Levi. The people on the train were fine, although it was a crush – well, the more the merrier – and somehow we all managed to get some sleep . . . We arrived at about 1 o'clock. I ran home to take a shower; then I had some lunch and was asleep by 4 o'clock. I got up at 8 but haven't really woken up since then and soon I'm going to bed again. I found two of your latest letters and one from Oleg, which is a cry from the depths and addressed to you . . . Not a single person had flowers on the train, of course. I carried mine all the way home, although I couldn't put them in water while I was travelling – they partly had to go on the side luggage rack and partly on the floor just under the seat . . . Well, Levi, that's all for now. Look after yourself.

The day after she left, Lev wrote to her:

My dear Svetin, it always seems so much bleaker without you when I have to get up at an ungodly hour; just now I went to switch over the substations, and I can see and hear you everywhere. There was a fair amount of work to do today and I did it all as though in my sleep. Tomorrow I'm on duty on my own, so it will be hard for me to write and even harder not to be thinking about you. But I'm feeling fine, all the same, my darling.

As before, Lev was buoyed by Sveta's visit. 'I've felt fine over the last few days,' he wrote on 23 August. 'The work is easy and I'm not being annoyed by anything, and if I do growl from time to time it's only for form's sake and not out of annoyance.'

Sveta, by contrast, found herself deflated after her return. 'It's been exactly a week since I arrived home and just as long since my last letter to you,' she wrote on the 28th.

> The Moscow climate is having a bad effect on me. First, it's stuffy everywhere – in the cinema, at work, in the underground, on the train, on the tram. Second, all I want to do is sleep. Third, my head is somehow empty. It's unlikely that the climate is to blame for that one. What is to blame, if not the head itself, is the fact that I'm tormenting it with impossible questions. Even on the train back, everything was gnawing at me: what should I do – say a firm 'no' [to a new research project at the institute] and put paid to my 'scientific' career? Or try to summon up the strength to do it? I know I have to try, but I can't see any realistic chance . . . So I'm walking around every day with a headache and full of apathy for the work going on at the laboratory.

Sveta was feeling so discouraged that she even thought of giving up photography. 'What a wretched person you are, Sveta,' Lev replied on 12 September, 'always looking for something else to scold yourself about.'

> I haven't seen any recent products, of course, and they may well be bad. But if they turn out to be good, you still won't be pleased – you'll say it's an accident and that the next photographs are bound to be poor. Anyway, I'm hoping that you're not going to neglect photography and that I'll get some samples of your work. I would

prefer to have pictures where you're in the passive mode [being photographed] – those you'll have the least use for, so, you see, my selfishness is moving contrary to your own interests [to take the photos] here – but I like your other work as well. You can send your pictures to me without fear – I won't show them to anybody, even if they turn out well . . . I want them to be just for me.

That autumn, Sveta worked long hours, writing up reports for the All-Union State Standards (which monitored the quality of manufactured goods), inspecting factories in Leningrad and joining labour teams to help bring in the harvest at collective farms in the Moscow area. Her administrative burden increased further when Tsydzik became ill and went into hospital for the early months of 1952. Sveta had a bad attack of hives and could hardly hold a pen. 'Hives are not a skin disease at all,' she wrote to Lev. 'They're painful and unpleasant. The only comfort is that it's not cancer, it's not tuberculosis, it's not etc. etc.'

Depression closed in on her again. Encouraged by her mother, Sveta went to see a homeopathic doctor, who prescribed Anacardium, widely used for memory loss and irritability. 'It seems to work,' she wrote to Lev. 'Everybody knows me at the institute but I struggle to remember the names of the new girls every autumn . . . and I'm always cursing at people.' Lev himself didn't always escape her anger. On 19 March, Lev had told her about a letter he'd received from Uncle Nikita, in which he wrote how his only solace was the thought of Lev and all his sterling qualities, and his only wish that he could live with him. 'I don't know how to reply without sounding falsely modest,' Lev had written to Sveta. She replied on 26 March:

I wish someone would give you a good whipping, Lev! To my mind it would be better not to write to N. K. on the subject. First, he won't believe what you say, and second, even if he did believe it, why do you feel it's necessary? So that there won't be any lies? It's still far from proven that the truth is always better out. To satisfy your own vanity ('Oh, look how honest I am'), you'd deprive someone of his ideal, that is, you'd cause another person pain. To be disappointed now so that there's no disappointment later on – great logic! Especially since you don't know whether it actually will be any harder later on. Sometimes I too get the urge to destroy people's illusions. But that's when I'm feeling evil; otherwise I think it's better to let the children amuse themselves. Honest to God, Levi, I'm being serious . . . Besides, your shortcomings won't decrease just by your counting them. I mean that not for you, Levi, but generally: and probably more for myself . . . You're a good man, Lev. As for me, I could write at length about how I'm not good (but then I think that's clear from many of my letters, and it's not worth wasting a separate letter on the subject).

Lev, meanwhile, was struggling to survive his sixth winter in Pechora. Once again the labour camp was unprepared for the cold. There were power-cuts. Many of the barracks in Lev's colony were badly in need of repair. Prisoners were languishing in the infirmary following a flu and scurvy epidemic, for which there were no medicines or necessary vitamins. The doctors could not cope. Between 120 and 130 prisoners (roughly 10 per cent of the prison population of the wood-combine) reported sick each day in January 1952. Lev visited the hospital to see a number of his bunk-mates from the barracks. 'There isn't enough food or ascorbic acid,' he reported to Sveta, 'so people are quite weak.' Hepatitis was equally widespread. Konon Tkachenko spent eight months in the infirmary with a severe strain of it. 'He is barely recognizable – just yellow skin on bones,' Lev wrote to Sveta, who had brought him the condensed milk. 'He can hardly move or talk.' Strelkov too succumbed to hepatitis – a further complication to the gallstones and liver disease that had made him so ill for the past few years – though he gradually got better by eating vegetables grown on the 'collective farm'. By 1952, Strelkov was living on a diet of green cabbage and vegetable oil.*

---

* Green cabbage was regarded as a cure for liver disease, hepatitis and ulcers.

Every year, Lev wrote to Sveta on 8 March to congratulate her on International Women's Day. In 1952, he sent his greetings late, on 12 March, but his letter was a special one. All the most important people in his life had been women – his grandmother, his aunts, Sveta, to whom he wrote with reverence and gratitude:

Svetlaya, my darling, I haven't yet sent you my congratulations for the 8th March, though nobody deserves the honour more than you. Actually, modesty probably holds you back from acknowledging that any special reverence is due on this occasion. I, on the other hand, am completely unhindered in this regard and without fear of admonishment can confess how very glad I am that the female sex exists on this earth. I'm full of the highest respect for you all, higher than my respect for mankind in general. It's difficult to put this feeling into words if one lacks the talent since it inevitably ends up sounding like empty rhetoric, but I would like to try nonetheless, even after Nekrasov.* Because in my life, from early childhood on, the good people to whom I owe the most have been women. I'm still tortured by the awareness that I will never be able to repay not only those who took care of me without any thought for themselves, like my grandmother, but also those who served as models of humanity, combining kindness with fortitude in all life's trials, quiet wisdom with lively humour in their perception of reality, tirelessness at work with a constancy of affection.

There have been so many women in my life whose qualities I admire that no number of negative examples, either observed at first hand or reported, could change my views. It's true that for every good person in the world there are several bad ones, but there is so much that is wonderful in that one person that it makes up for all

* The Russian poet Nikolai Nekrasov (1821–78). Lev is referring to his poem 'Russian Women' in praise of two princesses, Maria Volkonskaya and Ekaterina Trubetskaya, who had followed their husbands into exile in Siberia, where they had been sent for their participation in the Decembrist uprising of 1825. Lev is drawing a comparison between Sveta and these two famous heroines.

the bad in the others. I can't think of those women – my grandmother Lydia Konstantinovna, her sister, Aunt Liza, Eliz[aveta]
Al[eksandrovna] [Uncle Nikita's wife], Aunt Lelya and many others –
without the most profound reverence. How much sadness Lydia
Konstantinovna endured, how many misfortunes that could have
crushed her and destroyed her spiritual strength. How much fortitude she must have summoned to avoid succumbing to despair, to
remain magnanimous and spiritually pure while keeping a clear head
and continuing to support those without the strength to withstand
such difficulties on their own. How many women there are like that!
Women like my grandmother. And how much darkness there would
be in the world if they did not exist! Sveta, do I really need to tell
you that I see in you the qualities of all the finest women I have ever
known.

My darling, dear Sveta.

From the spring of 1952, the population of the wood-combine
began to decline. Prisoners were starting to be released in significant
numbers as their sentences came to an end, and there were no more
mass arrests to replace them. This was a nationwide phenomenon.
The Gulag system was slowly shutting down. As a result of these
departures the web of friends and relatives connecting the remaining prisoners to supporters in the outside world expanded in size
and importance. Once returned to society, newly released prisoners
could help those left inside the camps. These informal networks
were equally essential to the many prisoners who had no family, no
home or no job to which they could return on their release. Former
prisoners were usually barred from living in the larger towns, where
it was feared they might demoralize the population with their disaffected views, so they needed help from relatives and friends to find
places to settle and money until they could find work.

In March 1952, Rykalov came to the end of his eight-year sentence and left for Moscow, where his sister led a 'family council' to
decide where and how he ought to live. His health was poor; he had
not fully recovered from TB. Lev asked Sveta to help him:

He has only one lung and even then not a whole one. He walks with difficulty, becomes severely out of breath and feels very weak. He's thinking of moving to Kyrgyzstan (though he's not sure about the climate) or perhaps to northern Kazakhstan. His personal affairs, aside from his relationship with his mother and sisters, don't make him very happy. He didn't tell me the details, there wasn't time, and a telephone conversation doesn't lend itself to candour, but he has promised to write. If he has time, he'd like to call and see you. I told him that he shouldn't make a special effort, since every kilometre costs him dearly; but I promised on your behalf that if you were feeling well enough you would go and visit him yourself.

Ten days later, Sveta had not heard from Rykalov. He had disappeared. 'Maybe it's too early,' she wrote to Lev on 26 March, 'I'll try to find him tomorrow or the day after . . . I think his sister is called Marusia. I'll have to guess the flat but I definitely remember the building and staircase.'

Anisimov was the next to be released. 'Lyoshka has received his clearance papers,' Lev wrote to Sveta on 5 March. 'It will be boring without him. Of all our contemporaries here, he is the only one – after Liubka [Terletsky] – with whom I can have a really interesting conversation.' Anisimov was a Muscovite.

If he manages to overcome his shyness he'll drop in to see you for some tea on his way through [to his place of settlement beyond Moscow]. He's a fine fellow, as I've told you more than once, straightforward and sensible, but when he's with people he doesn't know he becomes very shy and reticent. He loves drinking tea with raspberry jam (I'm telling you that in confidence).

Anisimov departed on 12 March. Lev was worried that he would be too embarrassed to visit Sveta in the shabby clothes of a newly released prisoner. Anisimov arrived in Moscow on 16 March and wrote to Sveta from the Yaroslavl station to say that he was unable to see her as he had the flu and a stomach ache. Sveta had made jam for him. 'If I'd known he was sitting at the station, I could have gone there myself. Ifs and buts,' she wrote. 'Maybe he'll manage to come when the weather is a bit warmer.' She kept the jam on the sideboard, but Anisimov did not appear. Five months later he wrote to Lev with an explanation: 'I got to the station, sat down on a bench for an hour and a half, said farewell [to Moscow] and went on my way.' Anisimov was a qualified engineer but his status as a former prisoner made it hard for him to find a job, except as a fitter in a factory, so instead he looked for casual work as a repairman.

As the exodus of prisoners increased, the labour camp began to fall into decline. 'More and more people are leaving,' Lev wrote. 'Because of shortages of raw materials the profitability of the wood-combine has dropped and the staff must be reduced. Sadly, it's those who work badly who are still here.' Everywhere the story was the same: labour shortages and inefficiencies, falling productivity and mounting expenses, mainly for guarding prisoners, who became more rebellious the harder they had to work. The economics of the Gulag system no longer made sense. By 1953, the MVD was spending twice as much on the upkeep of the Gulag as it received in revenue from the camps' output. Several senior MVD officials were seriously questioning the effectiveness of forced labour. There was even talk of dismantling sections of the Gulag and reclassifying the prisoners as partially civilian workers. But Stalin was a firm supporter of the Gulag system, and none of these ideas was seriously proposed.

The decline of the Gulag system was clearly visible at the wood-combine. The Party archives of 1952 are dominated by discussions of waste and inefficiency, thefts, riots and refusals to work by prisoners who had not been paid. In the first half of 1952, more than 5,000 man-days had been lost, and only 60 per cent of the plan had been fulfilled. The administration responded by pushing the prisoners even harder, extending their shifts to fourteen hours, or forcing them to work when they were ill. The only results were more riots, strikes and slowdowns, and more losses of able-bodied men. Three group escapes from the wood-combine were attempted (two of them successful) in the first six months of 1952.

Physically the place was showing signs of degradation. For years, little had been done to clear the labour camp of scraps of wood, bark, sawdust, bricks and rigging that were piled high around the saw-mill and workshops. Some of it was burned in bonfires on the frozen river in winter, but the rest remained as a fire hazard. During his first years in the labour camp, Lev had noticed occasional signs of beauty around him. By 1952, these were gone. 'Objectively,' he wrote, 'little beauty remains in our area. It's all been built over, ruined by piles of rubbish and hacked down. In summertime there are no flowers or berries as there were three years ago, and you can't even see the grass. All that's left is the sky.'

Ever since he had come to Pechora, Lev had looked towards the sky. It was his only escape from the camp. He found beauty in the northern lights and the vast expanse of stars. 'Nature has blessed this meagre Komi land with a beautiful, not just colourful, and breathtaking sky!', Lev wrote to Sveta on 12 August.

Lingering sunsets, extending into even longer twilights full of such magical colours and effects that it's impossible to tear yourself away – you stand, head thrown back, until your teeth begin to chatter from the cold (autumn can already be felt). Today was cloudy and miserably grey. But in the evening the dull eastern clouds suddenly transformed themselves into such an intense, opaque blue that even the serene blue of the Caucasian mountains would probably have been envious. Then, after half an hour, the sun, already retiring over the horizon, suddenly sought out a delicate slit in the middle of the storm clouds and poured through it with such a vivid orange blaze that all the pines in its path suddenly began to glow – not with a red but with a pale yellow-green warmth. I've never seen anything like it – they were no longer trees but radiant silhouettes against a brilliant flame; and the smoke from the chimney that whirled among them, awash with the tenderest of tones and the colourless glassy undulation of the air, made them seem alive. The stars have emerged from their summer hibernation,* and I am grateful for this too.

The sky was the one aspect of the world that he could look at and imagine that Sveta was looking at as well. He would gaze at it when he longed for her.

In 1952, a new brick chimney was built at the power station. After it was finished, the bosses realized that they had forgotten to record its height, and called for volunteers to climb to the top with a measuring rope. Lev and Sergei Skatov, a stoker at the plant, climbed the stack by the small iron handles sunk into the brick and sat together on the narrow lip of the chimney top. They were almost 40 metres from the ground. Facing south, they looked out over the river and the pine forests, stretching as far as the eye could see towards Moscow. It was the first time in almost seven years that Lev had glimpsed the world beyond the labour camp. He recalled the episode:

> I wanted to find out what was outside, around the camp, how the river flowed, where it went, and what lay past it. We sat there for a while and then climbed down. As soon as I put my feet back on the ground, I felt a sharp pain in my back. It was a sciatica attack. I collapsed. If it had struck a few moments earlier, I would have been finished.

However profound their mutual trust and commitment, Lev and Sveta were vulnerable to enormous stresses at any breach of routine or communication. For the first year since 1947, Sveta failed to visit Lev in 1952. She had planned to come at the end of a work trip to Omsk and Kirov in June but had returned to Moscow because she needed treatment for her hives. The trip was rescheduled for September, but her mother Anastasia became ill, and Sveta needed to look after her. 'Mama still isn't any better,' she wrote on 19 July. 'If there's no one standing over her, making her eat, she'll stop eating

---

* The white nights of the North made the stars invisible.

and become worse again. It will be difficult for me to get away for a while and Mama should be taken somewhere later on as well.' Lev replied on 6 August:

> I really think you should cancel your trip north this year. Even if you were in full health it would require more effort than usual since you have so many demands on your time and you can't possibly do everything. You need to look after your mother and go somewhere with her, you need to get better yourself, you need to try to coordinate your holiday leave with Irina [Krauze]'s. And it's complicated sorting out holidays at work, with yours and M. A. [Tsydzik]'s. Sveta, maybe we can somehow wait out the rest of this year?

Sveta spent the summer accompanying her mother to various surgeries and hospitals. In August, Anastasia was diagnosed with spinal osteoarthritis. She cried constantly and could not sleep at night. Then, in September, it was said she had TB. Anastasia took to what she believed was her death-bed, leaving Sveta to look after both her mother and her father, Aleksandr, who was sick with an undiagnosed liver ailment. 'Papa has lost a lot of weight (4 kilograms this summer),' Sveta wrote on 28 September, 'and has pains in his side.' From July to October, Sveta was run off her feet, coming home from work to attend to her parents, dashing between home and the hospital, where her father had gone for tests, shopping for the family and writing to Lev late at night, by which time she was exhausted and in tears. Her letters read like medical reports.

Even in October she was still hoping to find time to visit Lev. But he again dissuaded her. 'I think it will be hard for you to take a holiday,' he wrote on 20 October, 'if you are not sure about your mother . . . It would be best to wait until she's better and then take a proper holiday and do something like skiing, which will help you to relax. In any case, don't use it to come here. Everything this year is against us – your health and your mother's and the time of year.' Four days later he wrote to his Aunt Katya to tell her his concern: 'Sveta wrote that you had promised to visit her on Sunday, but you didn't come. She was worried that you may be ill, but she could not come herself, because her mother's sick. Things are very difficult for them at home.'

In November, Sveta at last took time off: she spent all of it at home, looking after her mother. 'My holiday is going very quickly,' she wrote to Lev on 8 November. 'A week has gone by, a quarter of my time already. That is bad. Mama is getting used to having me around. Yesterday she complained that I had forgotten her, because I was away for a while. And today, when she woke up, she asked me not to go anywhere. She is just like a small child.'

The longer Lev went without Sveta, the more he saw her in his dreams. 'I miscalculated, Sveta,' he wrote on 24 December. 'There was no letter from you today. I've started dreaming about you again, frequently, but my dreams don't bring me any joy, because the feelings that come with them are so depressing and I can't rid myself of them after I wake up.' Three days later, he wrote again:

> When I put aside my books and papers and, having closed my eyes, expel from my head all thoughts of electric fields, centrifugal regulators and coherent rotations, I see you. I see you so clearly that my throat gets dry and I want to take your hands and weep, burying my face in them and lamenting that you are so far away. I see your red knitted jacket (which you don't even have any more), a strand of hair struggling free by your cheek, the speckles in your eyes and your moist eyelids. I see every detail of the lines on your palms resting in your lap. I want to tell you again and again that there is nobody better than you, that one thought of you eclipses everything for me, makes everything else seem trivial and insignificant.

Lev spent another New Year's Eve with the usual group of friends in Strelkov's laboratory. He wrote to Sveta about it on 2 January:

> The frosts have been unmerciful here all week, from minus 42 down to minus 47 degrees, and the workshops aren't in operation. Being outside without mittens is impossible for more than a minute or

two. The sparrows are freezing. One of them has warmed himself up in our barrack and has been living here for two days now. He's a jolly little thing. We saw the New Year in with G. Y. [Strelkov], just the three of us, since Tall N. [Litvinenko] is still in the hospital and K. [Tkachenko] was fearful of the cold and didn't come. Valya sent G. Y. a fine pipe, tobacco and a cap. I was just as pleased for him as he was for himself. It really cheered him up.

Lev had not received a letter from Sveta for three weeks. His dreams were becoming more anxious. 'Svetloe, it's so dreary without your letters,' he wrote on 6 January.

I've seen you in my dreams for three nights in a row. I dreamed that we were delivering some equipment to your institute and you'd arrived to receive it but I wasn't able to say anything to you, and then I couldn't find you, you'd already gone, apparently; and all that was left behind was your signature on the delivery receipt. But then it turned out that the signature wasn't even yours.

Another week passed without a letter from Sveta. On 10 January, Lev wrote:

Svetka, why aren't you writing to me? There are so many things I start to think when your letters stop coming – oh, so many – and the most rational logic, which in rare moments I still seem to be capable of, is unable to disprove the most illogical assumptions, especially as not everything in life is logical. It doesn't need to be much – just two lines.

And three days later:

The post comes tomorrow; I now wait for these days with something like a low dose of despair whereas before, after every one of those days I used to think – well that's all right, today's drawing to a close but perhaps there'll be a letter tomorrow.

Lev's worst fear was that Sveta had abandoned him. In fact, she had been away on a work trip to Sverdlovsk and Omsk that had lasted longer than she had anticipated because of problems at the tyre factories. She had been so busy that she had not found the time to write even a short note. Finally, she wrote to Lev on her return to Moscow on 18 January:

I don't know why, but I don't find it easy at all to write 2 lines. In fact it's easier for me to write a long letter, although it takes me longer. My work trip was meant to last 7 days (of which 5 were purely travel) but I think I wrote to tell you that. And even though I thought that a week was nothing to worry about, I still took envelopes and paper with me and carried them around with the aim of writing, but somehow I didn't get around to it . . . As so often happens, you make up your mind to do something the next day, but then when 'tomorrow' comes, you find yourself working even harder, and you tell yourself you'll do it in 3 or 4 days . . . The only thing I took comfort from was that you wouldn't be angry with me as long as you love me. That's one of the privileges of love, that you can do stupid things. All the same, I'm sorry. I was trying so hard to be good . . . When I got home and read your letters, I just wanted to cry, but I had nowhere and no time to cry.

Lev replied on 27 January:

My dear darling Svetloe, forgive me – again. I know myself that the business with the letters is all down to my foolishness. My dear Svet, my love, I lost my head, I just didn't know what to do with myself or what to do in general; I just knew that I shouldn't howl or get angry, but there was still everything else – anxiety for you, the fear that you might not love me any more, my longing for you, more anxiety, then jealousy, anger at myself for my stupidity, the desire to complain to you about it all. None of it would submit to my self-control, until I almost reached the point of despair . . . I'm ashamed to write it, Sveta, but I thought – forgive me, my dear Svet – that maybe it wasn't because of lack of time that you were finding it difficult to write. But Svetka, Svetinka, I still didn't know anything: I didn't know how long you planned to be away – you probably forgot to mention your schedule to me and I was only able to work out that your trip should end in December, since that had been the plan back in 1952; and I didn't know about the problems in Sverdlovsk or about the situation in O[msk]. Obviously in principle I could have guessed all that, and I did, in fact, in my more sensible moments. But what can I do when these are so few?

Sveta, my darling, it pains me that I almost reduced you to tears, but that can't be altered now, as much as I want to have behaved better.

I got your letter dated the 18th an hour ago just as I was leaving work. Sveta, I'll write to you about everything else later on, although there's not much at the moment. My darling Sveta. We'll try to make sure that everything will be all right with us, won't we?

II

Stalin died on 5 March 1953. He had suffered a stroke and lay uncon-
scious for five days before he died. His illness was reported in the
Soviet press only on 4 March. 'How unexpected the news report
was,' Lev wrote to Sveta two days later. 'On such occasions the
impotence of modern medicine becomes tragically clear. It's only
when important people are affected that the impossibility of pre-
serving human health a little longer than nature will allow becomes
fully evident.'

Stalin's death was announced to the public on 6 March. Until the
funeral, three days later, his body lay in state in the Hall of Columns
near Red Square. Huge crowds came to pay their respects. The
centre of the capital was mobbed by tearful mourners, who had
travelled to Moscow from all corners of the Soviet Union. Hundreds were killed in the crush. The loss of Stalin was an emotional
shock for the Soviet people. For nearly thirty years – the most trau-
matic in their country's history – they had lived in his shadow. Stalin
was their moral reference point – their teacher, guide, paternal pro-
tector, their national leader and saviour against the enemy, their
guarantor of justice and order ('There is always Stalin,' Lev's Aunt
Olga used to say when some injustice had occurred). The people's
grief was a natural reaction to the disorientation they were bound
to feel upon his death, almost regardless of their experience under
his regime. Even Stalin's victims felt sorrow.

Like everybody else, Lev and Sveta heard the news on the radio
on 6 March. In a state of fearful shock and excitement, neither could
say what they really felt. 'The death of Stalin was so unexpected,'
Lev wrote on 8 March, 'that it was hard at first to believe that it
could be true. The feeling was the same as in the first days of the
war.' He had nothing more to add about the momentous news,

although he must have hoped that it might lead to a change in policy towards the labour camps and possibly to his early release. Sveta, too, was guarded, although she could not conceal her joy that they had been united by the radio at this possibly life-changing moment. 'There has never been anything like there was in Moscow this past week,' she wrote to Lev on 11 March. 'And many times I thought how good it is that the radio was invented so people can hear the same things at the same time. And it's also good that there are newspapers. I'll try to tell you more sometime, but not now because I need to think about how to say what I feel in a few clear words.'

The one place where the death of Stalin was welcomed with undisguised rejoicing was in the Gulag's labour camps and colonies. There were, of course, exceptions, camps where the vigilance of the authorities or the presence of informers prevented prisoners from showing their happiness, but generally the news of Stalin's end was greeted with spontaneous outbursts of joy. 'No one cried for Stalin,' Lev recalled. The prisoners had no doubt that Stalin was to blame for their misery, and were not afraid to express their contempt for him when it was safe to do so. Lev recalled an incident from October 1952 when the prisoners in his barracks were listening to a radio broadcast of the results of the election to the Presidium of the Central Committee. The votes received by the candidates were read out in turn, and after each the announcer said: 'Za Stalina! Za Stalina!' ('Long Live Stalin!'). Some of the prisoners began to chant instead 'Zastavili! Zastavili!' ('They were forced!'), meaning that the vote was rigged. Everyone joined in and enjoyed the joke.

Among the prisoners it was commonly assumed that they would be freed on Stalin's death. On 27 March, the government announced an amnesty for prisoners serving sentences of up to five years, those convicted of economic crimes, men over fifty-five, women over fifty, and convicts with incurable diseases – a dispensation that would lead to the release of about one million prisoners in the next few months. At the wood-combine the amnesty halved the prison population (from 1,263 to 627) during 1953. Most of those released were criminals. They went on a rampage, looting stores, robbing houses, raping women and spreading terror throughout the town. 'Some of our people are already out and wandering at will in Pechora,' Lev wrote to Sveta on 10 April.

> They are taking every chance to rob and steal. The worst types are going free. Makarov, a fine-looking fellow with a beard . . . He has served 8 years for armed robbery. Kolya Nezhinsky is also leaving – he got ten years when he was already here in 1947 for stealing 6 kg of kasha. Then last year he stole 300 roubles from one of the men and pilfered bit by bit what he could from N. and his other neighbours. Despite all that, one can only pity him for the stupidity and injustice of his original sentence, without which he might not have become a thief.

Lev was hopeful that the amnesty would be extended to 'politicals'. Some of the technicians at the power station had been encouraged by the MVD to apply for their release. They had all been sentenced under Article 58-11 (belonging to an anti-Soviet organization), a clause not as serious as Lev's, though close enough in kind to give him hope that if they were covered by the amnesty he might be freed as well. He was soon disappointed. 'It turned out,' he wrote to Sveta on 14 April, 'that it was all a mistake by the local guards. There'll be no widening of the amnesty . . . Such a cruel mistake! People already had their hopes up, and their families were expecting their release.'

The reduction of the prison population resulted in a chronic shortage of labour at the wood-combine. Without enough prisoners to cut and haul the timber, the supply of fuel and raw materials declined dramatically. The administration of the labour camp, transferred from the Gulag to the Ministry of Transport in May 1953, tried to make up for the loss of manpower by keeping newly freed prisoners in Pechora. The MVD officials who oversaw the release of prisoners employed various strategies: they denied them exit papers, refused to give them money for train tickets or warned they would not be able to find work elsewhere and instead proposed incentives for them to stay on as hired labourers. Some were offered training to replace the skilled workers, craftsmen and technicians released by the amnesty. By the end of the year, 224 former prisoners were being trained as drivers, carpenters, machine-operators, mechanics and electricians (Lev was involved in preparing some of them to take over shift work at the power station). But despite these efforts there was a sharp decline in productivity at the wood-combine. The plan was not fulfilled, wages and rations were reduced, and free workers disappeared in search of better conditions at other labour camps (which were experiencing similar problems). 'Here in Pechora there are general cut-backs,' Lev wrote, 'and people don't know what to do with themselves, especially those who have a mackintosh in their baggage [i.e., former prisoners].'*

The newly released prisoners who returned home did indeed have a difficult time finding work. Soviet officials were generally mistrustful of former prisoners, and many employers continued to regard them with suspicion as potential troublemakers and 'enemies of the people'. The problem of unemployment was so acute that some ex-prisoners ended up returning to the labour camps. Without family or friends to help them back on their feet, they had little choice. The camp was the only place they could be sure of getting work, as free or semi-free workers (who were paid a wage but not allowed to leave the settlement). By July 1953, there were more than 100 former prisoners employed as semi-free workers in the wood-combine; by the end of 1954, that number had risen to 459. Many lived in the barracks of the former 1st Colony just outside the fence of the industrial zone. They were paid about 200 roubles a month, a minimum wage without the 'northern bonus' to attract free workers to the Arctic zone, but they received it only if they reported twice a week to the administration of the labour camp. One such worker was Pavel Bannikov, a prisoner from Lev's barrack who returned to the wood-combine after he failed to find a job in

---

* Lev and Sveta used code words for the Gulag associated with the rain (e.g. 'umbrella' and 'mackintosh').

the Moscow area. '[Bannikov] has been back with us for four days now,' Lev wrote to Sveta. 'He sees it as a temporary stopping point and plans to leave again in the autumn in search of something better. He told me his impressions of Moscow, which were interesting, both as a reminder of details sanctified by memory and as a portrait of the new.'

Bannikov had been to see Sveta. She put up many prisoners who came to Moscow after their release from Pechora. Lev would give them her address and alert her with a request to help them in the capital. 'Darling Svetloe,' he wrote on 12 June, 'Konon Sidorovich [Tkachenko] perhaps told you – but if not, then I surely did – that Vitaly Ivanovich Kuzora would visit you. So here he is. He is very orderly, and modest too. I don't know how things in Moscow will work out. He might need putting up for a night or two. It is inconvenient, I know, especially at the moment: but this won't go on for much longer, another year and a half at the most.' It must have been frustrating for Sveta to receive these strangers from the camp when Lev still had eighteen months of his sentence left to serve. She had not seen him for two years, their longest separation since their reunion in 1946.

It was not just prisoners who slept on the Ivanovs' floor. Many of the free workers who had helped Lev and Sveta stayed with her when they came to Moscow. In the more relaxed conditions after Stalin's death, travel was generally easier and these workers' wages had increased significantly with the addition of 'northern bonuses' to keep them at the labour camp. Stanislav Yakhovich, the Polish mechanic at the power station who had smuggled letters in and out of the industrial zone for Lev, was planning to pass through Moscow on his way back to Pechora from a holiday in the Crimea. 'He'd like to take advantage of a mattress and a couple of square metres of floor space for 8 hours of the day,' Lev wrote. 'He'll let you know by postcard what day he's going to arrive. If you've forgotten him, he's easy to recognize by his squinty eye and his Polish pronunciation of the letter "l" ("wouse" instead of "louse").'

Lev Izrailevich, who had smuggled Sveta into the prison zone on her first trip to Pechora, was one of several visitors in June 1953. That month, Sveta also put up the Bashuns. Ivan Bashun, a senior mechanic at the power station, had carried letters for Lev. The couple's provincial ways got on Sveta's nerves – she made no effort to conceal her disdain – but she did her best to entertain them nevertheless. 'Nina and Iv[an] have been staying with me for a week,' she wrote to Lev on 3 July.

> I told them I'm giving them a mark of 3 out of 5 (slightly below average) for their conduct in Moscow, but in all fairness it should've been a 1. They haven't been anywhere except shops. If I hadn't insisted on taking them to the [Lenin] Mausoleum and the University, they wouldn't have bothered to see them at all. Nothing has made an impression on them – not the Metro, or the tall buildings, or the view of the city from the Lenin Hills, or the Bolshoi Theatre. I was at a complete loss, exhausted by my efforts to find something to interest them. They didn't buy anything, except for a couple of shopping bags and something for Slavik, since they're convinced that everything you can get in Moscow you can also get in Kotlas and anything they don't have there can't be found here either.

For the prisoners who remained in Pechora, Stalin's death brought some improvements. As the population of the prison zone declined, the barracks became less cramped. In 1953, new barracks were built with individual beds instead of the double-row bunk beds that had been standard when Lev arrived in 1946. There were more cultural activities for the prisoners – regular films, plays and concerts in the club-house, even bands for dancing – and more outings to the Palace of Culture and the football stadium in the civilian sector of Pechora (which was itself becoming much more of a town, with a population of 25,000 inhabitants, shops and market stalls, a restaurant, a bus service provided by lorries and a radio station broadcasting through loudspeakers on the streets). In the wood-combine the separate radio station for the prisoners was improved as well: for the first time national broadcasts could be heard in the barracks. Prisoners were allowed more letters, and the censors paid them less attention than before.

In January 1954, the authorities of the wood-combine posted a new law by the Supreme Soviet prohibiting guards from using violence against prisoners and promising court hearings to judge complaints about such behaviour: guards found guilty would be punished with prison sentences and even, in extreme cases, with death. In the past there had been instances of prisoners being killed or beaten by guards – sometimes in revenge for a perceived insult or challenge to their power, more often just for sport – but no guard had ever received more than a 'severe reprimand' or a cut in wages. The new decree brought about a dramatic improvement in the treatment of prisoners. The number of guards was decreasing in any case as labour camps were closed or transformed into special economic zones employing nominally free labour.

This more humane atmosphere did nothing to resolve Lev's long-running problems with his boss, the head of the power station. A brutish, barely literate man, Ilia Sherman had risen to the rank of engineer-lieutenant in the MVD despite his minimal understanding of engineering. Lev described him as a 'small-minded person who finds fault with everything . . . and is suspicious of everyone'. Sherman saw every setback at the power station as sabotage. He usually tried to pin the blame on Lev, to whom he had taken an instant dislike. He bullied Lev, gave him orders that could not be fulfilled and threatened several times to send him on a convoy to another camp to work as a general labourer. It was Lev's worst fear.

Strelkov intervened to rescue Lev. In June 1953, his laboratory assistant Tkachenko was due to be released and would need to be replaced. An engineer and chemist, Tkachenko was in charge of monitoring the water quality in the boiler system of the power station, a position of great responsibility since wrong calculations could lead to serious accidents. Lev had worked as a chemistry assistant in his student days and so could do the job, which had the added benefit of putting him under the authority of the Department of Technical Control (OTK), a higher body outside Sherman's domain. With Strelkov's assent, Tkachenko started training Lev. 'Before he leaves,' Lev wrote to Sveta on 13 April, 'K. S. [Tkachenko] is planning to pass on to me some of his wisdom on the control of feed water. Starting this very night, I'm going to be reading his notes and any literature that he has. Then he's promising to teach me some of the more practical aspects.' On 1 June, Lev took over the new job. Although he went on working at the power station, where Sherman was in command, his new position as a water chemist under Strelkov and the OTK protected him from being sent away on a convoy. Lev wrote to Sveta on 9 June:

> I am feeling very calm, compared with last month, and also much better than last year despite the huge amount of work. Nikolai [Lileev] for some reason thought that it would be difficult to work for G. Ya. [Strelkov], and for me especially. I never believed that, and the very idea seems strange to me. In any case, I can't imagine a serious misunderstanding between G. Ya. and me, no matter what the circumstances. The arguments we had in the past were sometimes loud but never serious and always on account of some lack of intelligence on my part. My awareness of this fact will surely help me to control myself, although perhaps my respect for G. Ya. – which has grown every day since then – is enough to ensure it.

But if Lev felt less stress working for Strelkov, he showed increasing signs of impatience with his other friends and nearly all his barrack-mates. After so many years of being cooped up in a confined space, it was hardly surprising that prisoners became irritable and fell out with one another. Even the best friendships came under strain.

Lev's relations with Nikolai Lileev, his oldest friend in the labour camp, became tense towards the end of 1952. They had been together for seven years, arriving in Pechora on the same convoy, and Lev had a very high regard for Lileev's kindness, honesty and bravery. Lileev had displayed extraordinary courage on at least two occasions: once when he stopped a horse stampeding through the labour camp; the other when he saved Strelkov's life by chasing away three armed criminals who attacked him in revenge for an earlier incident when Strelkov had defended his laboratory from them. Yet in spite of his fondness and respect for Lileev – and perhaps because of them – Lev would express irritation more often

Lileev (left) and Lev, 1949.

about him than about anybody else. He complained about his 'childishness', 'flippant views on life' and 'lack of tact', especially in the barracks. 'N. annoys me more with every passing day,' Lev wrote to Sveta on 24 December.

> It seems we're just bored with each other. I really can't find anything to talk to him about. He's not interested in the practical challenges of manufacturing. He's indifferent to any type of machinery, including electrical, both on a practical and a theoretical level; he's even fallen behind on his mathematics and is spending all his time playing table tennis or chess or studying German with Vadim. There's no doubt

that language is a useful thing but for Vadim, just as for N., electrical engineering and mathematics would be more useful; that's why Nikolka's lessons seem like pure self-indulgence to me; and it's all I can do not to tell him. If there were no G. Y. [Strelkov], Ivan [Valiavin]* or A. M. [Iushkevich], I would still find it ten times more interesting to talk to a machine operator or anyone at all who looks life square in the eye than I would to N.

Lev was being unfairly critical. What was so wrong with a prisoner wanting to relax by playing chess or table tennis or learning German instead of maths? Lev's serious-mindedness had grown alongside his annoyance with his fellow prisoners.

Everything about his barrack-mates exasperated Lev: their talking in their sleep at night; their herd instinct; their practical jokes and noisiness; their incessant games of dominoes; their sentimental reminiscing; and the 'excessive tenderness' that he noted in several prisoners and found particularly 'repulsive'. Lev was disgusted by the feelings of affection that naturally developed between men inside the labour camp. He had not encountered it before, and he was disturbed by it. 'Regarding the family ideal,' he wrote to Sveta,

> it seems to me that it's really wrong when it's in a friendship between men. In my opinion, it's more than wrong – it's an abnormality that for me is repulsive to the point of being loathsome. I'm sure that my friendships with Andriushka [Semashko], Zhenka [Bukke], Nat [Grigorov] and Vaska Gusev [all student friends before the war] were sincere and solid, the kind without which each one of us would have found life more difficult. Whatever affected one of us was felt by all of us, and everyone was always happy for everyone else – but outwardly this was expressed with nothing more than a handshake.

---

* Lev's bunk-mate in the barrack. Ivan was a student at the Odessa Shipbuilding Institute in 1950, when he was arrested and sentenced to ten years in Pechora.

Far from merely irritated, Lev was appalled by the human degradation he saw all around him. People who had once been decent were now brutal, selfish, mean, hardened and insensitive. 'There is an unavoidable psychological evolution in the human being here,' he wrote to Uncle Nikita. 'Its extent depends on the individual, but the direction is a general one – the dulling of all feeling . . . What develops is an acceptance of qualities and actions that before would not have been acceptable.'

The first thing Lev noticed was the breakdown of fellow feeling. 'The infinite mutual hostility that chokes all human relations here amazes me,' he wrote to Sveta.

> There's no trace anywhere of solidarity among friends, or even of solidarity at work – everyone mistrusts everybody else and tries to ride on their back; everyone is on their guard and lying in wait. There are still, it seems, some little groups of workers who are united by common interests into something like friendship, but this connection is easily broken because of the distrust which eats away at all relationships.

Enterprising individuals were invariably thieves:

> Watching the people around me, I'm once again disgusted that no sooner do you meet someone who's energetic and quick-witted than he's almost always on the make to the point of theft, the scale of which is determined only by opportunity. If he's a cobbler, he's stolen and sold material, and the higher-ups have taken part in it. If he's an electrician, he's earned money on the side in a similar way. There is no need to even talk about the drivers.

The labour camp had taught him to believe, as he put it, 'that in 999 instances out of 1,000, the common principles of decency lead the average person to ruin or starvation in the struggle to survive'.

Lev was worried by the changes he noticed even in himself. 'Once again I am overwhelmed by the fear that I thought had disappeared,' he wrote to Sveta: 'that in the course of time you really do become a savage and malicious animal, and slow-witted besides, so that a joke doesn't make you smile and you aren't even capable of telling a story to a Liudmilla or Taniushka.'

What kind of father would he make after all these years in labour camps? Lev thought a great deal about that question. His experience had changed his views on what mattered in raising children. Lev was not a violent man, but there had been moments in the camp when he had been forced to defend himself. After one such incident, he had written to Sveta that the camp had taught him the importance of physical strength, something he had tried to develop by lifting weights (he made them out of axles from the railway wagons in the yard). He thought that strength was especially important for children growing up in a cruel world:

> Physical strength is the most necessary condition in life. Those parents who aren't making their children develop physically, whether they want to or not, should be subject to punishment. At any rate, physical development should play a far larger role than is mandated in schools. It's a crime that Nikolai Lileev, who is nearly twice as tall as me, is no better than I am at weightlifting and that in a fight only his height would be of any advantage. To look at him you would have thought him strong enough to play *gorodki* [a kind of skittles] with telegraph poles.

Lev's experience had also taught him that children needed practical skills to survive:

> What is a person suitable for, having completed, as I have, a university-style course of study or graduated from an institute of higher education? If that person doesn't remain at the institute and doesn't become a teacher, he still has merely the raw material to develop into a future professional, although the raw material itself isn't bad. It seems to me that children should go to school for only 7 years. They should then spend 3 or 4 years in a vocational college – construction,

electrical engineering, vehicular, mechanical etc. – and then 1 or 2 years in an apprenticeship gaining practical experience. An education of this kind, fostering intensive knowledge of a special field, will help them get through difficult situations . . . Planning for such rainy days is important even in our radiant times – you don't have to go far for examples. To raise a child, you must be prepared to punish him severely for all kinds of things – to punish him when his friends hit him but he doesn't hit back and to punish him even more if he still refuses to fight . . . What I say relates to the female sex as well – with the exception of fighting, naturally.

Lev had witnessed many prisoners lose what had been good in their character and become nasty, violent, alcoholic or insane. Psychologically, there was nothing more disturbing for a prisoner than watching the deterioration of another prisoner, not least because of the terrifying implications for himself. This accounts for Lev's rather harsh response to the changes he observed in Oleg Popov, the half-Latvian he had liked so much who had been sent on a convoy to break stones and become obsessed by bread. Lev and Sveta had continued sending parcels to Oleg. They were encouraged by his interest in literature – it seemed a sign of hope to them – and discussed between themselves what books he might like. Oleg could not write to Lev from the stone quarry (where there were rules against his writing to another prisoner) but he could write to Sveta:

I am very grateful to you for all the trouble you have taken over me, for your efforts, attention and friendship. I cannot express what is in my heart, and maybe such feelings should not be expressed. Sometimes I think that Lev must be a very lucky person, at least it seems that way to me, because it is not often that you find someone as good as you.

In December 1952, Oleg was sent back to Pechora. He wrote to Lev from one of the forest camps. 'I received a note today,' Lev wrote to Sveta, 'and you'll never guess from whom – from Oleg! I was indescribably happy. He's now only 3 kilometres away from here and feels as if he's been released from Hell.'

For the next year, Lev tried to get Oleg transferred to the wood-combine by talking to the bosses there, and in January 1954 he finally succeeded. Oleg was put into a hauling team made up of prisoners from the Baltic area. 'Yesterday Oleg came to visit us – after 6 years of destitution in the wilderness,' Lev wrote to Sveta on 8 January. 'Against expectations, he appears to be well – in good health and young. Only his look is more serious and there are signs of inner disturbance.' Within days, though, Lev's excitement turned to dismay. 'The more I really get to know him, the less I like Oleg,' Lev wrote to Sveta on 24 January.

> More and more I think that he has absolutely nothing on the inside – no kind of serious opinions, principles or feelings. All there is is ostentatious 'originality'. It's in quote marks because in actual fact he doesn't have any; it's been a long time since he was original. He never uses plain language and when he speaks it's always with pre-tensions to wit . . . None of this was noticeable before, evidently because his audience over the last few years has broken him of the habit of a more subtle camouflage . . . It's all really sad, of course, because it's yet another example of my disillusionment with people – even more unpleasant because it's not the first. Having noticed falsity in one person, I'm now seeing it in many.

Five days later, Lev wrote to tell Sveta to break off relations with Oleg. 'We have all fallen out with him – not only I but both the Nikolais. G. Ya. [Strelkov] never liked him much – and now dislikes him even more.'

Frightened at the thought of what might happen to himself if he remained much longer in the labour camp, Lev had frequent night-mares about not being able to leave: there was always some obstacle getting in his way and stopping him from going home, from being reunited with Sveta, the focus of his hopes.

They had not seen each other for two and a half years. She had been unable to come to Pechora in 1952 and 1953. Her mother was bed-ridden with TB, her father weak and frail, and she had to care for them. At work she was struggling to cope with an extra burden of administrative duties because of Tsydzik's illness. 'Everything's weighing on me, Levi,' she wrote in March 1953. 'I can't relax at home, but I can't go to any kind of sanatorium or holiday retreat either. I'd cry there just the same as I do at home.' Lev encouraged her to take a holiday – there was the possibility of a camping trip in the Altai region of Siberia – and told her not to come to Pechora. He was expecting to be released at some point during the next year, possibly in July 1954, though maybe not until the following December, depending on the final decision of the MVD. 'Sveta,' he had written in June 1953,

> you mustn't turn down the opportunity of a holiday in the Altai or in Erevan, whatever the circumstances . . . All other routes [i.e., to Pechora] are too complicated; if we have to wait another year, or a year and a half at most, we can do that. It's not so bad any more, Sveta.

In some ways, it was Lev who was supporting Sveta through this last year or so of separation. Their roles had changed. Despite his anxieties, Lev was getting stronger as conditions in the labour camp improved and the date of his release approached, while she was increasingly exhausted from coping with her parents and her work.

At the start of August, for the first time in her life, Sveta found herself in hospital. She had septicaemia and was running a fever. When she had recovered, she took Lev's advice and went on a walking holiday in the Altai. She wanted to travel to Pechora afterwards, but did not feel up to it. Lev was anxious about her.

> Svetloe, thanks to our postal system and the delivery of your telegram, I wasn't as frightened as I should have been by Aunt Katya's letter about your illness. That's also why your letters from the hospital didn't throw me into more of a panic. Still, I'm just a little

worried that you might suffer a relapse of this incomprehensible ailment during your travels.

It was agonizing for him to go so long without seeing her, but he found a paradoxical consolation in the wait:

Sveta, increasingly I want to say all kinds of needless – and perhaps even hurtful – words to you, and I'm always trying to hold my tongue. About how it is so difficult seeing your face only in a photograph for such a long time. And how the very fact that it's difficult is a source of joy. And how it becomes even more difficult with each passing year and therefore all the more joyful. And how, consequently, time and distance are not only able to destroy what there is but also to nourish it.

Writing on 22 September, around the time of her previous visits to Pechora, he begged her not to feel bad about missing yet another year. By this time he expected to be released in November 1954. He told her to be strong:

Sveta, my darling, you must not take yourself to task – don't put at risk your future or happiness, or your health. You mustn't tear your-self to pieces with journeys, work trips, caring for your mother, your father, domestic chores, and your own problems. All the more so, since the administrative scoundrels here are this year four times more stupid, bureaucratic and malicious than before. Svetin, when all is said and done, there are only 14 months to go – that's not so many any more. Try to be healthy, Sveta, and don't torment your-self with doubts and worries.

Sveta replied:

Of course, Lev, it's 14 months, not 14 years, to go. And in my brighter moments I remember this, but when I'm feeling bad – then it's bad. One shouldn't tear oneself to pieces, but one should be able to do things quickly, easily, successfully, without so much effort. And that I haven't managed to do.

For the moment her main task was to plan for Lev's release, to think about where they might build a life together. Lev would learn his options only when he received his release papers from the MVD – they would state the towns in which he could not live – but it was unlikely that he would be permitted to return to Moscow (newly released prisoners were nearly always barred from living closer than 100 kilometres to any of the major cities). The further away from the capital he settled, the easier it would be to find work that made use of his scientific skills, but the harder it would be for Sveta to see him, unless she left her parents in Moscow.

Lev and Sveta had discussed these issues as early as 1949. At that time she had suggested he might think about Poltava, in Ukraine, or some other town in the provinces, where he might find work as a teacher and where she could join him:

> Levi, why do you dismiss the idea of teaching? I don't know how it is around Poltava, but in my opinion the more remote places offer more opportunities. Obviously, Levi, I'm not planning to talk seriously about such topics now, since we know absolutely nothing about how things will be in half a dozen years.* Maybe everything will be the same but maybe it won't, and maybe we won't, either. If it's the same, then you know I'm ready for any possibility – only ideally with snow.

By the end of 1953, Sveta had come to favour Yaroslavl, which she had visited on a work trip to inspect a factory. It was only a night's journey from Moscow – so she could see her parents easily – and it had industries in which both of them could be employed. She wrote to Lev from the northern Volga city on 15 December:

---

* In 1949, there were six years remaining of Lev's prison term.

Yaroslavl is a nice town – not as rural as Omsk is. It's a city with long, straight streets, a decent number of boulevards and gardens, and 2- to 3-storey buildings. There are 4-storey ones in the centre and near the factory. The people aren't so provincial, at least I didn't see any preposterous dresses at the theatre or any garishly made-up girls. They don't go to the theatre wearing boots and don't chew sun-flower seeds. Provisions are also better here. There are lots of dairy products – both at the market and in the shops (cheese, cottage cheese, sour cream and cream). The situation with meat is not so good, but there are all the vegetables you could possibly want, and there's always kasha, flour, sugar and confectionery, etc. There are even different kinds of wine (not just one vermouth, as in Omsk). The bread is really good and tasty and people eat well in the cafeterias.

Voronezh was another alternative. Four hundred kilometers south of Moscow, it was twice as far away as Yaroslavl, but it had some advantages, and Tsydzik recommended it. Sveta wrote to Lev on 10 December:

M. A. says that Voronezh is better than Yar-l, that the climate is milder (which I'm not sure about – summers there are very hot), that there's always a light breeze, and no smell of rubber in the air (the factories are located outside the centre) as there is in Yaroslavl. I'll have a look at Voronezh in the spring or the summer. It takes about 10 hours to get there (also a night journey). Papa used to like Voronezh – he and Mama quite seriously discussed resettling there (before the war).

'I've been told good things about Voronezh,' Lev replied, 'but I think that while your parents haven't yet resolved to settle there them-selves, we should make sure that getting to them, that is, to Moscow, won't take any longer than from morning to evening or from evening to morning.' Lev was pessimistic about the possibility of actually liv-ing with Sveta and did not want to settle so far away that it became a burden for her to travel between him and her parents.

Sveta discussed the idea of Voronezh with relatives and friends. 'So, Levi,' she wrote on 19 January,

> no matter whom I ask about which is better, Voronezh or Yaroslavl, everybody without a moment's hesitation answers Voronezh. First, it has a lot of educational institutions, which inevitably leave their mark on a town, and it has more culture as well. Apparently the people are more friendly than in Yaroslavl. The streets are more beautiful. It's warmer. I don't know whether the latter is a plus or not. It seems that winters there are still winters. I'd be sorry if that wasn't the case. I really love winter. But it would undoubtedly be quite hot there in the summer.
>
> And the minuses: it's twice as far and, although it's been restored [it was badly damaged in the war], there is still so much damage that it will probably be more difficult to find a place to live, although everyone from here [the institute] who got a job at the factory was given a room and some even got an apartment. They have more need of engineers, so they'll probably take greater care of them. I'm making wild guesses, though.

Lev favoured Yaroslavl – it was closer to Moscow – though his main concern was not to be a burden on anybody and to track down his university diploma so he could get his career back on track. 'As regards the possibility of settling in Yaroslavl,' he wrote to Sveta,

> I still have no definite information. Many have been forced to settle in the outskirts of similar towns. But others live in places like Lvov. It's unclear what accounts for the difference – whether it's the whim of those in charge or personal resources, including the ability to make use of vitamins [pay bribes]. In any case, I think it will be possible to settle some 10 to 15 km from Yar[oslavl]. I can base myself at friends of Nikolai [a prisoner at the wood-combine], where I'll be able to leave my suitcase and spend a few nights until I find myself a corner and somewhere to work. Regarding the latter: I don't want and I'm not going to visit family or friends before I've found work

and a place to live. I can't count on anybody finding my diploma. I think the best thing would be for me to get it myself, once I've got myself organized wherever God is going to send me. In the meantime I'll look for work as a fitter or something else in any electrical facility, with no requirements except ≥ 500–600 roubles a month. With the diploma in hand, I'll be able to get different work – in the same enterprise or department – or leave to go somewhere else . . . This 'transition period', I imagine, could last 6 months to a year.

Lev had already warned Sveta that during this 'transition period' he would be able to visit her only occasionally for a few hours at a time. It was unlikely that the terms of his release would allow him to spend more than twenty-four consecutive hours in Moscow, and if he found a job in a provincial town, he would have to work six days a week, like everybody else in the Soviet Union. But he was hopeful that 'further down the line', once he had obtained his diploma and got a better job, he might 'finally be allowed to return home'. Until then, Lev was adamant that Sveta remain with her parents. Having waited all these years to be reunited with her, he had learned to be patient.

My darling Sveta, the things I'm going to write now are only tentative thoughts so don't get upset if you think that something is not as it should be. Sooner or later, in one way or another, we'll find something that's not too bad. But if it's not completely wonderful – well, it can't be helped. It will still be better than what we had before or have now. Sveta, of course you need to be near your mama and not just in case she or your papa becomes worse – how they are at the moment is bad enough; and your departure might cause their conditions to worsen . . . Which means there's really only one solution – for me to try to find work as close to you as possible so that if we can't be together all the time we can at least be together for one day out of seven. And that's already infinitely better than it's been for the past 13 years.

Lev's hopes were raised by the early thaw of 1954. 'Spring has been here for three days now,' he wrote on 25 March. 'After the freshly fallen snow of the day before yesterday, everything is already grey and muddy and our feet keep sinking in.' This year Lev found promise in the spring. The release of prisoners was gaining momentum, and he was expecting to be free at some point in the next months. The prospect of release got him citing poetry, Pushkin in particular:

> In the hope of glory and good
> I look ahead without fear.

Sveta, too, was buoyed by the anticipation of Lev's return. 'My darling,' she wrote, 'I've been planning to tell you how good I've been feeling lately; I'm being kind to everyone. My spirits are so high. I feel as if you'd greeted me this morning, as you used to do, on my way to catch the tram, and that we still had the whole evening ahead of us.'

Where and how would they meet at last? Sveta wanted Lev all to herself for the first few days. To make that happen she was prepared to travel anywhere, even to Pechora to collect him and bring him home. 'I can imagine,' she wrote to him, 'that eventually I'll be able to leave you for a month or two, but right now I don't want to let you out of my sight, even for an hour.'

> You must tell me if I should come for you. If I do, then later on I'll be able to hand you over to all the aunts for whole minutes at a time . . . There's no reason for you to be on your own, ever. I could see to that – I could walk behind you everywhere, I'd be like a tail, but at least I wouldn't be worried about losing you again. I don't want our first meeting to take place in front of other people and I'm not making an exception for anybody – not for your aunts, or my parents, or any friends. I have a horrible nature.

Lev too wanted to see Sveta straight away. He hoped to come to Moscow directly from Pechora, 'if only for a day or two', he wrote to her on 10 May, 'and only to see you'.

Lev was pessimistic about his chances of returning to Moscow on a more permanent basis. To live in Moscow he would need a 'clean' passport, which could be obtained only if he was officially rehabilitated or received a pardon on his release, but there was little hope of either. 'I don't think – as far as I understand the essence of the matter – that any efforts at the present time will produce anything positive,' he had written to Sveta on 11 April. 'Complete rehabilitation is impossible and a pardon won't provide any benefits for the future, if previous convictions aren't removed.' Lev had no illusions that his crime against the state could be negated by appeal. Even if the full facts of his conduct in the war had been taken into account at his trial in 1945, he now thought, he would still have been convicted, albeit with a shorter sentence, since he had allowed himself to be used as a translator in the German camps. The fact that he had been sentenced would remain on his passport.

Lev's acceptance of his partial guilt was something new in his thinking. In their earlier discussions of an appeal (in 1946–7) he had not acknowledged it or used it in his arguments against Sveta's suggestion that they try to get his sentence overturned. Perhaps the long years in the camp had worn him down to the point of accepting the injustice done to him. They had certainly taught him that there was nothing special about his own situation. There were many others just like him. 'I could apply for a change in circumstances if I thought I could make a case as a war hero, let's say, or at least of having merited a medal,' he explained to Sveta on 10 May.

But even I don't believe that. On the contrary, I think I'm guilty – just not to the extent recorded [in the sentence]. If everything had been written down and taken into consideration correctly, then maybe I would have been given 5 or 3 [years], or even less. But there would still have been something, 'with all its consequences'. And since that's the case, it's impossible to demand that something should be done as if nothing had happened. What should be done? And on what grounds? You see, it's been difficult for many people, but that's not grounds for making it easier for everyone. And if it's made easier for one person, why should that be me? There's nothing special about me to warrant it. Because I can do more interesting and beneficial work? Actually, I think I can be more useful in my latest profession (electrician) than through scientific work, much less research-based scientific work. I'm never going to turn into any kind of scientific researcher now, but a passable technician – possibly.

By this time, Sveta had resigned herself to the probability that she and Lev would live apart on his release. It was hard for her to accept after all these years of separation, but her parents needed her to look after them. The best they could hope for, she believed, was for Lev to be allowed to settle somewhere not so far from Moscow so that she could visit him. She wrote to him on 2 May:

For a long time now I've really needed to write you a serious letter and I keep putting it off because it immediately makes me feel depressed, since deep down I just don't believe that in 6 months everything will somehow get settled and our life together will work out. Either Mama will start to feel even worse, or Papa too will come down with something, or the housekeeper will leave, or there'll be something else on a global or local scale and I won't be able to move anywhere, just visit you from time to time. Yes, I need to be prepared for that. So it may not even be necessary to think about my work, just about proximity. What's closest? Kalinin, I guess. But the closer it is, the more difficult it'll be for you to find work. In Aleksandrov, for example (even suburban commuter trains travel there), it's apparently almost impossible to get work because of the abundance of all kinds of specialists. And yet, I suppose if we really are going to live together one day, we should keep my work in mind . . . There's no need to think about it straight away as there are other things of more immediate interest – your arrival and our being together, as close as possible, absolutely free and not so tied to work that you can't come here at any time. You'll need to arrange some meetings here to clear out all the rubbish of the old umbrellas hanging over you [to remove restrictions from the Gulag]. If that means not working for a while, then so be it. You wouldn't be the first person in the world to live without a job for a few months . . .

Lev was intrigued by the idea of Kalinin, or Tver, as it had formerly been called, a provincial town not far north of Moscow on the railway line to Leningrad. He, too, had been thinking about it as a possible place to settle after Pechora, if the authorities would allow it. 'I should have also written about Kalinin,' he replied on 10 May.

I don't know what I could find there and whether conditions are the same as in Aleksandrov. But given how tentative our plans are, do we really have to focus on a particular town? So long as there's a railway station, by which I mean a convenient transport system, then the rest doesn't really matter that much. What made you think of Kalinin in particular? At any rate, I'll try to find some natives of Tver here and make inquiries. It's probably a good place, and there's always the Volga. But that might also mean it's overcrowded.

Sveta had mentioned Kalinin 'almost accidentally, but not completely'. She had heard that a new tyre factory was going to be built there and thought that she and Lev might both find work in it. 'The town is growing overall and the suburban electric train will go there soon (although it's on a good line with at least 6 long-distance trains a day). It's 167 kilometres [from Moscow] and only a 4-hour journey. Shurka [Aleksandra Chernomordik] went there last summer and says she liked the town.'

Meanwhile, Sveta found out more about the factories in Voronezh and Yaroslavl. She did not like the Yaroslavl tyre factory: it was 'so vast and individuals get lost there'. But that might turn out to be an advantage, if Lev got work there, as he would not be noticed as a former prisoner, whereas in Voronezh he would 'stand out more'. On the other hand, the factory in Voronezh had fewer specialists, which would make it easier for Lev to get a job. 'At home, I casually asked my parents whether they would like to move to V[oronezh],' she wrote to Lev on 1 June.

Papa said 'Why?' and Mama, 'No.' I didn't continue the conversation because I have no idea how to discuss such personal matters with them. And why upset them? The decision doesn't have to be made right away, and we all need to stay alive until that 'later on'.

Sveta looked into the railway timetables and drew up a list of towns with their distances from Moscow to consider for the shorter term. 'So there you go,' she wrote at the bottom of the list. 'And what do I know about them? Nothing. But there are factories and electric power stations everywhere. After this, all that's left is to read the coffee grounds.' She then laid out the alternatives:

Possible options:
1. If the radius is < 100, I can either live and work here and travel to see you or live with you and travel to work and home again. The shorter the radius, the more convenient either option would be.
2. If the radius is < 200, but >100, the only possibility is for me to live and work here and just come to visit you.
3. With a radius > 200 there's still that possibility but visits will obviously be less frequent, and for me to carry on working and live with you, then Yar[oslavl] would still be the best. And with this there are also possible sub-options: either my parents live here or (something that Shurka thinks is completely feasible but that I don't think Mama would agree to) I move them with me. Then the radius could be even greater, but if Papa doesn't want to give up working, it's once again got to be either Yar[oslavl] or Vor[onezh]. We've got so used to M[oscow] that I don't know whether it's worth moving my parents . . . The provincial calm and purer air would be much better for them than all the commotion and running around here. But M[oscow] is still better for supplies and medicines (although Shurka says that they have morphine everywhere) . . . The best option for me – for my peace of mind and so I don't burst – would obviously be for everybody to live together, otherwise my hives are just never going to go away and I'll never stop lashing out at people. And it

would be easier financially as well. It's always more expensive living in two homes . . . In truth, I don't know what I want.

Sveta was torn between her duty to look after her parents and her desire to be with Lev. The conflict was making her feel agitated and depressed. All the anxiety about where they would live only partially masked a bigger worry: what would life be like with Lev? She had waited for this moment for fifteen years, but now that it was almost upon them, she was consumed by doubt:

I'm already falling headlong into a hole and there I am wallowing at the bottom, thinking how I didn't study well, how I'm a bad daughter, how I work badly – the only thing that's left is my service to myself and to the one called God (and even then somebody else would have managed to do it better; and if I'm allowed into heaven it will only be because of you). And if it now turns out (as is very probable) that I'm even going to make a poor wife – and will be no better as a mother – then all that's left for me is to hang myself. I'll stop eating and sleeping. Perhaps my fear of leaving Mama is covering up the fear that I won't be fit to be a wife. Honestly, I'm scared.

Lev, too, felt nervous, but his doubts were not about Sveta:

Sveta, my darling, there's not going to be any need for you to hang yourself, you silly creature! And right now there's no need to stop eating and sleeping. What does 'bad' mean in this or any other sense? In every way you'll be yourself, and what else do I – do we – need? How is it possible that there is something you're not fit for? No matter what you turn out to be, you'll be good at it. Do you really think that any set of skills, like being a housewife, can ever be the most important thing – that their absence cancels out the unique, priceless thing that makes us want to wait for each other? . . . And you mustn't leave your mother. I'm just as scared as you, if truth be told, Sveta, only I'm scared for myself and not for you; because according to friends and their recollections of me, I'm difficult to live with. But that's not why I say you should stay with your mother. It's that I don't think we'll ever stop worrying if we leave them. And if I'm already feeling guilty towards her now (and not just this minute but all the time), how could I possibly reconcile your leaving her with my conscience? All I can think of for the time being is to wait and try to set up a situation – in terms of an apartment and location – that would be acceptable to your mother and where we could all finally settle together. What more can we hope for when there's still absolutely no information?

Lev had no idea when he would be released. 'My leaving is still obscured by shadow,' he wrote on 4 June,

> but I've already started thinking about sending my books home little by little. The only thing I don't know is where to. I've got 2 suitcases full of all kinds of books. I'm going to try to cut the amount down to one and a half and send them in small parcels since I don't know where I'm going to be going first and it will be awkward to drag them along with me everywhere. But if I send them in small parcels then where to? To you or to Uncle Nikita?

Six days later there was 'no more certainty about the future'. There were 'no official statements or signed documents' about the procedures of release, Lev wrote to Sveta, 'and those leaving go through the formal procedures one way today and a different way tomorrow'.

In this limbo state, Lev decided on a temporary plan to optimize his chances of living within 50 kilometres of Moscow by travelling first to Uncle Nikita's at Malakhovka and trying to obtain his diploma, which he thought would help him find a better job and place to live.

> I'll go about tracking down my diploma from Uncle N.'s and look for work. And I'll visit everybody who's expecting me, of course. I'm promising myself that I'll control my obstinacy [about not

wanting to depend on people] for a month, for the sensible reason that a person has the right to take a month off after such a period of labour, and if he doesn't die over the course of the following year he'll be able to pay off his debts . . . If, at the end of the month, or near the end, it finally becomes clear that it's not working out [with the diploma and the search for a job near Moscow], then I'll go to K[alinin] or somewhere that seems right for both of us and try to find work there and four walls and a ceiling, where I'll be able to wait for you to visit, pending better times.

On 7 June, Sveta's father went to a sanatorium in Shirokoe, not far from Kalinin, to spend the summer recovering his health. On 1 July, he had a stroke. Ten days later, he had another. Sveta rushed to be with him. There was no paralysis but he was very fragile and had problems with his speech. Sveta sent a telegram to Lev: 'Papa's condition complicated by secondary stroke. Now slowly improving. I'm staying at Shirokoe Bologovskoe.'

Lev was expecting his release in the next few days. Now that the moment was upon him, he felt none of the euphoria he might have expected. In some ways, he was sad to be leaving. There were friendships he had made that he would miss, people like Strelkov who were sick, whom he did not want to leave behind, as he explained to Sveta in his final letter from the labour camp. If he had numbered all his letters over the past eight years, it would have been the 647th.

9 July 1954   No. 29

Svetloe, after your telegram I received your letter dated the 29th. I'm hoping there'll be something else tomorrow. How's Aleksandr Alekseevich [Sveta's father]? And your mother? The past week has been really full for me – I've had to help Strelkov 'pay old debts' in the form of all kinds of orders and promises. Strange as it may seem, in a week's time I'm going to be parting from old friends. And – this is less strange – I have some regrets. Only about people, of course, or rather their company, although with some there will be the possibility of meeting up again, probably quite soon. Incidentally, Strelkov has more freedom of movement than the rest of us at the moment, which is obviously improving his mood. Financially, the last two months have been three times better for him, first because of general changes to his pay-rate and second because he's currently substituting for one of the workshop's managers who has gone on holiday . . .

I have not managed to find anyone from K[alinin]. Well, it doesn't matter. If I'm not able to stay at Uncle N[ikita]'s for longer than a couple of days, I'll go to K[alinin] anyway. I still don't know how much longer I'll be here. In any event the delay is hardly going to be more than a week. For more than 10 days now we've had a heatwave here, and yesterday it was nearly 38 degrees, but I only managed to go swimming for the first time today.

The day before yesterday, when I was with A. M. [Iushkevich], I allowed a doctor to tap on my chest and have a good listen – it was the same doctor who put me in the hospital 4 years ago. He found that I still don't have any particular grounds for complaint or worry, which I agree with completely.

I still haven't written anything to my aunts. I'll write to Uncle N. tomorrow.

Look after yourself, Svet.

12

Lev was released on 17 July 1954. It was eight years and four months since he had arrived in Pechora, but under the credit system introduced in 1948 he had managed to reduce his ten-year sentence by one year and eight months. In preparation for his departure he had made two wooden suitcases in the workshops, one for his clothes, his linen and other personal items, the other for his tools – the pliers, spanners, hammers and screwdrivers that he would need to work as a mechanic or electrical engineer. With one heavy suitcase in each hand, he left the barracks zone. He was free at last.

But he could not leave right away. First he had to get his exit papers processed by the MVD and this took about a week. While he waited for his papers Lev stayed at the Aleksandrovskys inside the industrial zone, in the same apartment where he had met Sveta in 1947. 'Send your letters here for the time being, as before, but starting with your next letter, it will be better to send it to Marusia [Maria Aleksandrovskaya],' Lev had written to warn Sveta not long before his release.

He spent these last days in Pechora saying farewell to his friends and sorting out his things. He packed his books into parcels and sent them to his Uncle Nikita, who had room to store them at his house in Malakhovka. He also went to the market at Kanin, the settlement neighbouring Pechora. On his day trip there he took Igor, the eleven-year-old older son of the Aleksandrovskys, who had never been anywhere out of Pechora. It was very hot, and Igor got a headache on the long walk to Kanin. At the market Lev bought the boy an ice-cream. It was the first time he had ever eaten an ice-cream – an 'unheard-of delicacy in Pechora', recalls Igor. While he was enjoying it, a boy dressed in rags began to badger him and would not go away. He could not take his eyes off the miracle of the ice-cream. Taking pity on the boy, Lev spent the money he had saved so carefully and bought an ice-cream for him too.

Once he had his exit papers, Lev was at last ready to leave Pechora. He said a final farewell to his friends and exited the camp through the main gate of the wood-combine. Carrying his wooden suit-cases, he turned left on Moscow Street and then right into Soviet Street, the long main avenue that ran through the town to the station, 4 kilometres from the wood-combine. At the station he waited for the Moscow train coming in from Vorkuta, along the railway built by Gulag prisoners. The MVD had given him a ticket that would enable him to travel all the way to Kalinin, where he had chosen to go in search of a place to live.

Lev's first aim was to find Sveta. His train arrived in Moscow late at night. It was dark everywhere. From the Yaroslavl station he went to Sveta's house but 'the lights in the windows were out' and he did not want to wake the family. The last train for Malakhovka was about to leave from the Kazan station, so he went there and stayed the night at his Uncle Nikita's house. The next morning he returned to Moscow and knocked on the door of Sveta's apartment. He had not been there for thirteen years, since before his departure for the front in 1941. Now, as then, the door was opened by Sveta's mother. 'Anastasia Erofeevna, herself ill, said that Aleksandr Alekseevich had had a stroke and that Sveta was with him at the sanatorium,' recalled Lev. The scene that he had pictured in his head a million times – his knocking on the door of Sveta's home and her opening it to embrace him – was not to be.

Lev returned to the station and got on a train to Bologovskoe, the nearest stop to the sanatorium at Shirokoe, which he reached on foot. Dressed in the clothes in which he had left Pechora, thin, pale-faced and exhausted from his long train journey in the heat, he had the unmistakable appearance of a newly released prisoner, which attracted the attention of the staff at the sanatorium. Lev found Sveta in the ward with her father. She had wanted them to be alone at this moment. 'I don't want our first meeting to take place in front of other people,' she had written six months earlier. But that did not matter any more: they were at last together and that was all that counted now. During these first hours Aleksandr was the focus of their emotions. They sat together by his bed. Sveta's brother, Yara, had joined them at the sanatorium. Lev now felt that he belonged to Sveta's family. More than fifty years later Lev recalled a moving gesture of kindness that made it clear he had Sveta's father's blessing as a son. Aleksandr was in bed. He could not sit up, but beckoned Lev to him. Lev kissed him, and he kissed Lev. Aleksandr told him that he had 30,000 roubles in his savings account – enough to buy a home. 'That money is for you and Sveta,' Aleksandr said.

That evening Lev wrote to Sveta's mother from the sanatorium. He wrote as if he had been her son-in-law for years:

Dear Anastasia Erofeevna!

Svetka told me to write everything to you just as it is, objectively, which I'm going to try to do. Firstly, Aleksandr Alekseevich was in better form than I expected from your report . . . He's in good spirits and making jokes. The clarity of his thoughts and his memory is impeccable but his speech is still causing problems: he speaks somewhat indistinctly, though always coherently. If he wants to emphasize something he articulates the phrase very clearly but with obvious effort.

Svetka is probably exhausted but it's not noticeable. I think she's looking well, but I don't have anything to compare it to. We've been given lodgings: Yara is in the 5th dacha, 1½ minutes' walk away, and I'm here with Aleksandr Alekseevich and Svetka. There haven't been any complications so far.

Svetka thinks she'll bring Aleksandr Alekseevich home on the 29th if there's a definite decision about his release by then . . . It's rather cool here at the moment with intermittent rain showers, but we've been able to drag ourselves out of our room every so often. Svetlana and I tried to set out for some raspberries but were frightened off by the waterlogged bushes and so just settled for a walk for an hour and a half and an overview of the surrounding countryside.

It's a really beautiful place. It would still leave an enormous impression on one, even if it wasn't coming in the wake of such a dramatic change in scenery – and that's all there is to say for now. Well, it seems as if it's a full report.

Look after yourself. All of us send all of you our greetings. L.

Three days later, Aleksandr was transferred to a hospital in Moscow, and Sveta went with him while Lev set off for Kalinin, where he was obliged to register his place of residence with the police. It was difficult for them to separate after such a brief reunion. But they knew they were together now.

Before he left Pechora, Lev had found someone to help him get set up in the Kalinin area, a stoker in the workshops who came from nearby Kuzminskoe. He gave Lev the address of a woman who, he said, would put him up. Kuzminskoe was a run-down settlement of fifty houses with a ruined church, a small brook, a pond and a few fields, a half-hour walk from a railway station on the Moscow–Kalinin line. Maria Petrovna and her children lived in a dirty peasant hut with a small orchard garden on the edge of the village. Her eldest son, who was supposed to help Lev find a job, was not there when Lev arrived: it was harvest time and he had left to work on a collective farm. Lev had hoped to rent a room, but the one he was now offered by Maria was so filthy that he chose to stay instead in the hayloft and find another place to live. On 1 August Lev explained his situation to Sveta:

I found the woman quickly but her son, who's going to help me get settled in K[alinin], is on a kolkhoz until 4 or 5. So I'll try tomorrow to sort things out myself, get a passport* and so on. But today I'm going to go to Kalinin to buy some tea, sweets for the children and spoons and other things for the household where I'm taking refuge for the moment. They're good people – the mother, from Karelia, about 50–55 years old, and her younger sons, 18 and 14 – but they keep the house according to the principle of indifference and

---

* Soviet passports defined where a person was allowed to live and work.

inattentiveness, so that even I, who am after all used to anything, can hardly bear to stay here any longer than basic politeness requires, which is about 3 days. After that I'll try to find a place with somebody else in a different hut. It's difficult, if not impossible, to get a separate room (bearing in mind the most important of our requests). I'm going to consider the situation carefully tomorrow but for now I'll settle for Maria Petrovna's hayloft . . . The area is rather monotonous – near the village at any rate: a field with gently sloping uplands and some emaciated-looking villages every 1 to 2 km. There are gardens in the villages – as in ours – with apples, cherries and berries. Vegetable gardens, obviously. Cherries are 6–7 roubles per kg, cucumbers – 2.50. I was fed with a baked potato and cucumber yesterday and goose eggs and milk today.

Lev could not begin to look for work until he had a passport, but he had left Pechora before one had been issued by the MVD, so now he had to spend a lot of time trying to get hold of one from the police in Kalinin, a task complicated by the fact that he had none of the required documents to hand except for his birth certificate. 'As a way out of this vicious circle,' he wrote to Sveta on 4 August,

I went to the head of the local MVD administration's passport department yesterday. He was suspicious at first, but then I guess he saw that my face showed nothing but suffering. They can't decide about authorizing the passport without consulting 'Moscow' first. Fortunately, it turned out that one of Moscow's representatives is here at the moment and they suggested that I call on him. But at the appointed 16:00 hours, another meeting had already started and he put me off until this morning. It's now 10 o'clock and I'm waiting at the main post office before I go and see him. So that's what's happening.

The next day, Lev moved out of the hayloft and became a lodger in a neighbouring house owned by an elderly couple, the Roshchins. He hoped that the move would allow him to register as a resident with the local soviet and thus qualify for a passport. 'I'm going to go to the soviet first thing tomorrow morning,' Lev wrote to Sveta, 'it's in a village with the inexplicably evangelical name of Emmaus. We should find out what kind of jokers the landed gentry were who called it that.' Lev set out on the road to Emmaus. The passport desk was closed, so he was given a receipt and told to come back the next week. The chairwoman of the village soviet, once she found out that he had worked as an electrician, offered him a job at one of the smaller power stations in the area, but Lev rejected the offer, intending to apply for a job instead in Kalinin.

The delay was frustrating. Lev had been planning to visit Sveta, but the problems with his passport meant that 'my journey has to be postponed', as he wrote to Sveta on 7 August.

I called you today (some girl came to the phone) to let you know as soon as possible. My passport will be ready 'perhaps today after 4 o'clock in the afternoon', but most likely I won't have it until the next day the passport desk is open, which is Tuesday. After that it's supposed to be taken to the village soviet for registration, and from there to the police on the next day they're open – possibly Wednesday or else Saturday again (the office is open only 3 days a week). What a lot of tedious red tape. Damn those Pechora cretins from the special department.

Meanwhile Lev occupied himself in Kuzminskoe. He liked the Roshchins, but as an urbanite he found their peasant way of life, shared by much of the rural population, strange and primitive. He described it to Sveta:

My old couple – Petr Kuzmich and Marfa Egorovna – are illiterate and childless. Their wooden hut is made up of small anterooms and one large room, approximately 6 × 6 m, with a little kitchen off to the side. It's relatively clean; in comparison with the previous place it's even very clean. There is a smell of ammonia – the pigsty is next door (under the same roof which stretches over the interior courtyard) and doubles as the toilet. This is new to me but, if you believe a certain folk rhyme I heard a long time ago, it is characteristic of villages in Tver. After 20–30 minutes you don't notice the smell, and you take great pleasure in the silence and spaciousness and the illumination of the table I use for writing (with one window in front and another to the left) and the tranquil nature of the hosts.

The old couple are letting me sleep on a day bed in their main room for 10 roubles a day, with full board, which consists of:

1) Breakfast – eaten with them just like all the other meals – made up of something like potatoes with cucumber, cottage cheese and tea.

2) Lunch – I still don't know what this consists of.

3) Dinner – either soup or kasha and milk. There's no tea in the evenings.

They don't have any bedclothes; laundry wasn't agreed on but it's hardly likely that the grandmother is going to do the laundry since she's 70 and doesn't work on the kolkhoz. The grandpa repairs saddles on the kolkhoz. He drinks vodka, smokes and has tuberculosis. But on the whole he seems like a good fellow. I should also buy them some knives and forks because all they have in the house is a samovar and a couple of plates and spoons. It's really quite surprising.

From Kuzminskoe Lev could walk to Kalinin, only 12 kilometres away. He visited the town and reported on its merits as a place to live. He considered it a 'handsome' place with lovely squares and streets, well-maintained historical buildings and 'none of the tasteless mix of styles or pretensions to style of certain buildings on Gorky Street in Moscow, for example', he wrote to Sveta. The housing situation was not good, however. It was practically impossible to find an apartment. There were many 'new arrivals' in the town, released prisoners attracted to Kalinin's proximity to the Soviet capital. They were paying 7 roubles a day just for a bed in a hostel. Thinking of the money Sveta's father had given the two of them, Lev wondered about the cost of purchasing a house.

A mere cubbyhole in a house on the outskirts of Kalinin costs 14,000. From that I assume that it isn't possible to find a governor's house for 30,000. It may be better not to look in Kalinin at all and to try somewhere in Yar[oslavl] or Vor[onezh]. But if we're being serious I

The Roshchins.

think your father himself needs to look, though there's no great rush. Half a hut here in the village was bought recently for 10,000, which was considered a good deal, even though it's going to need repairs at the new owners' expense.

Sveta, who had made another work trip to inspect the factory in Yaroslavl, wrote to Lev about prospects in the northern Volga town:

Right now is still a very bad time for finding work – they're expecting cutbacks everywhere. The management is being cut by 12 per cent here . . . So don't take it personally, Levi. You yourself have written

275

that in the majority of cases they just reply 'We don't need anyone' without asking a single question. And don't lose heart, even if all this drags on, or else I'll also start sinking just by looking at you.

By the end of August, Lev had at last managed to get his passport from the Emmaus soviet. He was registered to live (and therefore work) in the Kalinin area. But in the passport was the stamp, 'Art. 39', which told prospective employers that he was a former prisoner. Lev looked for work in more than twenty factories. He applied for jobs on construction sites, in schools, even in a theatre and a museum. But everywhere the answer was the same: 'We absolutely don't need anyone.' After three months of searching, Lev was becoming despondent. 'Svetloe,' he wrote on 23 November.

The day hasn't really yielded anything new, unless you count the frail hopes for work at 3 of the 9 places I've visited over the last 24 hours. I've been to the trade school, the textile training college, the textile factory (a different one – named after Vagzhanov), the knitting factory, the silk-weaving factory ('Proletarian'), the Kalinin construction materials testing laboratory and the construction site for the printing plant, but nobody has anything. Three of the places asked me to check back again: the Voroshilov textile factory, which needs a heating engineer, and the Volodarsky garment factory, where there's a vacant position for a chemical treatment engineer (or a foreman) – my 'crowning role' over the last year and a half, as you know. Both places are cutting back on staff and they weren't sure whether they'd fill these posts with their own employees, so they're going to consult among themselves and give me an answer during the day tomorrow. The third place is the industrial training college correspondence department, where the teachers of theoretical mechanics and higher mathematics have been complaining to the director that they're overworked. The director is intending to find out whether these teachers really mean to cut back some of their hours, in which case he's going to recommend me to take up the slack. But there's huge difference between abstract complaints about being overworked and an actual refusal of money, so I'm not really expecting too much on Monday (or Tuesday), when I'm to call in for the results of the director's negotiations. That's all for the time being.

In the end Lev gave up looking for a job altogether. Instead Sveta found him freelance work as a translator through Sergei Rzhevkin ('Uncle Seryozha'), his father's friend who had been a professor of acoustics at Moscow University. Rzhevkin had good contacts at *Physics*, a Moscow-based journal that needed translations of articles from German, French and English – all languages that Lev had learned at school or picked up in the labour camps. Sveta would bring the articles to Kuzminskoe and take the translated texts back to Moscow, where she would type them out on a typewriter borrowed from a neighbour in her block of flats. Rzhevkin would present the translations to the editorial board of the journal in his own name and give Sveta the payments, which she would pass along to Lev. Had it been found out that the translations had been done by a former prisoner prohibited from working in the Soviet capital, there would have been a scandal. Soon Lev was also writing book reviews and articles that Rzhevkin signed with his own name, though again all the money went to Lev.

Lev came frequently to see Sveta in Moscow. He often stayed for days, sometimes even longer than a week. He had no legal right to be in the Soviet capital; that was what the stamp in his passport meant. If he had been caught by the police, he would have been expelled and possibly sent back to a labour camp. At first, the thought of entering Moscow filled him with anxiety. But he took comfort from the thought that Sveta would be there to support him. 'Sveta,' he had written in anticipation of his first visit, in August,

Sometimes when I'm in crowded places or on the street I suddenly start to feel ill at ease, but then I imagine that you're next to me and right away I can lift my head higher, the awkwardness passes, and everything seems simpler and easier.

What did Lev make of Moscow? He had not seen it for thirteen years, and all that time he had yearned to return to it. He had loved to talk about it with his fellow Muscovites in the labour camp, to hear news about it from Sveta. He had even seen it in his dreams. Looking back on his return to Moscow, Lev recalled that the city did not seem so greatly changed. There were more cars on the roads, the Metro was much busier and people were better-dressed, but otherwise it felt like the 'same old Moscow' he had known until the age of twenty-four.

By the end of 1954, Lev was practically living at the Ivanov apartment. During the day, while Sveta was at work, he would do his translations and look after Sveta's mother, who was now in the advanced stages of TB. Sveta's father was at home as well and in need of care, so Sveta had employed a housekeeper, who slept in the kitchen, the only space for her in the apartment. Lev took Yara's room – Sveta's brother was now in Leningrad – and Sveta slept with her parents so that she could tend to her mother at night.

Anastasia died on 28 January 1955. Lev was with her when she passed away. He had just raised her in bed to make her more comfortable and was embracing her, as she had embraced him all those years ago before his departure for the front, when she said her final words, 'Thank you, God.'

Because he was staying in Moscow illegally, Lev was careful to avoid Sveta's neighbours on the stairs, although some of the more trusted ones had known about him for years. He also had to avoid the police on the street – not an easy task given his propensity for crossing in places where he was accustomed to from his student days without knowing whether they were legal crossings any more (post-war Moscow had strict new laws against jaywalking). He never took his passport when he left the house, in case he was stopped by the police. Instead he took an empty bag, a shopping list and money, so that he could say he lived around the corner and had nipped out to the shops. Sometimes he put a bottle of vodka into the bag as a prop he could claim to have bought for a friend who had come to stay: it added credibility to his story and gave the police something to confiscate while they let him continue on his way. Everything went smoothly until one day there was a knock on the Ivanovs' door. It was a policeman. He asked who was living there without a right of residence. Hearing the conversation in the hall, Lev prepared to make a run for it. But the policeman was interested in the housekeeper, who had indeed not registered with the police. The situation was resolved and Lev could breathe more easily.

On 17 September 1955, Lev had some good news. The Soviet government declared an amnesty for Soviet servicemen who had collaborated with the Germans during the war. The announcement came unexpectedly a week after Konrad Adenauer, the Chancellor of West Germany, visited Moscow and asked for the release of German nationals from the Gulag. To improve relations with West Germany, Nikita Khrushchev, the Soviet leader, ordered the release of 9,000 German POWs imprisoned in the Gulag for 'crimes against humanity' under article 58 of the Soviet penal code. But since it was absurd to liberate the Germans and go on punishing their 'collaborators' in the Soviet Union, the amnesty was soon extended to Soviet servicemen like Lev, sentenced under article 58 for 'treason against the motherland'.

The amnesty meant everything to Lev – far more than the formal recognition of his rehabilitation by the government. It allowed him to return to Moscow as a legal resident and look for work with a clean passport; it let him start a new life with Sveta as his wife. The day after the amnesty's announcement in *Izvestiia*, Lev went back to the Emmaus soviet and got the 'Art. 39' stamp crossed out in his passport. His status now reverted to the legal basis of his pre-arrest passport, whose number was recorded with a statement of this fact on the same page as the crossed-out stamp. With his sentence cancelled from the record, Lev could openly live with Sveta in her apartment, if they were registered as man and wife. Until they could live together legally, they had not planned to get married.

They registered their marriage on 27 September 1955. Both of them were thirty-eight years old. There was no wedding ceremony, no special dress or suit that either of them wore for the occasion, no invited guests or witnesses. They didn't even have wedding rings. Lev and Sveta simply took their passports to the local office of the civil registry, a 'gloomy basement room', as Lev recalled, and registered themselves as man and wife. Lev's name was then added to the list of residents at Sveta's house. The young woman in the office who recorded their marriage understood that Lev was a newly released prisoner; the police had issued his passport in Kalinin, well known as a place of temporary settlement for ex-prisoners, and there was that crossed-out stamp in it. Thinking she might prevent Sveta from ruining her life by marrying a former prisoner, the woman said to her, 'I wouldn't recommend you marry him.' Sveta smiled. 'Never mind,' she said. 'Just put his name down as my husband.'

Lev and Sveta went home and told her father that they were married. 'Let me kiss you both,' Aleksandr said. 'That was all our wedding was,' Lev recalled. 'There was no celebration.' But eventually relatives and friends arrived with wedding gifts, food was put on the table, and toasts were drunk to the couple. There was no best man to make a speech, but a few days later Strelkov came to congratulate the newlyweds, and no one was better suited for that role. It was Strelkov who had saved Lev's life.

Strelkov had been released in November 1954. The old Bolshevik had served sixteen of the twenty-five years of his sentence. Dedicated to the Soviet cause, Strelkov had decided to continue working at the wood-combine, taking on the relatively well-paid post of deputy head of works at a time when the labour camp was being turned into an industrial enterprise under the control of the Ministry of Transport. Strelkov no longer lived in the laboratory but in a room in the communal block on Soviet Street, although he kept his books and other things with the Aleksandrovskys, inside the industrial zone. At the time of Lev and Sveta's wedding, Strelkov was in Moscow to see his daughter, Valya, and his seven-year-old grandson, whom he had never met.

'Lev, I need your advice,' Strelkov said when he came to see him and Sveta. 'I need to buy a present for somebody, and you have an artistic sense, so you can help me choose something.' Strelkov took

Lev to an antique shop in Stoleshnikov Pereulok, just off Gorky Street in the centre of Moscow, and asked him to choose one of the boxed sets of silver-plated cutlery as a gift for his unnamed friend. Before Lev had a chance to make his choice, Strelkov picked out a copper-nickel set that turned out to be by far the most expensive on display. Lev suggested that they buy a cheaper one. He did not want his friend to waste his hard-earned money. But Strelkov would have none of it. He paid the shop assistant, then turned to Lev and said, 'This is a wedding present for you and Svetlana.'

Lev and Sveta began their married life together. She went on working at the institute, and Lev went looking for a job. The amnesty had not made employers any less suspicious, and in Moscow he met the same prejudice as in Kalinin. He was turned away from factories and institutes – even from the Moscow Zoo, which was looking for an electrician – until finally he was hired as an engineer in a factory making scientific instruments. The job advertisement had called for an engineer with expertise in physics. The boss was so delighted to find someone with Lev's scientific background that he brushed aside Lev's warnings about having been a prisoner and sent him off directly to the chief engineer, who asked him how much he was earning from his translations and then offered more, a starting salary of 600 roubles a month. It was an average worker's wage, but enough to live on with Sveta's salary, which was almost twice that sum.

Lev and Sveta lived with her father at Kazarmennyi Pereulok, the newly married couple sleeping in the same large room as Aleksandr so that they could care for him at night. Sveta's father gradually recovered something of his health. Retiring from work, he read a lot and did odd chores around the house while Lev and Sveta were at their jobs. They all got along. For the first time since his childhood, perhaps for the first time ever, Lev experienced the happiness of family life.

In December 1955, at the age of thirty-eight, Sveta gave birth to a daughter, whom they called Anastasia (Nastia), after Sveta's mother. In January 1957 they had a son, Nikita, named after Lev's uncle. To have two children at their age, after all they had been through, must have seemed a miracle.

In 1945, after one of the most stressful nights of interrogration by the SMERSH investigators in Weimar, Lev had dreamed of Sveta in a white dress, kneeling by the side of a little girl. He had seen her in that vivid dream again in 1949, a few days after Sveta left him in Pechora.

In 1962, Lev and Sveta were staying with the children at Uncle Nikita's dacha at Malakhovka. One day, they were walking to the lake across a field that skirted the forest. Lev was in front, Sveta behind him with Anastasia, who was then six. 'As I reached the edge of the forest,' Lev recalled, 'I had this feeling . . . I turned around and behind me I saw Sveta in a white dress kneeling on the ground to adjust something on Nastia's dress. It was exactly what I had seen in my dream – Sveta on the right and, on the left, our little girl.'

Epilogue

In March 2008 I returned to Moscow to meet Lev and Svetlana. I wanted to record some interviews with them and ask them about the letters, which were hard to read and understand, even for a native Russian speaker, and full of details, code words, initials and hidden meanings that only they were able to explain.

I went with Irina Ostrovskaya from Memorial to their apartment on the fourteenth floor of a tower block in Yasenevo, a residential suburb in the south-west corner of Moscow. When we came out of the lift, we were met by Lev Glebovich, small and thin with a gentle weathered face, smartly dressed in a light-blue shirt and grey trousers, who introduced himself in broken English and showed us into the apartment with a natural courtesy. Lev was nimble on his feet for a ninety-one-year-old. As he moved the furniture in the narrow entrance-hall to make room for our equipment, I noticed he was strong. We made ourselves at home in the small kitchen whose windows looked out on the concrete towers and factory smoke-stacks of Moscow. Bread, sausage, sweets and biscuits had been placed on the Formica table for our visit. Lev told us that his grandson had been sent to buy more bread. He was anxious that we might not have enough – a worry I had come across on previous visits to survivors of the camps.

Once we were settled, Lev announced that he would fetch Svetlana Aleksandrovna. I was surprised to hear him use her name and patronymic in this rather formal way. I put it down to his old-fashioned gentlemanly manners, although later I came to understand that it was part of his veneration for the woman who had saved him. Lev soon reappeared with Svetlana in a wheelchair. He manoeuvred it into the kitchen with an ease suggesting years of practice and devotion. Svetlana had been ill for a long time: heart disease and a series of small strokes had left her unable to walk. Her grey hair and pebble glasses made her appear very old. But once she began to talk, she displayed a liveliness, her playful blue eyes sparkling when she made a joke and smiled.

Svetlana had retired from the institute in 1972, and six years later she and Lev had moved to Yasenevo, at that time a new suburb beyond the reach of the Metro. They lived with their daughter, Anastasia, who suffered chronically from bipolar depression and was unable to work. Their son, Nikita, a medical researcher, later moved with his wife and three children into an apartment in the same building.

Despite his fears that he would 'never turn into any kind of scientific researcher', Lev in fact returned to the world of Soviet physics. In 1956, he joined the Cosmic Rays Laboratory, part of the Scientific Research Institute of Nuclear Physics at Moscow University, on the invitation of its new director, Naum Grigorov, Lev's friend from the Physics Faculty before the war. Grigorov had recommended Lev to the Lebedev Physics Institute in 1940, and had written to him in the labour camp, even though, as a Party member, he had much to lose by doing so. Lev worked in the Cosmic Rays Laboratory for the next thirty-four years. He helped with the design and installation of the equipment and recorded observations from experiments. But it was too late for him to build a career as a researcher in his own right. Too many years had passed since he had worked at the Lebedev Institute, years of huge advances in the field of subatomic particles.

Lev's main focus was his family. Unusually, he shared the care of the children with Sveta, did the shopping, the cooking and cleaning at Kazarmennyi Pereulok, where they lived until the move to Yasenevo, and looked after Aleksandr Alekseevich, who died in 1962. Sveta was the dominant personality in the household, and made all the practical day-to-day decisions. But in important matters she deferred to Lev.

They had the same philosophy of how to bring up their children. It was something they had discussed in their correspondence over many years, and their experience had made their common values clear. According to Nikita, they were not strict parents in the usual sense. 'They did not try to control our behaviour,' he explained. But the family held to a strict code of ethical principles:

> The moral authority of our parents was very great indeed. It induced in us a certain self-control: we limited our wants and learned to see the world as they saw it. They taught us through personal example and by talking to us openly and with respect. My father, in particular, tried to spend as much time as he could with us. He told us stories from his life, evaluating how people had behaved in the circumstances they had faced.
>
> Looking back on their influence today, I would say that it was definitely positive, although they did to some extent impose on us the values they'd taken from their own experience and try to shape our consciousness. As we grew up, we needed to free ourselves from some aspects of their rather strict didactic view. The education of children is a difficult process, and it's hard to say what is good or bad.
>
> The main thing about our parents is that they were always ready to listen and help us correct our mistakes rather than punish us. In our family there was an atmosphere of complete trust. If someone said something, it meant that it was true (or that the person believed it sincerely). To doubt the word of someone in the family, including ours, was unthinkable. We were never afraid that our parents would punish us, or that they would not believe what we said. But we were afraid of their judgement.

Lev and Sveta talked freely about their past to their children – a rare phenomenon in families that had been swept up in the mass arrests of the Stalin period. Litvinenko and Lileev, for example, did not talk about the labour camp to their children. Like millions of former prisoners, they wanted to protect them from the truth, which could burden them for life with the stigma of their 'spoilt biography'. Perhaps they also wanted to protect themselves from the judgement of their children, who were taught at school to believe in enemies of the people. Lev and Sveta took a different view. They thought that it was wrong to conceal anything from Nikita and Anastasia and wanted to prepare them for the difficulties they were bound to face. As Sveta had once written, it was not enough to love: 'One must be able . . . to live in this world, which will probably always remain cruel'.

As a child Nikita took his parents' story for granted. He thought of it as normal, ordinary. It was only in his later teenage years that he came to understand how exceptional it was. He was always aware, however, that his parents' history was not something he should talk about at school or anywhere outside the trusted circle of relatives and friends. 'From an early age I understood that we had two different lives – one lived in public and the other privately – which we somehow needed to combine yet keep apart.'

It was mainly Lev who talked about the past. Sveta did not like to dwell on it. Lev was proud of her and liked to tell the story about how she'd waited all those years for him. It was his way of reminding the children – who often bore the brunt of her bad temper when she got tired or depressed – that their mother was wonderful, no matter what.

There were also lessons that he wanted them to learn. 'My father did not talk to us about the horrors of the Gulag,' recalls Nikita, 'but he tried to give us advice and guiding principles, illustrating them with examples from his life inside the camps. The first was never to feel sorry for yourself, a commandment he would reinforce by telling us about fellow prisoners who never once complained. The second principle was that wherever you may find yourself, if only temporarily, you should always try to live as if it's permanent.'

Nikita and Anastasia heard about the camps from the many former prisoners who visited their parents, whose home was always open to friends from Pechora. The connections established in the Gulag lasted for generations, uniting families across the Soviet Union. The Mishchenkos would stay with the Lileevs when they went to Leningrad, with the Litvinenkos in Kiev and with the Terletskys in Lvov; and all these families would stay with them in the

Soviet capital. After his release, at the age of thirty-three, Lileev studied at the Polytechnic Institute in Leningrad and then became a teacher (he is still alive). Terletsky went to the Arts Institute in Lvov and became a sculptor (he died in 1993). Strelkov also kept in touch with Lev and often came to see him in Moscow. Nikita remembers him much as he appears in the photographs from Pechora, only older: 'He was very charming, full of energy, with curly white hair, and smoked a pipe.' Strelkov died in 1976.

Lev retired from the Cosmic Rays Laboratory in 1990, at the age of seventy-two. In 1998, he wrote a short account of his time in the labour camp and sent the typescript to the Historical-Regional Museum in Pechora, which at that time was collecting memoirs of the camp by former prisoners. In 2006, he published his memoirs, *Poka ia pomniu* ('While I Remember'), which were mainly about his war years. The book contained a section at the end about Pechora, similar to the earlier typescript, and in an appendix Sveta's brief account of her visits to the labour camp. In 2007 the couple gave their archive to Memorial, which had carried out a series of interviews with Lev about his experiences in the war.

We spent two days in their apartment filming interviews. Lev had a photographic memory and a remarkable ability to reflect on his own recollections of the past. Svetlana had less to say. But she sat with Lev and held his hand, and when I asked her what had made her fall in love with him, she thought for a few moments and replied: 'I knew he was my future from the start. When he was not there, I would look for him, and he would always appear by my side. That is love.'

Lev Glebovich died on 18 July 2008; Svetlana Aleksandrovna on 2 January 2010. They are buried side by side in the Golovinskoe Cemetery in Moscow.

In 1980, the wood-combine in Pechora finally burned down. No one was surprised. Only the iron entrance gate, the power station's brick chimney and a few buildings were left standing. By decree of the Ministry of Transport the wood-combine was liquidated shortly after the fire. It has since become a wasteland inhabited by a few people and wild dogs.

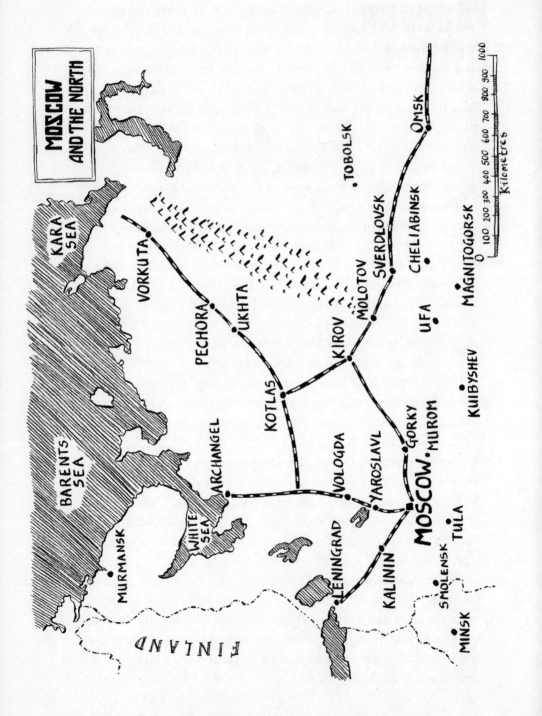

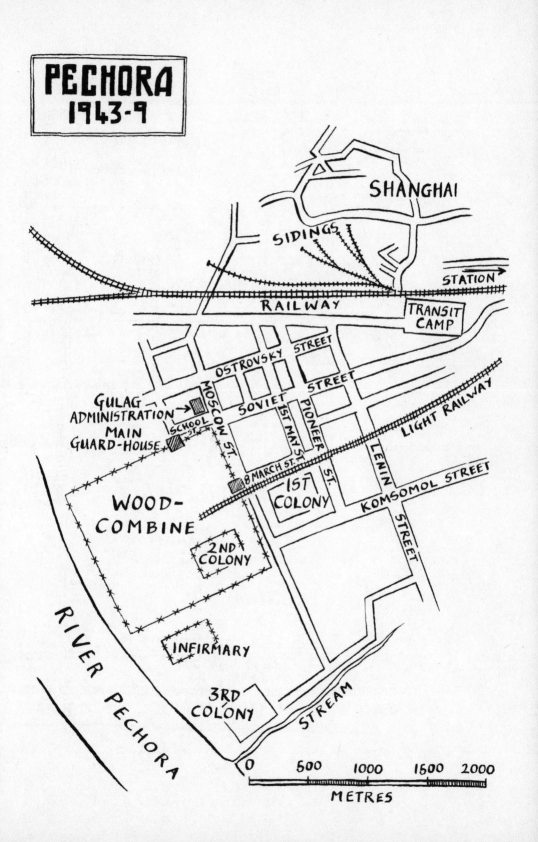

PECHORA
1943-9

SHANGHAI

SIDINGS

STATION

RAILWAY

TRANSIT CAMP

OSTROVSKY STREET

STREET

SOVIET STREET

GULAG ADMINISTRATION

MAIN GUARD-HOUSE

SCHOOL ST.

MOSCOW ST.

1ST MAY ST.

PIONEER ST.

LIGHT RAILWAY

8 MARCH ST.

1ST COLONY

KOMSOMOL STREET

LENIN STREET

WOOD-COMBINE

2ND COLONY

INFIRMARY

RIVER PECHORA

3RD COLONY

STREAM

0   500   1000   1500   2000
METRES

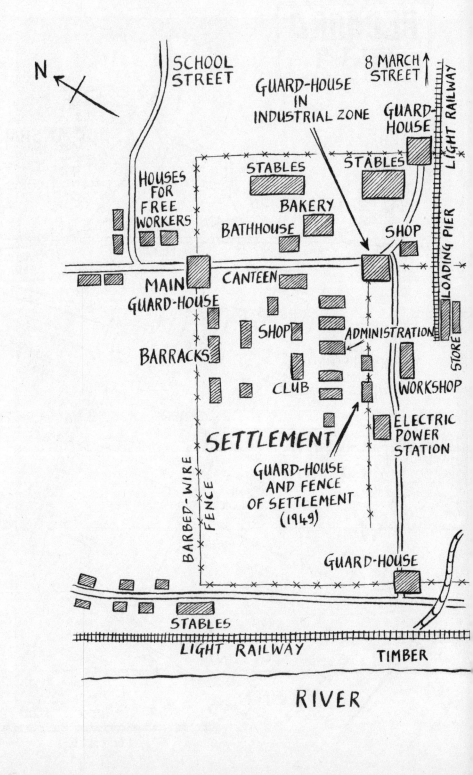

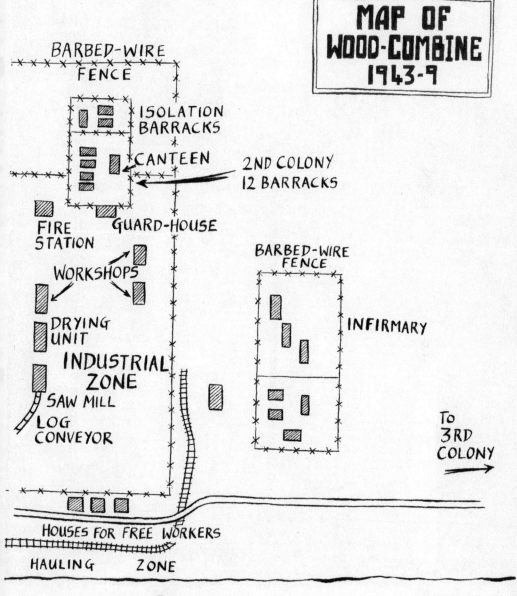

MAP OF
WOOD-COMBINE
1943-9

BARBED-WIRE FENCE

ISOLATION BARRACKS

CANTEEN

2ND COLONY
12 BARRACKS

FIRE STATION

GUARD-HOUSE

WORKSHOPS

BARBED-WIRE FENCE

INFIRMARY

DRYING UNIT

INDUSTRIAL ZONE

SAW MILL

LOG CONVEYOR

TO 3RD COLONY

HOUSES FOR FREE WORKERS

HAULING ZONE

PECHORA

Acknowledgements

This book really belongs to the Mishchenkos. It is their story, and without their help it could not have been written. Lev Glebovich and Svetlana Aleksandrovna were supportive from the start of this project. I am only sorry that they did not live to see its fruition, but hope their family will accept this book as a token of my debt of gratitude to them. Nikita L'vovich read the drafts in Russian, added valuable insights and commentaries, and made criticisms with touching gentleness and tact. I am also grateful to his children, Ilia, Lida and Vera Mishchenko, all three rightly proud of their grandparents.

In terms of the research and writing of this book my greatest debt is to Irina Ostrovskaya, Senior Researcher at Memorial, who knew and worked with Lev Glebovich and Svetlana Aleksandrovna for many years before the discovery of their letters. Irina persuaded them to give me access to their archive, conducted most of the filmed interviews, supervised the transcription of the letters, provided biographical notes, answered endless queries and read my drafts in Russian, correcting my mistakes with tireless patience and challenging my views on many things.

At Memorial in Moscow I would also like to thank Alyona Kozlova, Elena Zhemkova and the members of the academic council, who read sections of the draft.

In Pechora I would like to thank Tatiana Afanas'eva, the director of Memorial, who gave up a great deal of her time to help my research, and Boris Ivanov, who provided invaluable information about the town and wood-combine. Special thanks are owed to him for his extraordinary drawing of the convoy outside the 1st Colony.

In Syktykvar I would like to say a special thanks to Anton Niskovsky, a researcher in the People's Archive of the Republic of Komi, who helped me find, among many other valuable documents, the Gulag files of the wood-combine and the Pechora labour camp.

I owe a debt of gratitude to the BBC for two visits to Moscow: the first with Mark Burman, the radio producer, who was with me when we discovered the trunks at Memorial; the second with Ben Lewis and Paul Cox to film the interviews. I would like to thank Nick Fraser for investing in the project, and Ben Lewis for his efforts to raise interest in a documentary film. Thanks are also due to the UK Film Council for financing the copying of the dvds for the Mishchenkos and Memorial. I am particularly grateful to Tanya Seghatchian, whose support has helped me far more than she knows.

The Leverhulme Trust financed the transcription of the letters by Memorial. I am grateful to the Trust for its generous support.

Special thanks are also due to my friend Emmanuel Roman, who has been a keen supporter of this project and helped to finance it.

With the translation of the letters into English I was helped by Nicky Brown, who did the groundwork for my own translations of the letters in this book. I am very grateful to Nicky, a talented translator, who gave some precious insights into the letters. I am also grateful to Polina Haynes, who translated my draft chapters into Russian (so that they could then be checked by the Mishchenkos and Memorial) with tremendous care to detail and efficiency.

I would like to thank David Khmelnitsky for his gudiance in the world of Soviet physics; Emily Johnson for sharing her research on Gulag letters; Anna Rotkirch for her advice on matters of courtship; and Deborah Kaple for sending me an early copy of her *Gulag Boss*. Special thanks are also due to Rodric Braithwaite and Hiroaki Kuromiya, who read the draft in its entirety and provided valuable commentary.

I would like to thank my family – Stephanie, Eva, Lydia, Alice, Kate and Stoph – who read or listened to the early drafts and made helpful suggestions.

As ever, I owe a debt of gratitude to my agent, Deborah Rogers, who always believed in this book, a new departure for my work, and fought hard for me to write it in this form. At RCW Mohsen Shah, Stephen Edwards and Laurence Laluyaux have been fantastic over many years.

At Penguin I would like to thank Simon Winder, my ever supportive editor, Stefan McGrath, Jenny Fry, Marina Kemp, Penelope Vogler and David Watson, the copy-editor; at Metropolitan, the copy-editor Roslyn Schloss. But my greatest editorial debt is to Sara Bershtel at Metropolitan, whose wise guidance and rigorous attention to detail have made this a better book.

London, January 2012

A Note from Memorial

Letters have a special value for the historian of daily life. Kept in private family archives, they offer direct evidence of a lived reality, written at the time, and letting us into the interior world of the people writing them. Through letters we can follow the stories of individuals, families and even whole generations against the background of historical events. They are particularly valuable when they are written during periods of turmoil in the lives of their authors.

Memorial has a large archive of correspondence from the time of the Gulag – letters to the camps and letters from the camps. Most of the letters are to the camps. For prisoners, a letter was the only thread connecting them to 'normal' life. They tried not to lose the letters they received, and after their release they preserved them as precious things. By contrast, few letters from the camp survive. It was dangerous to hold on to 'evidence' of contact with a prisoner.

The Memorial archive contains various collections of such letters. Sometimes just a single page – or only a torn fragment – has survived. In other cases there may be a few letters, rarely more, usually written within a few months or a year. To find both sides of a correspondence is extremely rare indeed: that is an enormous stroke of luck for a researcher.

All of which is to underline the extraordinary significance of the eight-and-a-half year correspondence between Lev Mishchenko and Svetlana Ivanova. Preserved in its entirety in the Moscow archive of Memorial, it is the biggest known collection of private letters relating to the history of the Gulag. From the period of Mishchenko's imprisonment in the Pechora labour camp there are 1,246 letters: 647 from Lev to Svetlana; and 599 from her to him.

Memorial's acquaintance with the Mishchenko family began in

2000, when Lev Glebovich was working on his memoirs. There were lots of questions our researchers wanted to ask him about his reminiscences, and in the course of many conversations he told us the story of his life. In these interviews Lev often mentioned the letters, but he gave them no importance, thinking they were simply private documents of little general interest. But as he wrote his memoirs and reflected on the past, Lev began to see himself from another perspective, as a witness of twentieth-century history. It was only in 2007, after overcoming many doubts, that he and Svetlana Aleksandrovna decided to give their family archive, including the letters to and from the camp, to Memorial.

The correspondence is unique in its size and quality. Remarkably, it is a complete run of letters – from the first written by Lev from the camp on 12 July 1946 to the last he sent from Kalinin on 23 November 1954. All the letters were carefully dated and numbered by their authors, and at the start of every year the numbering began again. Lev and Svetlana kept a strict account of the correspondence and told each other about the receipt of each letter.

It is no longer possible to tell which letters were sent by the normal post and which through official channels: there are no censors' marks or stamps. Most of the letters did not pass through the censors but even these cannot be thought of as entirely free: their authors understood and always bore in mind that they could be intercepted by the authorities, so in the letters there are many silences, hinted meanings and allusions.

To store the letters he received Lev made a small hiding place underneath the floorboards of his barrack. When he had collected a large number of letters, he sent them in a parcel back to Svetlana in Moscow with the help of the voluntary workers who had delivered them to him.

The letters written from the labour camp by Mishchenko contain:

1. Information about life inside the camp: the relations
   between the prisoners; their work; conditions in the

barracks; their relations with the administration of the camp; details about feuds, intrigues, denunciations and slander.

2. Information about his fellow prisoners, their life-stories, misfortunes, joys.
3. The thoughts and feelings of Mishchenko: what interests or disturbs him; his ideas on science and his work; his opinions on the books sent to him by Svetlana; his reaction to events outside the camp.

The letters from Svetlana Ivanova tell about:

1. Her daily life – her work and studies, her professional, material, intellectual and emotional concerns, her relatives and friends.
2. Events in her life and in the lives of people close to her during the war.
3. Muscovites in the post-war years – their return to the capital from evacuation, their material problems, working conditions and leisure pursuits.
4. Post-war Moscow – new buildings, shops, urban transportation, holidays, theatrical premières, new films, etc.
5. Public events and her participation in them.

Svetlana responds not only to Lev's needs but also to the needs of his fellow prisoners. From her letters it is clear that many of her friends and relatives were involved in helping Lev. Svetlana lists the contents of the parcels she has sent to the labour camp. She worries that the parcels may have gone missing. From the contents of these parcels we can learn a lot about conditions in the camp. Foot-wraps, underwear, combs, toothbrushes, pillows, clothes, medicines and bandages, needles and thread, pens and pencils, books and newspapers – all these were sent to prisoners. Svetlana sent spectacles, scientific textbooks, cereals and vitamins. Her letters often came with blank sheets of paper, envelopes, postage stamps – and apologies that she had been unable to send a parcel because she didn't have a box.

Svetlana's letters also give us a remarkable account of post-war daily life in the Soviet capital. Their intimate descriptions of every-day reality – from Komsomol activities to the long queues at shops and railway offices – allow us to understand the lives of Muscovites and to sense the atmosphere of the late 1940s and early 1950s.

Svetlana's letters were written in the conviction that everything that took place in Moscow was of direct concern and importance to Lev and his fellow prisoners. She asks Lev for his advice, shares her doubts with him and actively involves him in the daily routines of her life, in order to help him feel less isolated from the normal world. It is as if she is living life for the two of them. She tells him her impressions of the latest films and plays, recounts meetings with her friends and writes to him about events in Moscow so that Lev might escape, if only mentally, from the barbed-wire confines of the prison camp and find some diversion from the monotony of his labour.

At the same time the events in the camp become part of her own life. Morally she tries to support Lev, to counteract his pessimism and despair, to stop him from sinking into hopelessness.

The Mishchenko–Ivanova correspondence is thousands of pages, and every page is filled with love, though the word itself is hard to find in the letters. Both Lev and Svetlana wrote sparingly about their romantic emotions. Neither wanted to burden the other by 'opening up their hearts'. But at times these feelings burst on to the page, and then it becomes clear that these are the letters of a man and woman who love each other passionately.

In 1947 Svetlana decided to travel to Pechora without official per-mission. She did not think how such a journey – by a member of the Komsomol to visit a convicted 'enemy of the people' – might destroy her career and bring her to the attention of the political police. She was not Lev's wife, nor his relative. She had already been questioned by the police and threatened by them. A journey to the camp was difficult and dangerous: she risked severe punishment and even arrest, and she had no certainty that she would be able to see Lev. Yet she went to Pechora, and an illegal meeting with Lev did take place with the help of those same friends who had smuggled the couple's letters.

The Mishchenko–Ivanova correspondence spans a decade in the lives of two people who kept their love intact despite the repressive grip of the Stalinist system. They lived apart with only hope in their future together to sustain them. Their letters should be read as a historical drama, as a dialogue between protagonists who listened to each other lovingly and understood each other's slightest hint. They tell the story of two people who were both extraordinary and yet typical of Soviet society. For a historian the content of those trunks is a unique archival treasure revealing a hidden world of emotions and connections few documents can match.

Irina Ostrovskaya
International Memorial

Sources

Archives

The Mishchenko–Ivanova correspondence is housed in the archive of the Memorial Society in Moscow. The letters of Lev (LM) and Svetlana (SI) between 1946 and 1954 are identified by year and number (for example, SI 46-20, the first letter cited in the book, is by Svetlana to Lev, her twentieth to him in 1946). Lev and Svetlana numbered all their letters very carefully, and their numbering has been retained. Letters between them from the period before 1941 are identified by their author and date (e.g. LM 39-28.10). Other documents from the Mishchenko–Ivanova archive are cited individually. The Mishchenko–Ivanova correspondence will be opened to researchers in 2013.

APIKM   Archive of the Pechora Historical-Regional Museum
               (Memorial), Pechora
GU RK NARK   People's Archive of the Republic of Komi, Syktykvar
MSP   Archive of the Memorial Society, St Petersburg

Interviews

Aleksandrova, Irina Vladimirovna (Moscow, 2008)
Aleksandrovsky, Igor Aleksandrovich (Pechora, 2010)
Ivanov, Boris Borisovich (Pechora, 2010)
Lileev, Nikolai Ivanovich (St Petersburg, 2004)
Mishchenko, Il'ia Nikitich (Moscow, 2008)
Mishchenko, Lev Glebovich (Moscow, 2006, 2008)
Mishchenko, Lida Nikitovna (Moscow, 2008)

Sources

Mishchenko, Nikita L'vovich (Moscow, 2008)

Mishchenko, Svetlana Aleksandrovna (Moscow, 2008)

Mishchenko, Vera Nikitovna (Moscow, 2008)

Serditov, Iurii Zotikovich (Pechora, 2010)

Yakhovich, Alla Stepanovna (Pechora, 2010)

Published Works and Dissertations

Applebaum, A., *Gulag: A History* (London, 2003)

Azarov, O., 'Po tundre, po zheleznoi doroge', *Martirolog: Pokaianie*, 2 vols. (Syktykvar, 1999)

—— 'Zheleznodorozhnye lageria NKVD (MVD) na territorii Komi ASSR (1938–1959 gg.)', Kand. diss. (Syktykvar, 2005)

Begin, M., *White Nights: The Story of a Prisoner in Russia* (London, 1977)

Braithwaite, R., *Moscow 1941: A City and Its People at War* (London, 2006)

Chivanov, V., 'Pechora glazami Priezzhego', in *Vygliadyvaias' v proshloe* (Pechora, 2009)

Fizicheskii fakul'tet MGU v gody Velikoi Otechestvennoi Voiny (Moscow, 1975)

Gregory, P., 'An Introduction to the Economics of the Gulag', in P. Gregory and V. Lazarev (eds.), *The Economics of Forced Labour: The Soviet Gulag* (Stanford, 2003)

Herling, G., *A World Apart*, trans. J. Marek (London, 1986)

Ivanova, G., *Labour Camp Socialism: The Gulag in the Soviet Totalitarian System* (Armonk, NY, 2000)

Khochu byt' liubimoi: Russkaia zhenskaia poeziia ot Zolotogo i Serebriannogo veka do nashikh dnei (Moscow, 2008)

Mayakovsky, V., 'Unfinished Poems', trans. Bernard Meares, in *Twentieth-Century Russian Poetry*, selected with an Introduction by Yevgeny Yevtushenko (London, 1993)

Mishchenko, L., *Poka ia pomniu* (Moscow, 2006)

—— 'Poka ia pomniu', in *Vygliadyvaias' v proshloe* (Pechora, 2009)

Mochulsky, F. V., *Gulag Boss: A Soviet Memoir*, trans. and ed. D. Kaple (Oxford, 2011)

Morozov, N., *Gulag na Komi krae 1929–1956* (Syktykvar, 1997)

Sources

Moskva voennaia, 1941–1945: memuary i arkhivnye dokumenty (Moscow, 1995)

Pechorstroi: Istoriia sozdaniia (Pechora, 2000)

Rossii, J., *Spravochnik po GULAGu*, 2 vols. (Moscow, 1991)

Sakharov, A., *Memoirs*, trans. R. Lourie (London, 1990)

Serov, B., 'V Pechoru pod konvoem', in *Vygliadyvaias' v proshloe* (Pechora, 2009)

Sokolov, A., 'Forced Labour in Soviet Industry', in P. Gregory and V. Lazarev (eds.), *The Economics of Forced Labour: The Soviet Gulag* (Stanford, 2003)

Vsesoiuznaia perepis' naseleniia 1939 goda: Osnovnye itogi (Moscow, 1992)

Vygliadyvaias' v proshloe (Pechora, 2009)

Source Notes

Chapter 1

p. 7   First meeting: Interview with Lev and Svetlana, 2008.

p. 7   Sveta's clothes: SI 46-20.

p. 7   Sveta's and Lev's heights: SI 51-37, LM 54-11.

p. 8   'student club': Sakharov, *Memoirs*, pp. 88–9.

p. 9   'Sveta's such a lovely girl': Interview with Lev and Svetlana, 2008.

p. 10   'Let's go that way': Interview with Lev and Svetlana, 2008.

p. 11   'A plump, slow-moving woman': *Poka ia pomniu*, p. 21.

p. 11   'thought his notes were very good': Interview with Lev, 2008.

p. 11   'I took it as a lawful pass': *Poka ia pomniu*, pp. 21–2.

p. 11   'daughter of a minor provincial official': Interview with Lev, 2006.

p. 12   'a small Siberian town': Interview with Lev, 2006.

p. 12   'Is that uncle a hunter?': *Poka ia pomniu*, p. 8.

p. 12   'Lev was taken to the hospital': *Poka ia pomniu*, p. 9.

p. 13   'The funeral': Interview with Lev, 2006.

p. 13   'He's come to say goodbye': *Poka ia pomniu*, p. 9.

p. 13   'Lev later visited his mother's grave': *Poka ia pomniu*, p. 9.

p. 13   'a second funeral': *Poka ia pomniu*, p. 9.

p. 13   'his grandmother': Interview with Lev, 2006.

p. 14   'Granovsky Street': Interview with Lev, 2006.

p. 14   'Almost every day': *Poka ia pomniu*, p. 10.

p. 14   'three of his parents' closest friends': Interview with Lev, 2006.

p. 14   'Lev went to a mixed-sex school': Interview with Lev, 2006.

p. 15   'It seems to me that I was more grown up': SI 49-83.

p. 15   Sveta's strict upbringing: Interview with Irina Alexandrova, 2008.

p. 15   'He had to work his way through school': *Poka ia pomniu*, p. 14.

p. 16   'The man wrote sad poems': *Poka ia pomniu*, p. 15.

p. 16   'Lev was living with his grandmother': Interview with Lev, 2008.

p. 16 'mainly maths and physics books': Listed in SI 49-86.

p. 17 'A strict church-goer': SI 50-11.

p. 17 'She's just my friend': Interview with Lev, 2008.

p. 17 'The one place': Interview with Lev, 2008.

p. 19 'Military training': Interview with Lev, 2006.

p. 19 'We have idiots': *Poka ia pomniu*, p. 18.

p. 20 'Their relationship had cooled': Interview with Lev, 2008.

p. 20 'black moods': SI 47-3.

p. 20 'How many times': SI 46-18.

p. 21 'The glow of your cigarette': LM 46-1 (poem translated by Nicky Brown). The original ('Ogonek tvoei papirosy') can be found in *Khochu byt' liubimoi*, p. 207.

p. 21 'Svetka!': LM 39-28.10.

p. 21 'Lev's grandmother died': LM 46-1.

p. 21 'Vagankovskoe cemetery': Communication by Nikita Mishchenko.

p. 22 'Sveta would stay late': Interview with Lev, 2008.

p. 22 'We climbed up': LM 40-15.8.

p. 23 'Do you know, there's a lovely square': SI 40-31.7.

p. 23 'Levenka, My first impulse': SI 40-3.8.

p. 24 'We're not going anywhere': *Poka ia pomniu*, p. 27.

p. 24 'Today, at 4 o'clock': Cited in Braithwaite, *Moscow 1941*, p. 74.

p. 25 'more than a thousand students': *Fizicheskii fakul'tet MGU v gody*, p. 12.

p. 25 'Lev was shaken': *Poka ia pomniu*, p. 27.

p. 26 'Svetik, we're living in the woods': LM 41-13.7.

p. 26 'fed and watered': LM 41-14.7.

p. 26 'second visit in early September': LM 41-7.9; SI 46-1.

p. 26 'a piece of paper': Interview with Lev, 2008.

p. 27 'There was one last visit to Moscow': Interview with Lev, 2008.

Chapter 2

p. 28 'Lev set off from Moscow': Interview with Lev, 2006.

p. 28 'eau de Cologne': Communication by Nikita Mishchenko.

p. 29 'At the end of the third night': Interview with Lev, 2008.

p. 29 'Lev was brought to a transit camp': *Poka ia pomniu*, p. 36.

p. 29 'In early December': Interview with Lev, 2008.

p. 30 'German captain': Interview with Lev, 2006.

p. 30 'Ich kann diese Aufgabe': *Poka ia pomniu*, p. 38.

p. 30 'The truck was going very fast': *Poka ia pomniu*, p. 40.

p. 31 'interrogated by the commandant': *Poka ia pomniu*, p. 42.

p. 31 'lectured on Nazi ideology': *Poka ia pomniu*, p. 43.

p. 32 Hladik episode: *Poka ia pomniu*, pp. 42–9.

p. 33 Vlasov recruitment episode: *Poka ia pomniu*, pp. 52–4.

p. 34 'The prisoners made their escape': Interview with Lev, 2006.

p. 35 'Lev once wrote to Prague': Interview with Lev, 2008.

p. 36 'Taxi drivers were charging': *Moskva voennaia, 1941–1945*, p. 478.

p. 36 'Their first stop was Murom': Sakharov, *Memoirs*, p. 43.

p. 36 'The railway cars': Sakharov, *Memoirs*, p. 44.

p. 36 'chemistry and oscillation physics': SI46-1.

p. 37 'It wore me out so much': SI46-4.

p. 37 'I was in a strange, unfamiliar laboratory': SI46-4.

p. 38 'It was very hard for everyone': SI46-20.

p. 38 'ill with brucellosis': SI46-1.

p. 38 'laboratory on the third floor': SI49-45a.

p. 38 'Many times she thought that she should run away': SI46-3.

p. 39 'summoned her for questioning': SI46-3.

p. 39 'Getting a bit angry': SI46-13.

p. 39 'All my relatives had come for my birthday': SI46-4.

p. 40 'It was what I needed to say to someone': SI46-21.

p. 40 'For a long time I stood on the threshold': SI46-8.

p. 41 'It's not for me to judge you': SI46-21.

p. 41 'Pittler ammunition factory': Interview with Lev, 2006.

p. 42 'transferred to Buchenwald': *Poka ia pomniu*, p. 66.

p. 42 'For each of these rooms': Geoffroy de Clercq, 'Buchenwald-Wansleben', www.jewishgen.org/ForgottenCamps/Witnesses/WanslebenEng.html.

p. 42 'For any misdemeanour': *Poka ia pomniu*, p. 73.

p. 43 'I remember that at 8 p.m.': Geoffroy de Clercq, 'Buchenwald-Wansleben'.

p. 43 Escape from convoy episode: Interview with Lev, 2008.

p. 44 'Ahead of us on the road': *Poka ia pomniu*, p. 76.

p. 44 'the only time during the entire war': Interview with Lev, 2008.

p. 44 'Throw away your weapons!': Interview with Lev, 2006.

p. 44 'tasted as good as restaurant food': Interview with Lev, 2008.

p. 44 'In Russia you have Communism': *Poka ia pomniu*, p. 77.

p. 44 'Sveta and her family': Interview with Lev, 2008.

p. 45 'Even if I had only one small chance': Interview with Lev, 2008.

p. 45 'We ate twelve times a day!': *Poka ia pomniu*, p. 78.

p. 45 'Happy Return!': *Poka ia pomniu*, p. 79.

p. 46 SMERSH interrogation: *Poka ia pomniu*, pp. 80–83.

p. 46 'I was not afraid of dying': *Poka ia pomniu*, p. 84.

p. 46 'say goodbye': LM 46-1.

p. 46 'I was dozing after an interrogation': Interview with Lev, 2008.

Chapter 3

p. 48 'The convoy travelled': Details from APIKM, f. 31, op. 14 (Mishchenko); MSP, f. 3, op. 15, d. 3, APIKM, f. 31, op. 50 (Lileev).

p. 48 'The prisoners were fed': Mishchenko, 'Poka ia pomniu', p. 31.

p. 48 'The most likely explanation': See Applebaum, *Gulag*, pp. 170–72.

pp. 48–9 'The guards employed', 'no longer human beings': Interview with Lev, 2006.

p. 49 'Lev was badly hurt': *Poka ia pomniu*, p. 92.

p. 49 'jogging pace': APIKM, f. 31, op. 50 (Lileev).

p. 49 'All along the line': APIKM, f. 23, op. 7 (Serditov).

p. 49 'sanitary point': MSP, f. 3, op. 15, d. 3; interview with Iurii Serditov, 2010.

p. 49 'Many of the prisoners were so frail': APIKM, f. 31, op. 50 (Lileev).

p. 49 'transit camp': B. Serov, 'V Pechoru pod konvoem', p. 13.

p. 50 '131,930 prisoners': *Vsesoiuznaia perepis'*, p. 229.

p. 50 'All the work was done by hand': Azarov, 'Po tundre, po zheleznoi doroge', *Martirolog*, vol. 2, p. 159.

p. 51 '55 per cent': GU RK NARK, f. 1, op. 2, d. 844. l. 43.

p. 51 '157,000 prisoners': Azarov, 'Zheleznodorozhnye lageria', p. III.

p. 51 'put the rails directly on the ground': Details from Mochusky, *Gulag Boss*, pp. 77–83, 91–3.

p. 51 'The crucial bridge': Details from Morozov, *Gulag na Komi krae*, pp. 87ff.

p. 51 '5 kilometres an hour': Statistics in Azarov, 'Zheleznodorozhnye lageria', p. 191.

p. 51 '200,000 tons of it a month': GU RK NARK, f. 1, op. 3, d. 67, l. 37.

p. 51 'ramshackle town': Details from GU RK NARK, f. 623, op. 1, d. 76; V. Chivanov, 'Pechora glazami priezzhego', pp. 52–66; APIKM, f. 23, op. 7 (Serditov); interviews with Boris Ivanov, 2010.

p. 52 '52 hectares': GU RK NARK, f. 173, op. 1, d. 1, l. 9.

p. 52 'fifty buildings', 'temporary wooden structures': GU RK NARK, f. 173, op. 1, d. 1, ll. 29, 155.

p. 53 'There were ten barracks': Mishchenko, 'Poka ia pomniu', p. 32.

p. 53 'Terletsky': Mishchenko, 'Poka in pomniu', pp. 39–40.

p. 54 'Anisimov': LM 46-26; LM 47-28.

p. 54 'eighty-three to be precise': GU RK NARK, f. 1, op. 3, d. 1081, l. 161.

p. 54 'The other colonies': Details from GU RK NARK, f. 1876, op. 7, d. 356.

p. 54 '500 [special exiles]': GU RK NARK, f. 1876, op. 7, d. 356, l. 61.

p. 54 'It is next to us', LM 47-39.

p. 54 'Conditions in the 3rd': GU RK NARK, f. 1876, op. 7, d. 358, ll. 22–4.

p. 54 'The work meant dragging': Details from GU RK NARK, f. 1876, op. 7, d. 358, l. 10.

p. 55 'standard uniform': Interview with Lev, 2006.

p. 55 'rations': Details from Mishchenko, 'Poka ia pomniu', p. 32. Similar figures are given by Lev in LM 47-39a.

p. 55 '60 cubic metres': Calculated from GU RK NARK, f. 623, op. 1, d. 80, l. 45.

p. 55 'Sickness and death-rates': GU RK NARK, f. 1876, op. 7, d. 355, ll. 11–12, 37.

p. 55 'According to a prisoner': APIKM, f. 31, op. 14 (Mishchenko).

p. 55 'We don't seem to care': GU RK NARK, f. 1876, op. 7, d. 355, l. 61.

p. 56 'looked like a peasant': LM 52-22.

p. 56 'Strelkov': Details from Serov, 'V Pechoru pod Konvoem', pp. 19–20; Mishchenko, 'Poka ia pomniu', pp. 35–7; APIKM, f. 31, op. 14 (Mishchenko).

p. 58 'the drying unit was in desperate need': GU RK NARK, f. 1876, op. 7, d. 355, ll. 76–9.

p. 58 'The room was kept at a minimum temperature': Interview with Lev, 2006.

p. 58 'spacious living area': Details from LM 46-18, LM 46-23; APIKM, f. 31, op. 50 (Lileev); MSP, f. 3, op. 15, d. 3, l. 24.

p. 58 'he would be hungry': Interview with Lev, 2008.

p. 59 'surrendered in a moment of weakness': LM 48-52.

p. 60 '2 June 1946': *Poka ia pomniu*, p. 124.

p. 61 'No. 2 Pechora, 1.VIII.46', *Poka ia pomniu*, pp. 124–6.

p. 61 'could not sleep', 'would not eat', 'drove her parents', 'longed for' 'would have changed everything': SI 47-3.

p. 61 '12 July 1946': SI 46-1.

p. 64 'Pechora, 9.VIII.46': LM 46-1.

Chapter 4

p. 66 'Letters and printed matter': *Poka ia pomniu*, p. 125.

p. 66 'only two or three times a month': Interview with Lev, 2008.

p. 66 Censorship by women: Details from interview with Lev, 2008.

p. 67 Sending and receiving parcels: SI 48-102, SI 52-22; APIKM, f. 31, op. 50 (Lileev).

p. 67 'So if you or Aunt Olya': LM 46-1.

p. 67 'My dear Lev', SI 46-2.

p. 67 'I too have become a fatalist': SI 46-3.

p. 68 'It was a present for me': LM 46-6.

p. 68 'I got your letter of the 26th': SI 46-6.

p. 68 'Sveta, you know that I'm never lazy': LM 46-3.

p. 68 'carried unfinished letters': LM 50-30.

p. 69 'There's no need for any kind of poste restante': SI 46-3.

p. 69 'so as not to attract attention': SI 47-42.

p. 69 'I need to be at home': SI 47-22.

p. 70 'Sentimental words about love': SI 47-37.

p. 70 'If the best decide to end their plight': Translated by Nicky Brown.

p. 70 'Muscovites wear whatever they have left': SI 46-20.

p. 71 'It's grey and overcast': LM 46-4.

p. 71 'No gold has been seen': SI 46-7.

p. 72 'The institute was a large complex': Details from SI 46-1, SI 47-25, SI 49-45a.

p. 72 'state secret': *Poka ia pomniu*, p. 118.

p. 72 'on the grey side of 50', 'I can talk with him': SI 46-2.

p. 72 'I've learned that it's very difficult': SI 47-20.

p. 73 'Sveta had a busy schedule': Details from SI 46-24.

p. 73 'On Sundays': SI 46-12, SI 46-20.

p. 73 'I don't often meet with our old friends': SI 46-1.

p. 73 'Today, after lectures': SI 47-21.

p. 74 'Dear Lev, hello!': A. Zlenko to LM, 19 September 1946.

p. 74 'Naum Grigorov': N. Grigorov to LM, 5 March 1947.

p. 74 'I was very surprised': K. Andreeva to LM, 8 April 1947.

p. 74 'I'm afraid of being an unwanted guest': LM 46-11.

p. 75 'On to the matter of umbrellas': SI 46-15.

p. 75 'I read your dressing-down': LM 46-16.

p. 76 'It's very good': LM 46-11.

p. 76 'Your two letters': LM 46-4.

p. 76 'When I see my name': LM 51-43.

p. 76 'covering my head': LM 47-4.

p. 76 'Listen, Lev, in order to decide': SI 46-3.

p. 77 'Lev replied by acknowledging': LM 46-7.

p. 77 'You're right that I'm trying to breathe': SI 46-13.

p. 78 'Levi, I have always believed you': SI 46-18.

p. 79 'I finally need to start': LM 46-22.

p. 79 'As for the parcels': SI 46-15.

p. 80 'Sveta, it's obvious that God': LM 47-22.

p. 80 'there were several random killings': GU RK NARK, f. 1876, op. 7, d. 356, l. 66.

p. 80 'The autumn here is beautiful': LM 46-7.

p. 81 'Sometimes when I write to you': LM 46-8.

p. 81 'Time is moving on': SI 46-6.

p. 82 'I've finally managed to get moved': LM 46-5.

p. 82 'Nikolai Lileev': Details from MSP, f. 3, op. 15, d. 3; APIKM, f. 31, op. 50 (Lileev).

p. 82 'Viktor Chikin': Details from LM 47-20, LM 47-30, LM 47-38.

p. 83 'more than half the responsible positions': GU RK NARK, f. 173, op. 1, d. 2, ll. 49–50.

p. 83 'shortages of electricity': GU RK NARK, f. 1876, op. 7, d. 355, ll. 31, 73, 79.

p. 83 'train 212 more specialists': GU RK NARK, f. 1876, op. 7, d. 355, ll. 36–40.

p. 83 'Working in the power station': Details from MSP, f. 3, op. 15, d. 3; APIKM, f. 31, op. 50 (Lileev); Mishchenko, 'Poka ia pomniu', pp. 36–7.

p. 84 'Going through the guard-house': APIKM, f. 31, op. 50 (Lileev).

p. 84 'Lev was working the day shift': Details of routine from LM 46-6.

p. 84 'Lev could walk to work in eight minutes': LM to N. Mel'nikov, 21 October 1946; LM to E. A. Poltoratskaia, 18 January 1947.

p. 84 'Right now in my den': LM 46-12.

p. 84 'It's like a banya here': LM 46-26.

p. 85 'so dim and yellow': LM 46-27.

p. 85 'At the moment work is done': LM 46-5.

p. 85 'The time we spent': APIKM, f. 31, op. 50 (Lileev).

p. 86 'an excellent raconteur': LM 46-20.

p. 86 'Liubka is a wonderful, very special boy': LM 46-17.

p. 87 'Gleb is good at mathematics': LM 46-2.

p. 87 'I can't share you': LM 46-11.

p. 87 'Oleg is wonderful': LM 47-7.

p. 87 'an original': LM 46-23.

p. 87 'the two Nikolais', 'He is more modest', 'simpler and more direct': LM 46-2.

p. 88 'tactlessness': LM 47-10.

p. 88 'It's no longer such a boring world': LM 46-18.

p. 88 'Generally speaking': LM 46-14.

p. 89 'The wood-combine was not prepared': GU RK NARK, f. 1876, op. 7, d. 356, l. 130.

p. 89 'Sveta, I am drowning': LM 46-29.

p. 90 'What do I wish': LM 46-24.

p. 90 'He's putting a brave face on it': LM 46-29.

p. 90 'I'm tired of spending holidays without you': SI 46-28.

Chapter 5

p. 92 'more than a quarter': Gregory, 'An Introduction', p. 18.

p. 92 '445 free workers in 1946': GU RK NARK, f. 1876, op. 7, d. 356, l. 107.

p. 93 'just 1.8 square metres of living space': GU RK NARK, f. 1876, op. 7, d. 356, l. 132.

p. 93 'no running water or sanitary provision': GU RK NARK, f. 1876, op. 7, d. 360, l. 75.

p. 93 'We are surrounded by disaffected people': GU RK NARK, f. 1876, op. 7, d. 355, l. 89.

p. 94 'no real segregation': GU RK NARK, f. 1876, op. 7, d. 355, l. 72; d. 356, l. 107.

p. 95 'MVD was well aware of the smuggling': GU RK NARK, f. 1876, op. 7, d. 357, l. 21.

p. 95 'My darling Sveta': LM 47-16.

p. 95 'This is to tell you': LM 47-31.

p. 95 'My letters seem to be more punctual': LM 47-35.

p. 95 'I've become acquainted with an interesting gentleman': LM 47-32.

p. 96 'I saw Izrailevich again recently': LM 47-37.

p. 97 'L. Y. is really grateful for your efforts': LM 47-41.

p. 97 'Yesterday I[zrailevich] brought two letters': LM 47-48.

p. 97 'In future, as I have written': LM 47-49.

p. 97 'I learn from talking with him': LM 50-19.

p. 98 'The other day an opportunity': LM 47-21.

p. 98 'Aunt Katya came to see us today': SI 47-67.

p. 98 Aleksandrovsky: Details from interview with Igor Aleksandrovsky, 2010; GU RK NARK, f. 1876, op. 7, d. 358, l. 51.

p. 99 Details of Aleksandrovsky house: GU RK NARK, f. 173, op. 1, d. 5, l. 4.

p. 100 'The first time Lev met him': Interview with Lev, 2008.

p. 100 Yakhovich: Interview with Alla Yakhovich, 2010.

p. 101 'What, this? Just papers': Interview with Lev 2008.

p. 102 'obstinate persistence', 'clashed with Anatoly Shekhter', 'known to everyone as a slanderer and racketeer', 'subversively delaying the release': LM 46-22.

p. 102 'I didn't want to write about this': LM 47-5.

p. 103 'My darling Sveta, I need': LM 47-16.

p. 105 'nearly always look much worse': LM 47-39a.

p. 105 'I made your views known': SI 47-8.

p. 106 'The room is no longer mine': *Poka ia pomniu*, pp. 125–6.

p. 107 'As for what is taking place': SI 47-30.

p. 107 'Both are completely possible': SI 46-4.

p. 107 'It was true that the MVD had a policy': Ivanova, *Labour Camp Socialism*, p. 114.

p. 107 'I don't want you to waste your energy': LM 46-7.

p. 107 'You don't have faith': SI 46-22.

p. 107 'like student work': LM 47-11.

p. 108 'I won't think about the Maximum': LM 47-16.

p. 109 'I just don't know what to say': SI 47-30b/d.

p. 109 'I wrote to you in passing': LM 47-39.

Chapter 6

p. 111 'I know you will do all you can': SI 46-1.

p. 111 'You ask me about a meeting': LM 46-1.

p. 111 'good, conscientious, and high-tempo work': Applebaum, *Gulag*, p. 237.

p. 111 'invariably silent and irritable': Herling, *A World Apart*, p. 95.

p. 111 'possible in principle': LM 46-11.

p. 111 'to find out whether it is personally possible': SI 46-10.

p. 111 'Lev . . . even if it's only a possibility': SI 46-10.

p. 112 'I didn't expect a two-week journey': SI 46-13.

p. 113 'They say it's possible': LM 47-11.

p. 113 'As for meetings, Sveta': LM 47-16.

p. 115 'When I leave the station': LM 47-20.

p. 116 'The meeting was not a cheerful one': LM 47-39.

p. 117 'experienced traveller': SI 47-30.

p. 117 'Levi, Gleb's mother visited O. B.': SI 47-30.

p. 120 'for a few minutes': LM 47-8.

p. 120 'Natalia Arkadevna came to see me on Monday': SI 47-38.

p. 121 'Levenka, my darling': SI 47-43.

p. 121 'It's 28 degrees here': SI 47-47.

p. 121 'I asked about the photographic equipment': SI 47-47.

p. 122 'Since there are local trains': SI 47-48.

p. 123 'All my plans remain in place': SI 47-49.

p. 123 'Autumn has drawn near': LM 47-50.

p. 124 'Svet, your letter, as you supposed': LM 47-51.

p. 124 'The salute has just taken place': SI 47-50.

p. 126 'Nothing ever turns out': LM 47-51.

p. 126 'At the institute they gave me': SI 47-51.

pp. 126–7 'I have the details of the work trip', 'another 300 or 400 roubles', 'I'm very nervous about the preparations': SI 47-51.

p. 127 'so I wasn't able to let him know': LM 47-52.

p. 127 'All in all': LM 47-52.

p. 127 'The details of Sveta's journey': *Poka ia pomniu*, pp. 115–18.

p. 128 'prepared for an unsuccessful outcome': SI 48-31.

p. 128 'natural', 'How could I have gone there': Interview with Svetlana, 2008.

p. 128 'The dress saved me': *Poka ia pomniu*, p. 115.

p. 130 'about a hundred guards': Details from GU RK NARK, f. 1876, op. 7, d. 357, ll. 29–30, 68–72; d. 358, ll. 29–32; d. 363, ll. 78–81.

p. 130 Thieving by the guards: Details from GU RK NARK, f. 1876, op. 7, d. 355, l. 37; d. 356, ll. 1–2, 9–11, 62–5, etc.

p. 130 Drunkenness and 'reports of disciplinary hearings': GU RK NARK, f. 1876, op. 7, d. 357, ll. 26–7, 41–2, 69, 71–2; d. 358, ll. 29–30, 32–3, etc.

p. 130 'Prisoners had walked out': GU RK NARK, f. 1876, op. 7, d. 355, ll. 36–40.

p. 131 'let outsiders into the prison zone': GU RK NARK, f. 1876, op. 7, d. 356, l. 42; d. 357, l. 21.

p. 131 'what little street lighting there was': Details from GU RK NARK, f. 1876, op. 7, d. 356. l. 42.

p. 131 'Lev Izrailevich and Sveta reached the main gate': *Poka ia pomniu*, p. 116.

p. 132 'It was not jealousy': *Poka ia pomniu*, p. 117.

p. 133 'We had to restrain our feelings': Interview with Lev, 2008.

p. 133 'They brought two chairs for us': *Poka ia pomniu*, p. 117.

p. 133 'fight with somebody': Interview with Igor Aleksandrovsky, 2010.

p. 133 'Maria was due to work the night shift': Details from *Poka ia pomniu*, p. 117.

p. 134 'It was only when we were left on our own': Interview with Lev, 2008.

p. 134 'I asked him: "Do you want to?"': Communication by Nikita Mishchenko.

p. 134 'Lev and Sveta spent two nights': *Poka ia pomniu*, p. 117.

p. 134 'some sort of sanitary wagon': *Poka ia pomniu*, p. 118.

p. 134 'My darling Lev': SI 47-51a.

p. 135 'My own sweet Sveta': LM 47-54.

p. 135 'My own sweet, glorious Sveta': LM 47-55.

p. 136 'My sweet, my lovely Sveta . . . finally!': LM 47-56.

p. 137 'For 250 roubles': SI 47-52.

Chapter 7

p. 139 'The first snow fell tonight': LM 47-60.

p. 139 'Svetinka . . . the more I think about you': LM 47-58.

p. 139 'You once asked': LN 47-69.

p. 140 'It's a truism': LM 47-71.

p. 140 'good-natured', 'cultured': LM 48-22a.

p. 140 'it is safer for me here': LM 48-10/2.

p. 141 'intelligent, nice, not over-educated': LM 47-44.

p. 141 'There have been some changes at the plant': LM 47-59.

p. 141 'disturbing impression': LM 47-60.

p. 141 'Many of the women who have arrived': LM 47-61.

p. 142 'When I think of you': LM 48-10.

p. 142 'Life without the rationing system': SI 48-6.

p. 143 'So, my darling, foolish Lev': SI 48-25.

p. 143 'The patient is 49 years old': LM 48-17.

p. 144 'Sveta wrote back': SI 48-17, SI 48-29.

p. 144 'Liubka is gloomy and barely talks': LM 48-58.

p. 144 'My Liubka is very slowly returning': LM 48-61.

p. 145 'The endocrinologist': SI 49-29.

p. 146 'My darling Levi, I want to be with you so much': SI 48-9.

p. 146 'N. A. rang the other day': SI 48-19.

p. 147 'A depression has come over me': SI 49-2.

p. 147 'Having swallowed all kinds of pills': SI 49-45b.

p. 148 'At the moment . . . skiing is the one thing': SI 49-17.

p. 148 'Go somewhere': LM 48-22.

p. 148 'It is very hard for her': LM to N. Mel'nikov, 8 April 1948.

p. 148 'So why have I turned to Lydia?': SI 48-18.

p. 149 'over-acquaintance with geography': SI 49-45a.

p. 149 'too superficial', 'nice-looking, almost bland': LM 48-64.

p. 149 'I can imagine that Tamara likes': SI 49-27.

p. 150 'It's always difficult to bury someone': SI 47-28.

p. 150 'I didn't want to compromise her future': Interview with Lev, 2008.

p. 151 'Leva . . . Alik is turning seven, not eight': SI 48-25.

p. 152 'not know how children grow': SI 48-25.

p. 152 'Alik its capable': SI 48-104.

p. 152 'A young girl came to the power station': LM 47-57.

p. 153 'They were never stopped or searched': Interview with Igor Aleksandrovsky, 2010.

p. 153 Toys and town children: Interviews with Igor Aleksandrovsky, Alla Yakhovich, Boris Ivanov, 2010.

p. 153 'I was enlisted as a father again today': LM 47-64.

p. 154 'She is older and . . . acts more grown-up': LM 47-66.

p. 154 'I have lost faith in myself': LM 47-69.

p. 154 'machines were idle for almost a quarter of the working time': GU RK NARK, f. 1876, op. 7, d. 357, l. 82.

p. 154 'There is no rhythym in our work': GU RK NARK, f. 1876, op. 7, d. 357, l. 44.

p. 154 'idiots': LM 48-31.

p. 154 'stupidities': LM to N. Mel'nikov, 18 November 1947.

p. 155 'There's such a dreadful shambles': LM 48-28.

p. 155 'I'm unable to sit calmly': LM 48-69.

p. 155 'Yesterday one of our operators remarked': LM 49-10a.

p. 156 'So . . . we may be due a quarter of a day': LM 47-46.

p. 157 'escapes and even mass break-outs': GU RK NARK, f. 1876, op. 7, d. 359, l. 84.

p. 157 'large contingent of prisoners': LM 48-43.

p. 157 'Well, Svetishche, some instructions': LM 48-45.

p. 158 'Yesterday, M. A. asked': SI 48-31.

p. 159 'If the work trips fall through': SI 48-39.

p. 159 'might turn out to be difficult': LM 48-27.

p. 159 'The latest decision by those fickle': LM 48-46a.

p. 160 'Apparently, it's not going to add any particular restrictions': LM48-46b.

p. 160 'Party meeting on 12 May': GU RK NARK, f. 1876, op. 7, d. 357, l. 39ff.

p. 160 'The matter is resolved': SI 48-51.

p. 161 'the chief accountant of the institute informed her': SI 48-52.

p. 161 'until she had further news': SI 48-55.

p. 161 'Slowly they are introducing': LM 48-48.

p. 161 'Maybe 1949 will be a better year': LM 48-46c.

p. 162 'My darling Lev . . . week has already passed': SI 48-60.

p. 162 'I am interested, Levi': SI 48-63.

p. 163 'I haven't written for a week', 'In my last letter': SI 48-64.

p. 163 'the right to give life': SI 48-64.

p. 164 'On the one hand, chances diminish': SI 48-64a.

p. 165 'Goodness knows when I'm going to depart': SI 48-65.

p. 166 'It's a pity to stop': SI 48-65.

p. 166 'So, my darling Sveta': LM 48-61a.

p. 167 'On the stretch between Kirov and Kotlas': *Poka ia pomniu*, pp. 118–19.

p. 167 'they were eagerly awaiting': *Poka ia pomniu*, p. 119.

p. 168 'I waited the whole day': *Poka ia pomniu*, p. 119.

p. 168 'I thanked him enthusiastically': *Poka ia pomniu*, p. 119.

p. 168 'The meeting took place': Interview with Lev, 2008, *Poka ia pomniu*,
　　　p. 119.

p. 169 'My darling Lev . . . a second day': SI 48-66.

p. 170 'My dear, dear Levi, I'm home at last': SI 48-68.

p. 171 'I looked at myself in the mirror today': SI 48-69.

p. 171 'blissfully happy and kind towards everyone': SI 48-71.

p. 171 'I am full of happiness': SI 48-75.

p. 171 'My darling, lovely Sveta': LM 48-62.

p. 171 'My darling Sveta, tomorrow is your birthday': LM 48-63a.

p. 172 'My darling Svetinka, no letter has come from you': LM 48-67.

p. 172 'I was imagining the wildest things': LM 48-68.

p. 172 'The days are passing by very quickly': LM 48-73.

p. 173 'This evening they sent Liubka away': LM 48-78.

p. 173 'Liubka had become quite ill': LM 48-79.

p. 173 'I was never able to cry': LM 48-83.

p. 174 'Well, my friend': LM to Terletsky, 3 December 1948.

Chapter 8

p. 175 'My darling Sveta': LM 48-94.

p. 175 'Sveta had a great deal of work': SI 49-2, SI 49-5.

p. 175 'There is no joy in it': SI 49-5.

p. 176 'allowing something to be done': SI 49-2.

p. 176 'to calm my nerves': SI 49-39.

p. 176 'These pills are helping me': SI 49-37.

p. 176 'Pavel, an acquaintance': SI 49-4.

p. 177 'was planning to get married': SI 48-42.

p. 178 'As for the "best"': LM 48-40.

p. 179 'She loves me? She loves me not?': Mayakovsky, 'Unfinished Poems',
　　　p. 273.

p. 179 'For some reason': SI 49-15.

p. 179 'but also in reality': LM 49-62a.

p. 179 'Nikolai has had to switch': LM 49-15.

p. 179 'There will be more free days': LM 49-6.

p. 180 'I like being on my own at work': LM 49-7.

p. 180 'Today was an idiotic day': LM 49-8.

p. 180 '*Anna Karenina*': LM 49-8.

p. 180 'The people in our barracks': LM 49-9.

p. 180 'It was a sad day': LM 49-13.

p. 181 'Nobody has done as much as him': LM 49-9.

p. 181 'Only 25!': LM 49-28.

p. 181 'There was snow in May': LM 49-39.

p. 181 'first warm days': LM 49-47.

p. 181 'frequent power cuts', 'shortages of warm clothes': GU RK NARK, f. 1876, op. 7, d. 359, ll. 61–4, 87–92.

p. 182 Rates of illness in the 2nd Colony: *Vygliadyvaias*', pp. 119–20; GU RK NARK, f. 1876, op. 7, d. 359, l. 34.

p. 182 'an educated man': LM 48-60.

p. 182 'I found him dressed': LM 49-18.

p. 182 'Two or three days ago': LM 49-35.

p. 183 'it seems, not a native': LM 49-18.

p. 183 'a woman in her forties': LM 49-29.

p. 183 Nina Grin: Details from *Vygliadyvaias*', pp. 184–9.

p. 183 Svetlana Tukhachevskaya: Details from APIKM, f. 31, op. 50 (Lileev).

p. 184 'On 2 July 1949': Record of meeting in GU RK NARK, f. 1876, op. 7, d. 360, ll. 62ff.

p. 184 'government secrets': Thefts discussed in GU RK NARK, f. 1876, op. 7, d. 359, ll. 54–5.

p. 185 'How it's going to work out this year': LM 49-30.

p. 185 'The decision made little sense': SI 49-31.

p. 185 Complications with work trips: SI 49-40.

p. 185 'which up to now has been a lucky time': SI 49-40.

p. 185 'between 30 minutes and two hours': LM 49-13.

p. 186 'Wives are more interesting to me': SI 49-44.

p. 186 'You probably already received': LM 49-51.

p. 186 'It might be possible to think': SI 49-49.

p. 187 'It doesn't matter how long': LM 49-56.

p. 187 'I asked Mikhail Aleksandrovich': *Poka ia pomniu*, p. 120.

p. 187 'Sveta left by train for Ukhta on 30 August': SI 49-55.

p. 188 'They took me by car to the station': *Poka ia pomniu*, p. 120.

p. 188 'My darling Lev, the journey is fine': SI 49-56.

p. 189 'We made it to Kotlas': SI 49-57.

p. 189 'My darling Sveta . . . you are still everywhere with me': LM 49-66.

p. 189 'only now I see you without any features': LM 49-69.

p. 190 Dreams: LM 49-71, 72, 74, 76.

p. 190 'I understood that the most terrible thing in life': LM 49-82.

Chapter 9

p. 191 '1950. Half a century', 'Biting frosts': LM 50-2.

p. 191 '2,561,351 prisoners': Applebaum, *Gulag*, p. 416.

p. 192 'It's like an entire town': SI 50-53.

p. 192 'Great Construction Projects': SI 51-27.

p. 192 'for the whole hour': LM 53-30.

p. 193 'Every year about half a million': Gregory, 'An Introduction', p. 16.

p. 193 Pechorlag and building of the second track: *Pechorstroi*, p. 36.

p. 193 'At a series of meetings': GU RK NARK, f. 1876, op. 7, d. 361, ll. 1–10.

p. 194 'idea of paying prisoners': Sokolov, 'Forced Labour', p. 40.

p. 194 '90 roubles . . . double that amount': GU RK NARK, f. 1876, op. 7, d. 361, l. 117.

p. 194 'billboards': GU RK NARK, f. 1876, op. 7, d. 361, l. 103.

p. 194 'In the 11th Colony': GU RK NARK, f. 1876, op. 7, d. 361, ll. 115–16.

p. 194 'kiosk in the remote colony': GU RK NARK, f. 1876, op. 7, d. 361, l. 117.

p. 195 'They are threatening': LM 50-46.

p. 195 200 roubles for Katya: LM 50-81.

p. 195 'collective farm': LM 51-35.

p. 195 'fatherly pleasure': LM 52-39a.

p. 195 '1 per cent at best': LM 51-45b.

p. 195 'bred rabbits': LM 51-48, LM 52-18.

p. 195 'We've belatedly': LM 51-55.

p. 196 'small improvements': APIKM, f. 31, op. 15 (A. K. Nedel'ko).

p. 197 '600 metres of towelling': GU RK NARK, f. 1876, op. 7, d. 363, l. 131.

p. 197 'Why send me sugar': LM50-9.

p. 197 Shops in the main town: Interview with Boris Ivanov, 2010.

p. 197 'Palace of Culture': GU RK NARK, f. 1876, op. 7, d. 360, l. 37.

p. 198 football teams: Interview with Boris Ivanov, 2010.

p. 198 'training complex': APIKM, f. 31, op. 15 (A. K. Nedel'ko).

p. 198 Lev teaching: LM50-47, LM50-49.

p. 200 'financial aid is not needed', 'So he's undoubtedly': LM51-35.

p. 200 'His hands are covered', 'After Oleg came to see me': LM48-15.

p. 200 'Conditions in the camp': SI49-48.

p. 200 'letters with requests': SI49-65, SI50-20.

p. 201 Lev sending money: LM49-52, LM49-58.

p. 201 'spent on bread', 'he was allowed': SI50-22.

p. 201 'I received three letters': SI50-43.

p. 201 'It's not good': LM50-6.

p. 202 'I thought it was the end': K. N. Rykalov to LM, 25 December 1960.

p. 202 'I've stubbornly been making him': LM50-12.

p. 202 'Sharp pains in his bladder': LM50-3.

p. 204 '[Valya's mother] arrived': SI50-53.

p. 204 'Minin reflector': LM50-83.

p. 204 'I'm not crying any more': SI50-18.

p. 204 'walking round her room': SI50-62.

p. 205 'I expected to see 4 walls': SI50-27.

p. 206 'Thanks to them': LM51-38.

p. 206 'Yesterday I got a few letters': LM51-35.

p. 207 'House of Meetings': GU RK NARK, f. 173, op. 1, d. 3, l. 6.

p. 207 'My holiday leave finishes': SI50-46.

p. 208 'warmer clothes, a woollen blanket and a bedsheet': SI50-51c.

p. 208 Three days with Lev: *Poka ia pomniu*, p. 121.

p. 208 'met S.': LM to N. Mel'nikov, 26 September 1950.

p. 208 'Farewell, Levi': SI50-51b.

p. 209 'My darling Sveta': LM50-59.

p. 209 'I can't decide': SI50-54.

p. 210 'I agree with you': LM50-67.

p. 211 'My darling Lev': SI50-64.

Chapter 10

p. 213 'My darling Sveta': LM51-1.

p. 213 'My darling . . . I still haven't sent you the letter': LM51-4.

p. 213 'reparation generators': LM51-4.

p. 214 'of the need to feed the town': LM51-22.

p. 214 'power station was closed down for three weeks': GU RK NARK, f. 1876, op. 7, d. 363, l. 45.

p. 214 'twenty-nine "serious accidents"': GU RK NARK, f. 1876, op. 7, d. 364, ll. 32–3.

p. 214 'lorry carrying seventy men': GU RK NARK, f. 1876, op. 7, d. 365, l. 60.

p. 214 'We're living and functioning': LM51-36.

p. 215 8,000 metres of rigging gear, etc.: GU RK NARK, f. 1876, op. 7, d. 363, ll. 58–65.

p. 215 'severe reprimand': GU RK NARK, f. 1876, op. 7, d. 362, l. 42.

p. 215 'accommodating unauthorized persons': GU RK NARK, f. 1876, op. 7, d. 363, l. 152.

p. 215 Serditov's denunciation: GU RK NARK, f. 1876, op. 7, d. 363, l. 153.

p. 215 Arvanitopulo sacked: GU RK NARK, f. 1876, op. 7, d. 365, l. 1.

p. 216 'It is a catastrophe': LM51-60.

p. 216 Novikov plays dominoes: GU RK NARK, f. 1876, op. 7, d. 366, l. 80.

p. 217 'twenty-seven individual and group escapes': GU RK NARK, f. 1876, op. 7, d. 363, ll. 100–101.

p. 217 Guards bribed, GU RK NARK: f. 1876, op. 7, d. 366, ll. 121–2.

p. 217 Railway wagons, knives, saws, blades: GU RK NARK, f. 1876, op. 7, d. 366, l. 80.

p. 217 Koval'chuk uncovers conspiracy: GU RK NARK, f. 1876, op. 7, d. 366, l. 122.

p. 217 'many of them hostile': GU RK NARK, f. 1876, op. 7, d. 363, l. 78.

p. 217 Escape plans of 1 May: GU RK NARK, f. 1876, op. 7, d. 363, ll. 72–85.

p. 218 'We had a lot of fun': SI51-29.

p. 219 'Levi . . . conscience and grief': SI51-26.

p. 220 'I'd like to follow in the footsteps': LM51-20.

p. 220 'The final word is yours': LM51-21.

p. 220 'very pleased', 'go-ahead': LM 51-28.

p. 220 'special expeditions', 'Decisions like this': LM 51-28.

p. 221 'My conscience has been troubling me': SI 51-37.

p. 221 'no need for labour': LM 51-35.

p. 221 'Levi, I really want to go to sleep': SI 51-40.

p. 221 'Don't think I'm glad': LM 51-41.

p. 222 'My darling Levi . . . I received permission': SI 51-43.

pp. 222–3 'Welcome, Sveta', 'Incidentally, about the three trinkets': LM 51-45a.

p. 223 'Good morning, Svetlye': LM 51-45b.

p. 224 'Well, all right, Sveta – after seven': LM 51-45c.

p. 224 'So I'm home, Levi': SI 51-44.

p. 224 'My dear Svetin': LM 51-45e.

p. 225 'I've felt fine': LM 51-47.

p. 225 'It's been exactly a week': SI 51-45.

p. 225 'What a wretched person': LM 51-51.

p. 226 'Hives are not a skin disease at all': SI 52-30.

p. 226 'It seems to work': SI 52-15.

p. 226 'I don't know how to reply': LM 52-12.

p. 226 'I wish someone would give you a good whipping': SI 52-16.

p. 227 'Between 120 and 130 prisoners': GU RK NARK, f. 1876, op. 7, d. 365, l. 14.

p. 227 'There isn't enough food': LM 52-22a.

p. 227 'He is barely recognizable': LM 51-56.

p. 227 'diet of green cabbage': Interview with Igor Aleksandrovsky, 2010.

p. 228 'Svetlaya, my darling, I haven't yet sent you': LM 52-9c.

p. 230 'He has only one lung': LM 52-12.

p. 230 'Maybe it's too early': SI 52-16.

p. 230 'Lyoshka has received his clearance': LM 52-4.

p. 231 'as he had the flu', 'If I'd known': SI 52-15.

p. 231 'I got to the station': LM 52-35.

p. 231 'More and more people are leaving': LM 53-17.

p. 231 '5,000 man-days had been lost', etc.: GU RK NARK, f. 1876, op. 7, d. 366, ll. 76–82.

p. 231 'Three group escapes': GU RK NARK, f. 1876, op. 7, d. 365, l. 129.

p. 232 'scraps of wood, bark, sawdust': GU RK NARK, f. 1876, op. 7, d. 366, l. 64.

p. 232 'Objectively . . . little beauty remains': LM50-17.

p. 232 'Nature has blessed': LM52-34.

p. 233 'I wanted to find out': Interview with Lev, 2008.

p. 233 'Mama still isn't any better': SI52-34.

p. 234 'I really think you should cancel': LM52-32b.

p. 234 'Papa has lost a lot of weight': SI52-46.

p. 234 'I think it will be hard': LM52-42a.

p. 234 'Sveta wrote that you': LM to E. A. Poltoratskaia, 24 October 1952.

p. 235 'My holiday is going very quickly': SI52-53.

p. 235 'I miscalculated, Sveta': LM52-67.

p. 235 'When I put aside my books': LM52-69.

p. 235 'The frosts have been unmerciful here': LM53-1.

p. 236 'Svetloe, it's so dreary without your letters': LM53-3.

p. 236 'Svetka, why aren't you writing to me?': LM53-6.

p. 236 'The post comes tomorrow': LM53-7.

p. 237 'I don't know why': SI53-2.

p. 237 'My dear darling Svetloe': LM53-11.

Chapter 11

p. 239 'How unexpected': LM53-23.

p. 239 'There is always Stalin': Interview with Lev, 2008.

p. 239 'The death of Stalin': LM53-24.

p. 240 'There has never been anything': SI53-16.

p. 240 'No one cried for Stalin': Interview with Lev, 2008.

p. 240 incident from October 1952: Interview with Lev, 2008.

p. 240 'halved the prison population': GU RK NARK, f. 173, op. 1, d. 1, ll. 1–2.

p. 241 'Some of our people': LM53-32.

p. 241 'It turned out': LM52-34.

p. 241 'chronic shortage of labour': GU RK NARK, f. 173, op. 1, d. 10, ll. 55–7.

p. 242 '224 former prisoners': GU RK NARK, f. 173, op. 1, d. 13, l. 4.

p. 242 'Here in Pechora': LM54-10.

p. 242 'that number had risen to 459': GU RK NARK, f. 173, op. 1, d. 12. l. 97.

p. 242 'paid about 200 roubles a month': APIKM, f. 31, op. 15 (A. K. Nedel'ko).

p. 243 '[Bannikov] has been back with us': LM 52-38.

p. 243 'Darling Svetloe': LM 53-48a.

p. 243 'He'd like to take advantage': LM 53-84.

p. 244 'Nina and Iv[an] have been staying': SI 53-38.

p. 244 'barracks became less cramped': *Vygliadyvaias'*, p. 44.

p. 244 Cultural activities: Interview with Igor Aleksandrovsky, 2010.

p. 244 Pechora as a town: Interviews with Boris Ivanov, 2010.

p. 244 'radio station': APIKM, f. 31, op. 19 (I. Z. Serditov).

p. 245 'new law by the Supreme Soviet': APIKM, f. 31, op. 13 (L. G. Mish-chenko).

p. 245 Sherman biographical details: GU RK NARK, f. 173, op. 1, d. 13, ll. 12, 130.

p. 245 'small-minded person': LM 52-2.

p. 245 Tkachenko's job: *Vygliadyvaias'*, p. 43.

p. 246 'Before he leaves': LM 53-33.

p. 246 'I am feeling very calm': LM 53-48.

p. 247 'childishness', 'flippant views', 'lack of tact': LM 53-58.

p. 247 'N. annoys me more': LM 52-69.

p. 248 'talking in their sleep': LM 52-33.

p. 248 'Regarding the family ideal': LM 49-21.

p. 249 'There is an unavoidable psychological evolution': LM to N. Mel'nikov, 8 April 1948.

p. 249 'The infinite mutual hostility': LM 48-86.

p. 249 'Watching the people around me': LM 50-77.

p. 249 'that in 999 instances': LM 48-57.

p. 249 'Once again I am overwhelmed': LM 49-76.

p. 250 Weights made out of axles: Communication by Nikita Mishchenko.

p. 250 'Physical strength': LM 48-33.

p. 251 'I am very grateful to you': O. Popov to SI, 17 December 1951.

p. 251 'I received a note today': LM 52-67.

p. 252 'Yesterday Oleg came to visit us': LM 54-1.

p. 252 'The more I really get to know him': LM 54-4.

p. 252 'We have all fallen out': LM 54-5.

p. 253 'Everything's weighing on me': SI 53-19.

p. 253 'Sveta . . . you mustn't turn down the opportunity': LM 53-20.

p. 253 'Sveta found herself in hospital': SI 53-45, SI 53-46.

p. 253 'Svetloe, thanks to our postal system': LM 53-58.

p. 254 'Sveta, increasingly I want to say all kinds of needless': LM 53-58.

p. 254 'Sveta, my darling, you must not take yourself to task': LM 53-65.

p. 254 'Of course, Lev, it's 14 months': SI 53-61.

p. 255 'Levi, why do you dismiss': SI 49-17.

p. 256 'Yaroslavl is a nice town': SI 53-78.

p. 256 'M. A. says that Voronezh is better': SI 53-77.

p. 256 'I've been told good things': LM 54-6.

p. 257 'So, Levi . . . no matter whom I ask': SI 54-3.

p. 257 'As regards the possibility': LM 54-19.

p. 258 'further down the line': LM 53-77.

p. 258 'My darling Sveta, the things I'm going to write': LM 54-21.

p. 259 'Spring has been here for three days now': LM 54-13.

p. 259 'In the hope of glory and good': LM 54-1 (from Pushkin's 'Stanzas').

p. 259 'My darling . . . I've been planning to tell you': SI 54-8.

p. 259 'I can imagine': SI 53-81.

p. 259 'if only for a day or two': LM 54-21.

p. 260 'I don't think – as far as I understand': LM 54-15.

p. 260 'I could apply for a change': LM 54-21.

p. 261 'For a long time now': SI 54-26a.

p. 262 'I should have also written about Kalinin': LM 54-21.

p. 262 'almost accidentally, but not completely': SI 54-31a.

p. 262 'so vast and individuals get lost there': SI 54-30a.

p. 262 'At home, I casually asked': SI 54-30a.

p. 263 'list of towns': SI 54-30a.

p. 263 'Possible options': SI 54-31a.

p. 264 'I'm already falling headlong': SI 54-31.

p. 264 'Sveta, my darling, there's not going to be any need': LM 54-26.

p. 265 'My leaving is still': LM 54-24.

p. 265 'no more certainty about the future': LM 54-25.

p. 265 'I'll go about tracking down': LM 54-25.

p. 266 'Papa's condition complicated': SI 54-34a.

p. 266 'Svetloe, after your telegram': LM 54-29.

Chapter 12

p. 268 'two wooden suitcases': Interview with Lev, 2006.

p. 268 'Send your letters here': LM54-27a.

p. 268 Trip to Kanin: Interview with Igor Aleksandrovsky, 2010.

p. 269 Lev's arrival in Moscow: Interview with Lev, 2006.

p. 269 'the lights in the windows', 'Anastasia Erofeevna': *Poka ia pomniu*, p. 24.

p. 269 'I don't want our first meeting': SI53-81.

p. 270 '30,000 roubles': Interview with Lev, 2008.

p. 270 'Dear Anastasia Erofeevna!': LM54-30.

p. 271 Kuzminskoe descriptions: LM54-31.

p. 271 'I found the woman quickly': LM54-31.

p. 272 'As a way out of this vicious circle': LM54-32.

p. 273 'I'm going to go to the soviet': LM54-33.

p. 273 'my journey has to be postponed': LM54-36.

p. 273 'My old couple': LM54-33.

p. 274 'handsome', 'none of the tasteless mix': LM54-35.

p. 274 'They were paying 7 roubles a day': LM54-40.

p. 275 'A mere cubbyhole': LM54-40.

p. 275 'Right now is still a very bad time': SI54-48.

p. 276 'We absolutely don't need anyone': LM54-38.

p. 277 Freelance work as a translator: *Poka ia pomniu*, p. 107.

p. 277 'Sveta . . . Sometimes when I'm in crowded places': LM54-35.

p. 278 'same old Moscow': Interview with Lev, 2008.

p. 278 Anastasia's death, 'Thank you, God': Interview with Lev, 2008.

p. 278 'empty bag, a shopping list and money': *Poka ia pomniu*, p. 108.

p. 279 'It was a policeman': Interview with Lev, 2008.

p. 279 Amnesty of 17 September 1955: Rossii, *Spravochnik po GULAGu* vol. 1, p. 16.

p. 280 'gloomy basement room': Interview with Lev, 2008.

p. 280 'I wouldn't recommend you marry him': *Poka ia pomniu*, p. 110.

p. 280 'Let me kiss you both': Interview with Lev, 2008.

p. 280 Strelkov details: V. Aleksandrovsky to LM, 20 February 1955.

Source Notes

p. 280 'Lev, I need your advice': Interview with Lev, 2008.

p. 281 Lev's job searches in Moscow: Interview with Lev, 2006.

p. 282 'As I reached the edge of the forest': Interview with Lev, 2008.

Epilogue

p. 284 'never turn into any kind of scientific researcher': LM 54-21.

p. 285 'They did not try to control': Communication by Nikita Mish-chenko.

p. 286 'One must be able . . . to live in this world': SI 47-30.

p. 286 'From an early age', 'My father did not talk', 'He was very charm-ing': Communication by Nikita Mishchenko.

p. 287 'I knew he was my future from the start': Interview with Svetlana, 2008.

List of illustrations and Plates

Illustrations

1. Envelope of letter from Svetlana   2
2. Svetlana's 1st letter   3
3. Lev's 24th   4
4. Svetlana   8
5. Lev   9
6. Lev on Mount Elbrus   22
7. Hauling team at the wood-combine   56
8. Strelkov and his cat in the laboratory   59
9. Lev in the laboratory   85
10. Strelkov in his laboratory with Lev, Konon Tkachenko, Nikolai Litvinenko and Nikolai Lileev   88
11. Remains of the settlement   93
12. Aleksandr, Maria and Vladimir   99
13. Moscow illuminated   125
14. The station at Kozhva   129
15. Guards at the wood-combine   131
16 and 17. Lev Izrailevich's photos of Sveta   136, 137
18. Strelkov, Lev, Lileev and Litvinenko   196
19. The Pechorlag football team   197
20. Terletsky with Irina Evgenevna Preobrazhenskaya   199
21. Sveta with Lev's aunts   206
22. The administration of the wood-combine   216
23. Lileev and Lev   247
24. The Roshchins   275

(Credits: 1–6, 9, 13, 16–18, 20–24 courtesy of the Memorial Society in Moscow; 7–8, 10–11, 14–15, 19 courtesy of the Archive of the Pechora

Historical-Regional Museum (Memorial), Pechora; 12 with thanks to Igor Aleksandrovich Aleksandrovssky; 13 Ria Novosti)

Plates

1. Lev and Svetlana in 1936
2. Lev with Evgenii Bukke in 1936
3. Svetlana's and Lev's letters
4. The industrial zone of the wood-combine, 1956
5. View of the Pechora River
6. Club house in the wood-combine
7. Wood-Combine Street
8. Convoy outside the 1st Colony
9. Remains of the wood-combine in the 1980s
10. Train ticket from the Pechora railway
11. Lev's boots from Pechora
12. Svetlana with Anastasia
13. Lev with his children at Nikita's dacha
14. Svetlana and Lev, Moscow, 2002

(Credits: 1–4 and 11–14 courtesy of the Memorial Society in Moscow; 5–10 courtesy of the Archive of the Pechora Historical-Regional Museum (Memorial), Pechora; plate 8 drawing by Boris Ivanov; plate 9 photograph by Vladimir Chivanov)

About the Author

ORLANDO FIGES is the author of *The Crimean War*, *The Whisperers*, *Natasha's Dance*, and *A People's Tragedy*, which have been translated into twenty-seven languages. The recipient of the Wolfson History Prize and the Los Angeles Times Book Award, among others, Figes is a professor of history at Birkbeck College, University of London.